D1040803

LIVES IN THE BALANCE

Perspectives on Global Injustice
and Inequality

INTERNATIONAL STUDIES
IN
SOCIOLOGY AND SOCIAL ANTHROPOLOGY

Editor

S. ISHWARAN

VOLUME LXVI

PAT LAUDERDALE
AND
RANDALL AMSTER (EDS.)

LIVES IN THE BALANCE
*Perspectives on Global Injustice
and Inequality*

LIVES IN THE BALANCE

Perspectives on Global Injustice and Inequality

EDITED BY

PAT LAUDERDALE

AND

RANDALL AMSTER

BRILL

LEIDEN · NEW YORK · KÖLN

1997

This book is printed on acid-free paper.

Library of Congress Cataloging-in-Publication Data

Lives in the balance : perpectives on global injustice and inequality
/ edited by Pat Lauderdale and Randall Amster.
      p.   cm. — (International studies in sociology and social
anthropology, ISSN 0074-8684 ; v. 66)
      Includes index.
      ISBN 9004108750 (paperback : alk. paper)
      1. Equality. 2. Justice.   I. Lauderdale, Pat II. Amster,
Randall. III. Series.
HM146.L58 1997
305—dc21   97–16211
                                                            CIP

Die Deutsche Bibliothek - CIP-Einheitsaufnahme

Lives in the balance / ed. by Pat Lauderdale and Randall Amster. –
Leiden ; New York ; Köln : Brill, 1997
      (International studies in sociology and social anthropology ; Vol. 66)
      ISBN 90–04–10875–0

ISSN 0074-8684
ISBN 90 04 10875 0

© *Copyright 1997 by Koninklijke Brill, Leiden, The Netherlands*

All rights reserved.
No part of this publication may be reproduced,
translated, stored in a retrieval system, or transmitted in any form
or by any means, electronic, mechanical, photocopying,
recording or otherwise, without prior written permission
from the publisher.

PRINTED IN THE NETHERLANDS

CONTENTS

Articles

Introduction
Critical Perspectives on Justice
*The Persistence of Global Injustice and Inequality**

PAT LAUDERDALE** and RANDALL AMSTER**

W HEN WE RECEIVED the invitation in early 1996 to create this special issue for publication in 1997, four matters became immediately clear. First, we knew that the substantive topic would focus upon comparative studies of inequality and injustice. Second, we realized that it was crucial to find exceptional scholars who not only were actively engaged in the areas, but who could put aside major parts of their research agendas to meet a hard and fast deadline, particularly in light of the fact that many of them were working and traveling in different parts of the world. Third, we wanted articles from researchers who had both quantitative and qualitative knowledge of diverse peoples' struggles against inequality and injustice, rather than the popular but false dichotomy between homogeneous globalization (vulgarized as "McWorld") and secessionist self-determination (vulgarized as Jihad). And fourth, we wanted to challenge scholars by having them directly address the concept of justice in a meaningful way. This special issue has been compiled with these guiding principles in mind.

The study of justice has generally been considered the province of philosophers and legal scholars. Rooted in the tradition of classical social contract theory and

* We appreciate the support of David Goldberg and the School of Justice Studies at Arizona State University, as well as Cecilia Ridgeway and the Department of Sociology at Stanford University for providing technical assistance for this project. We also are indebted to those students and faculty members at both institutions who share our interest in the multifaceted, complex nature of the study of, and the diverse struggles for, justice.

We especially thank Janet Soper, who manages the Publication Assistance Center of the College of Public Programs at ASU, for her unfailing and precise work in directing and completing the copyediting process and her ability to keep us to the deadline without undue pressure. This task was extremely difficult, particularly as we had to request immediate responses from authors on their final drafts. She truly maintains a welcomed and unique sense of justice.

** School of Justice Studies, Arizona State University, Tempe, AZ 85287-0403, U.S.A.

informed by the actual or idealized social arrangements of a particular historical period, such work typically analyzes the role of the state in producing justice and maintaining social order through codified law and the political system. As seen through this lens, justice is the end of a process characterized by rationality, equality before the law, and concentrated power in enforcement and sanctioning. Often overlooked in such analyses, however, are the pervasive injustices and inequalities borne by peoples around the globe at the hands of state hegemony and the pressures of international corporate rationality. Simply put, there are intractable problems created by stating what justice should be rather than the sociological analysis of how different constructions of justice are employed for various ends. In many respects, then, much of the classical theorizing about justice amounts to little more than an ongoing apology for the modern state and its ideological cornerstones of linear progress, universal truth, and the domination of nature.

In contrast, comparative sociological research often focuses on injustice and inequality, operationalizing these concepts from the lived experiences of marginalized peoples throughout the world system; justice in this lexicon is not simply a detached ideal or a set of universal principles, but instead can serve as a comprehensive locus of inquiry for a study of social conflict and global change. From this perspective, concrete struggles against material stratification and political exclusion can inform the study of justice by bringing to light its failure to manifest in much of the world—in stark contrast to the monolithic models of progress and prosperity often invoked by entities such as the United Nations and other global organizations such as the International Monetary Fund. What a comparative, critical sociological analysis reminds us is that for most of the world's inhabitants, justice remains a desire that has gone unfulfilled; in this sense, we come to understand justice not as a transcendent universal ideal, but rather as dependent in part upon one's place in the hierarchical spectrum of global power, wealth, and status.

The articles collected in this volume all address these questions of justice, injustice, and inequality from a comparative, critical perspective. In view of the range of theoretical comparative approaches in sociology, we chose the widest variety of sophisticated perspectives that integrate theory, methodology, and analysis. The papers were selected for their unique but compatible approaches to a sociological study of justice, with each contributing to the state of confirmation or disconfirmation of a substantive theory. Common thematic threads include analyses of the alternative ways in which historically marginalized peoples have come to define the concepts of justice and injustice; how such peoples have fared in utilizing various means to attain justice; and the role of discourses surrounding class, race, ethnicity, and gender in shaping conceptions of what is just or unjust. Rationalization, for example, refers to an encompassing process by which exchange and authority are brought within the purview of intellectually calculable rules; authority promoted by increased rationalization becomes characterized by an impersonal, formal legal order with concomitant levels of bureaucratization, centralization, and national mobilization. All of the articles respond, albeit in different ways, to the impact of such changes in the world system. Taken together, these articles comprise a critique of nation-statism, rational capitalism, and concentration of power in the postcolonial world by focusing our attention on the cracks in the armor of the dominant western paradigm, and by illuminating the continuing struggles for equality and power among those who remain marginalized in the new world (dis)order.

In the first article, Francisco Ramirez and Elizabeth McEneany undertake an event history analysis of the global spread of women's suffrage and abortion rights, noting that the former have by now been almost universally institutionalized, while the latter have been increasingly extended yet still remain contested ground in many nations. The authors' institutionalist approach emphasizes the often neglected role of culture in studies of the world system, including both its ontological and significatory aspects. By uncovering a qualitative difference between franchise and abortion rights—namely that the former derive from rights originally extended to men while the latter do not—the article provides a fresh look at the difficulties brought to bear on a traditionally marginalized group in attaining equality. Concerning the implementation of franchise and reproductive rights for women, it remains to be addressed whether such rights are merely symbolic without expenditures that allow or facilitate women's access to voting or health care. Thus, set against a framework of a burgeoning "world culture" that facilitates the political incorporation of women, Ramirez and McEneany conclude that while legal inequalities are ostensibly diminishing around the globe, disparities nonetheless persist as "culturally coded" inequities.

The next two pieces require us to undertake a closer examination of schemes of interpretation and social structures. The connection between the two requires an understanding of how people produce the material structures and objective conditions of social existence that appear before them as external forces and laws beyond their making or control. The articles consider the related concepts of political assassinations and terrorism, respectively. Working with a data base of 87 political assassinations by Jews in Israel from 1882 to 1988, Nachman Ben-Yehuda analyzes such events as a form of alternative or popular justice invoked when assassins (usually organized groups and not individual actors) believe that they cannot get a fair result by pursuing formal legal or political channels. As such, the article argues that it is possible to characterize political assassinations conceptually as a method of conflict resolution or social control, and rhetorically as a form of claims-making activity. Annamarie Oliverio, by contrast, considers the discursive construct of "terrorism" not from the perspective of the actor/deviant, but as a tool of the state in producing and maintaining hegemony, domination, injustice, and order. Comparing two ostensible "cultures of terrorism" (the United States and Italy) and the distinct rhetorical mechanisms employed by each, Oliverio concludes that terrorism is best analyzed as a political construct and not an essentially expressive act, revealing terrorism not as the cause of fissures in the social fabric but as an index of a deeper hegemonic crisis sought to be deflected by the discursive practices of the state.

These two studies remind us that when justice is reduced to a juridical concept it becomes only of derivative interest. Both examine how institutional rules take the form of cultural theories, ideologies, and prescriptions concerning how society actually operates in contrast to how it should work to attain collective purposes, especially goals of justice and progress. In addition, the research suggests that if the state inculcates violence as a legitimate means to resolve problems then others may resort to it when reason fails and force prevails.

Also employing a comparative perspective on the state, Julia Maxted and Abebe Zegeye discuss the "disintegration" of the nation-state and the repercussions for human rights in Africa. Focusing their analysis on political crises in Liberia and Somalia, Maxted and Zegeye foretell a "long and painful . . . transition to new forms of federation and political community" in a region of the world long beset by famines, internal wars, and poverty. They suggest than in the quest for self-determination, reformers ironically might first have to strengthen the nation-state system in order to "bear the weight of the transition" away from statism and toward a more egalitarian and equitable set of political structures.

In a somewhat different vein, Richard Harris critically explores how capitalism and the modernity project have generated pervasive inequalities and injustices throughout Latin America. Grounding his analysis in the material conditions of existence, Harris uncovers the intractable effects of economic exploitation and social and political inequality on the inhabitants of this technologically developing region. Sensitive to the postmodern rejection of universalistic and totalizing discourses, Harris nonetheless effectively demonstrates the continued vitality of "political economy" as an analytical tool for the illumination of injustice and inequality as generated by the global corporate-capital world system. The article concludes by identifying potential forces of change that could yield new social structures based on sustainable development, popular democracy, and social justice.

Similarly, Claudia von Werlhof analyzes the most recent uprising in the Chiapas region of southern Mexico, exploring constructs such as democracy, power, autonomy, justice, freedom, the land, and especially p(m)atriarchy as they are manifested in the current "Zapatista" movement. Unlike earlier protests in the 1980s for example, this movement has received worldwide attention in raising important questions for future research on the facade created by popular media coverage and its role in ignoring or suppressing protest that is part of a more protracted struggle. While in prior work she has differentiated between matriarchy and matri-centered societies, here she uses matriarchy to bring the issue of hierarchy into sharper focus, as she does with her critique of the typically unquestioned concept of democracy and its foundation in the language of domination. The article analyzes how fundamental concepts such as dignity, compassion, and the rejection of progress and development have come to characterize the movement, examining the implications of this rebellion for our lives in the post-industrial West. Von Werlhof concludes that it may be the case that the first insurrection of the 21st century will bring about change from "below," with those on the "periphery" showing us in the "center" how the future will be.

Pat Lauderdale also considers the instructive potential of indigenous practices and ideologies, analyzing the jurisprudential methods of indigenous North Americans and contrasting these practices with those of the modern state. He explicates the relevance of diffusion rather than concentration of political power and its relationship to fundamental indigenous concepts such as "land," in which land as place represents history, culture, and religion. Assessing the restitutive nature of indigenous "lawways" as compared with the generally repressive methods of the state, the article sets forth a research agenda for a further consideration of the potential role of indigenous practices and wisdom in ameliorating the inequalities and injustices that pervade the modern statist paradigm with its emphasis on self-interest, linear progress, and the domination of nature.

We find ourselves in a world that reflects a tension between the hegemonic facade of global corporate capitalism and representative democracy on the one hand, and the contingent, fragmentary quality of postcolonial life on the other. How (indeed, whether) this dialectic will be reconciled in the new millennium is not merely a question for academic consideration, but has real implications for the lives of people in the "developing" world who are caught at the interstices of these conflicting trends. What a comparative, critical sociological perspective can provide is a window into the souls of people struggling for self-determination, equality, and justice. It is in this spirit that we present this work focusing on the study of injustice and inequality in the world system.

From Women's Suffrage to Reproduction Rights? Cross-national Considerations[1]

FRANCISCO O. RAMIREZ* and ELIZABETH H. McENEANEY*

ABSTRACT

While women's suffrage has become completely institutionalized around the world, liberalized abortion is one indicator of the status of women that remains contested. Moreover, abortion rights differ fundamentally from women's suffrage in that they are not derivative of rights originally extended to men. In this article, we summarize and compare the results of prior studies that assess the effects of independence era, international linkages, modernization, state activism, and status of women on the rate of the adoption of women's suffrage and reproduction rights. We argue that world cultural models of progress and justice foster expanded models of political citizenship; these then provide more compelling rationales for further women's rights.

COMPARATIVE STUDIES of social inequality increasingly include research on the status of women. Much of this literature presupposes that women are naturally citizens and persons, and proceeds to compare their life chances relative to those of men. The persistence of inequalities is an empirical generalization frequently reported in these studies and this generalization is in turn explained through some variant of patriarchal reproduction theory. Overlooked in this discourse is the degree to which egalitarian standards are now routinely invoked in assessing the status of women. The historical rise and elaboration of these standards facilitate the discovery of inequalities between men and women qua citizens and persons and the legal and moral classification of these inequalities as inequities. Egalitarian standards can and are activated by the more egalitarian social movements that are transforming the status of women throughout the world.

This paper reflects on two aspects of the changing status of women: the attainment of the franchise and the codification of reproduction rights. The right to vote and to seek public office is but one dimension of citizenship, a necessary albeit insufficient condition for its realization (Walby, 1994; Katzenstein, 1984). The

* Department of Education and Sociology, Stanford, CA 94305, U.S.A.

right to terminate a pregnancy or choose motherhood further adds to the citizenship status of women. The franchise is the classic example of a political right (Marshall, 1964); reproduction rights are best conceptualized as civil rights justified on privacy grounds.[2] However, reproduction rights, and in particular, the liberalization of abortion laws, differ from franchise rights in that the former uniquely apply to women and are not derivative from rights earlier extended to men.[3]

Both sets of rights, though, involve universalistic aspirations and claims carried by increasingly international forces. By universalistic we mean that advocates and critics alike invoke standards that apply to women worldwide. The rights of women, not just the rights of these women in this country, are debated and the debates are not limited by local or even national boundaries. Here, we address both the similarities and differences in these citizenship acquisition processes. We use these comparisons to highlight commonalties predicted by world culture theories and to discuss differences between more institutionalized versus more contested domains in the transformation of the status of women.

This paper examines worldwide patterns of both women's suffrage acquisition and the liberalization of abortion laws. The paper also highlights key findings from prior cross-national analyses of both women's suffrage acquisition (Ramirez, Soysal, and Shanahan, forthcoming) and the liberalization of abortion laws (McEneaney and Ramirez, 1996). In both sections we emphasize the changing and more inclusive models of political citizenship and the increasingly international character of the franchise and abortion rights movements. We conclude by reiterating the general world culture argument to further interpret the comparative evidence.

World Culture and the Political Incorporation of Women

Citizenship and Women

There is an enormous literature on the political incorporation of the working class through the extension of the franchise (Marshall, 1964; Bendix, 1964; Lipset, 1963; Rokkan, 1970). Contemporary sensibilities cannot but hear the theoretical silence regarding the disenfranchised status of women throughout this work. The situation of the latter was known but not considered relevant. Thus, Rokkan (1970) provides information as to the dates of early female franchise acquisition but only men enter into his explanatory schema. Whether in the realm of civil, political, or social rights, the incorporated actors were imagined to be men (Orloff, 1993) or women related to men solely as mothers or widows (Skocpol, 1992). The historical construction of gendered boundaries between the state and civil society or between the public and the familial domains is thus ignored.

The gendered character of the state and citizenship preoccupies feminist scholars but some have dismissed the franchise as irrelevant, or worse as negatively co-optive

(MacKinnon, 1983; but see Piven, 1985, for a contrary point of view). Part of the problem is the ease with which the false inference "nothing has changed" is drawn from the fact that "all has not changed." New inequalities are discovered as egalitarian expectations, rooted in citizenship status, expand. Furthermore the reciprocal relationship between citizenship development and social movements (Turner, 1990) is not well understood. Women's right to vote and seek office has thus been ironically ignored by both the earlier historical literature and by the current interest in examining (often ahistorically) gender-based inequalities. As a result "the most publicized battle in the history of feminism" (Sapiro, 1983) and more generally, the transformation of the status of women, has yet to emerge as a central issue in comparative sociological theory. Global trends in abortion legislation, for example, have been described in case history format (see Sachdev, 1988), but rarely studied empirically as a truly global process.

Our effort to address this important issue starts from three core assumptions in world culture theory:

1. Nation-states and nation-state candidates are increasingly constructed from and influenced by world models of progress and justice set forth as universalistic scripts for authentic nation-statehood (Anderson, 1991).

2. These models increasingly allocate to the nation-state ultimate responsibility for the attainment and management of collective progress and societal justice (Meyer et al., 1996).

3. These models increasingly define collective progress and societal justice as contingent on the development and activity of entities reconstituted as individual citizens (Thomas et al., 1987).

From these assumptions it logically follows that there should be an increase in the visibility and value of the reconstituted entities and an intensification of the universalistic discourse regarding their status. Thus, a national population is socially constructed and the status of a national population becomes the object of treatises and theories that increasingly emphasize their common value and association with progress and justice as well as their relationship to the nation-state. To be sure, the transformation of translational masses into national citizens is a dynamic that initially did not include women. But the transformation of the status of women—from wives and mothers to individuals and citizens—was the unintended consequence of a changing logic of individualization and citizenship.

The political incorporation of women, we argue, is a worldwide process deeply influenced by world models of progress and justice and strongly associated with becoming a legitimate nation-state. These models are articulated and transmitted through international organizations, social movements, and certified expertise. Through these carriers world models shape the constitution and activity of nation-states and inform policies regarding the appropriate status of women within them.

The net effect has been a proliferation of international organizations with a focus on women (Boli and Thomas, forthcoming) and the expansion and internationalization of women's movements (Smith, 1994; Berkowitz, 1994). There has also been a concomitant rise of certified expertise on women's issues, e.g., women and development, women in organizations, women's education, women's health issues. These worldwide developments make the rights and needs of women in multiple domains a recurring theme in international agendas and conferences today.

The historical movement from national struggles for enfranchised status to women's rights as an international regime (DuBois, 1994; Galey, 1984; Hevener, 1986; Reanda, 1984) is too complex to deal with in a single paper. Suffice it to say that even from the outset the quest for the franchise had a clear transnational dimension (see the papers in Daley and Nolan, 1994). Early victories in New Zealand, Australia, and Finland were not assessed elsewhere as examples of local color but as markers of transnational development of world significance. There was both an awareness of organizing efforts in other nation-states as well as efforts to create transnational organizational links among the franchise movements. The visibility and value of women as entities worthy of individual citizenship within legitimate nation-states increased. In contrast, the abortion rights movement was less overtly organized at an international level in the early stages. The initial push toward liberalization came from different spheres at the nation-state level: associations of medical professionals as well as feminist women's groups, eased by favorable court decisions (United Nations, 1995). Later in the process, as population became a worldwide development concern, reproduction policy was increasingly shaped at the transnational level (Barrett, 1995).

Moreover, a common discourse was forged wherein the franchise was tied to notions of autonomous and responsible adulthood. Not only was this idiom favored by proponents of the franchise, but opponents, by challenging the capacity of women to make autonomous decisions, also helped spread the common discourse. Interestingly enough, opponents included not only conservatives but also leftists who feared that women would be unduly influenced by conservative authorities, e.g., the Catholic church. (Offen's [1994] discussion of the late development of the franchise in France emphasizes the latter point.) While earlier discourse sometimes emphasized differences between men and women to make the case for women's suffrage rights—his head and her heart (Chafe, 1972)—over time the common profranchise discourse stressed the common personhood that the sexes shared.

At the level of international organizations a parallel shift occurred, away from protective legislation underscoring the motherhood status of women to legislation granting to women the same rights men had obtained (Berkowitz, 1994). The acquisition of the franchise led the way in the historical development of common rights based on common individual citizenship. The liberalization of abortion laws reflects a unique development, neither reinforcing common rights nor merely returning to the era of protective legislation. While the contradictions between the abstract individual and the gendered boundaries between the public and the familial domains gave rise to the women's franchise movements early on in the West (Connell, 1990), abstract individuals obviously do not preoccupy the abortion rights movement. The franchise movements sought to include women under the category of the abstract individual; the abortion rights movements focus on bodied individuals and challenge state legislation and social convention that link female sexuality to compulsory motherhood. We revisit these points in the concluding section. We turn now to directly examine the relevant worldwide patterns.

Worldwide Patterns of Suffrage Acquisition and Liberalized Abortion Laws

We employ minimal legal criteria to gauge the timing of both suffrage acquisition and the liberalization of abortion laws. The franchise data comprise dates taken from *The Handbook of International Data on Women* (Boulding, 1976), supplemented by information from Sivard's *Women: A World Survey* (1985). These dates refer to the first time the franchise was extended to all women in each of 133 countries throughout the world. At any point in time women have either acquired or not acquired the franchise in a given country. Changes in political regimes often result in the suspension of the franchise, but there are *no* cases where the franchise was withdrawn from women only. The right to vote and seek public office is indeed associated with the abstract individual. But our measure deals solely with legal capacity and does not take into account nonlegal obstacles to the exercise of the franchise, obstacles that vary both between and within nations. Since electoral surveys show that the voting gap between men and women has steadily declined in many countries,[4] the date of first enfranchisement for women is a reasonable measure of a necessary step in the process of acquiring equal franchise status.

Abortion law data are taken from the United Nations survey, *Abortion Policies: A Global Review* (1995), supplemented by a limited number of case histories in Sachdev (1988) and an early survey by the United Nations Fund for Population Activities (1979). To parallel our franchise data collection effort we consider the date of first time liberalization of abortion.

Following the United Nations survey we distinguish between eight levels of liberalization of abortion laws:

1. Abortion is officially prohibited under all circumstances.

2. Abortion is prohibited under most circumstances, except to save the life of the pregnant woman.

3. Abortion is permitted to preserve the physical health of the woman.

4. Permitted on "juridical" grounds (i.e., in cases of rape or incest).

5. Permitted in cases of fetal impairment.

6. Permitted in order to preserve the physical or mental health of the woman.

7. Permitted for social or economic reasons.

8. Abortion permitted on request.

As in the case of suffrage rights we recognize that legal capacity is not equivalent to practical feasibility. Formal liberalization is often decoupled from the availability and cost of abortion services, the geographical accessibility of facilities, and the range of discretion afforded medical professionals for implementing the pertinent legal code. In Italy, for example, about 70 percent of medical doctors chose not to perform abortions even after passage of liberalized provisions (United Nations, 1995). On the other hand, long before it enacted liberalized legislation, Switzerland had a reputation as a place where European women could obtain safe abortions from licensed physicians (United Nations, 1995). In general, though, we assume that more liberalized provisions create a more favorable climate for making choices regarding pregnancy continuation or termination.

We think of the eight levels as constituting a continuum—a Likert scale of liberalization. A nation permitting abortion at one level most typically permits abortions in circumstances outlined under lower levels. The path to a more liberal abortion policy often involves intermediate steps, permitting abortion where the mother's health is endangered, along with a mixture of provisions regarding cases of rape, incest, and fetal impairment. Cuba, for example, instituted legislation to permit abortion in just those cases (levels three, four, and five) in 1936 with further liberalization under Castro (abortion on request) in 1965.

Unlike suffrage rights, abortion rights may be attenuated on a variety of grounds. Among the 155 nations for which we have data, we find about ten countries that experienced major reversals after liberalization and many more that underwent minor retrenchment. In addition, government action on abortion policies is often incremental, typically involving a gradual sloughing off of restrictions on the practice. In contrast, the franchise is typically extended to women, all women, with a single stroke of the pen.

We define the liberalization of abortion as the extension of legal grounds to include any of the last three levels. A country is classified as having a liberalized abortion law if abortion is allowed to preserve the physical or emotional health of the mother, for economic or social reasons, or on request. This is a stringent criterion, going beyond the minimal set of permissible grounds for abortion: incest, rape, or to preserve the physical health of the mother. Thus, at any point in the time period considered, 155 countries are coded as being in one of two states: liberalized or not liberalized. This procedure, while masking the incremental and reversible nature of the process, allows us to directly compare worldwide patterns of franchise acquisition and liberalized abortion laws.

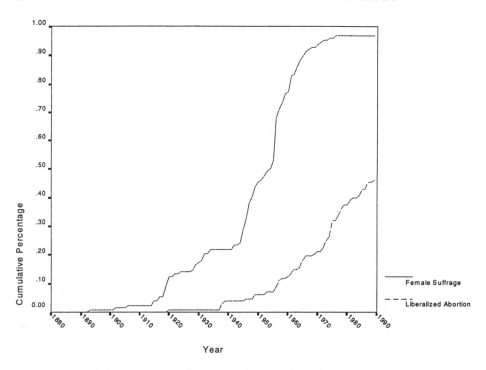

Figure 1. Cumulative Percentage of Nations with Female Suffrage and Liberalized Abortion.

Figure 1 plots the cumulative percentage of countries within which women have gained the franchise from 1890 to 1990. We start in the 1890s when women in New Zealand (1893) first gained the franchise. Figure 1 also plots the cumulative percentage of countries where a liberalized abortion policy has been enacted. The notion of liberalized abortion first emerges around the turn of the century, when Papua-New Guinea (at the time a French colony) instituted liberalized abortion policies. Russia was the first independent nation to liberalize in 1920.[5]

A clear pattern emerges in Figure 1. By 1900, women had gained the franchise in less than one percent of the countries of the world. From the turn of the century onward there is a steady increase in the percentage of countries that have extended the franchise to women. By 1990, women have suffrage rights in almost all countries. The only exceptions are those countries where men do not have franchise rights either and these are only a very few cases: Oman, Qatar, Saudi Arabia, United Arab Emirates, and Kuwait. What was a hotly contested issue in the late nineteenth century had become a thoroughly taken for granted right a hundred years later.

The worldwide pattern for liberalized abortion law runs in the same direction. By 1940, only about two percent of the countries of the world had a liberalized abortion policy in place. Seventy years later we find liberalized abortion policies in a little more than 50 percent. The magnitude of worldwide change in the liberalization of abortion law is less pronounced than the almost universal attainment of franchise status for women. Still, the number of nations that legally prohibit abortion under all circumstances has dramatically declined. At the beginning of this century, abortion was not a legitimate subject for state intervention: Only 12 nations had any kind of law pertaining to abortion in 1900. In each and every one of these 12 cases, however, abortion was either completely prohibited or allowed only to save the life of the pregnant woman. De facto restrictions on availability were severe nearly everywhere. As of 1990, nearly all nations legislate about abortion, but the list of countries totally prohibiting abortion has shortened, including only Chile, Djibouti, Egypt, Malta, Mauritius, Nepal, Panama, and Sao Tome. Thus, while "choice" is not a clear cut standard or regime worldwide, absolute prohibition is no longer the norm either.

The worldwide patterns depicted in Figure 1 do not mask any regional "deviants." Change starts earlier and moves faster in some regions, but in all regions the direction of change is the same. That direction involves both the institutionalization of the franchise for women and the liberalization of abortion laws, though with considerably more variability as to the appropriate level of liberalization. In both female suffrage and abortion liberalization, an upward bump may be observed in the post-World War II era, a period characterized by both rapid decolonization (Strang, 1990) and the further crystallization of world models of progress and justice in the United Nations and other international organizational carriers (Chabbott, 1996).[6]

World models of justice are reflected in the Universal Declaration of Human Rights (1948), followed by the Convention on the Political Rights of Women (1954). New nation-states would come of age at a time when the rights of women were better established as a feature of international discourse. New nation-states would also face development agendas where older pronatalist policies had for the most part been replaced by intensifying fears about population growth rates. World models of progress were more likely to extol the virtues of family planning (Barrett, 1995) and education for women (Bradley and Ramirez, 1996). More dependent on worldwide consensus for their legitimacy as nation-states, newer countries may move more quickly to enact world models, especially when enactment does not result in significant costs to them. Alternatively, long independent states may have greater institutional inertia to overcome in moving in the direction of both a *more inclusive* and a *more expanded* model of citizenship. These states came of age when citizenship was both more male-linked and citizenship rights more restricted. Thus, it is likely to take longer for these states to incorporate women as abstract individuals and to expand their view of citizens to include more "bodied" rights.

Figure 1 does not, however, clarify the relationship between the age of the country and the timing of the suffrage and the liberalization processes. Both world culture theory, as discussed above, and organizational imprinting theory (Stinchcombe, 1965) would lead one to expect longer gaps between dates of national independence

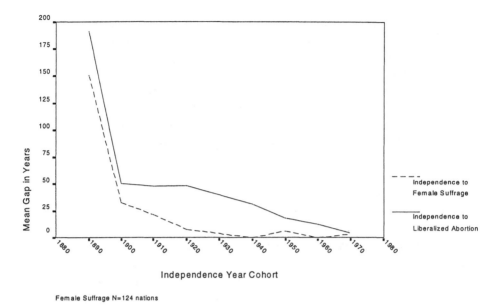

Figure 2. Mean Gap between Independence and Female Suffrage, Abortion Liberalization.
By Independence Year Cohort.

and the enactment of both the franchise and liberalized abortion policy among the
older countries. World culture theory emphasizes the increasing power of world
models of progress and justice and their more immediate influence on nation-states
born when these models are better established. Organizational imprinting theory
emphasizes the weight of history and organizational inertia as forces that are more
likely to affect older nation-states. To assess the prediction implied by both theories,
we turn to Figure 2.

Figure 2 attempts to illustrate a cohort effect, marked by date of independence,
among nations that have extended the suffrage to women and liberalized abortion
laws. At issue is whether countries "born" in different historical eras are more or
less likely to enact more inclusive and more expanded models of citizenship. Again,
the patterns are quite clear.[7] Prior to 1900 the average time lag between national
independence and female suffrage acquisition was 150 years. This gap suggests a
gendered—read male—logic of political citizenship among the older cohort. Note
how this gap dramatically declines in the twentieth century. Indeed, by 1960 suffrage
for women on average is extended prior to independence. This was the case in much
of Africa where suffrage movements were deeply embedded in national independence
struggles. This process is also illustrated by recalling that women in the United States
and Great Britain had to wait much longer after independence for the suffrage than
did their sisters in their former colonies, the Philippines and India.

A strikingly similar pattern is observed when we turn to the issue of liberalized abortion. The average time gap declines from about 190 years for countries in the earliest independence cohort to only a four-year gap for the 1970 cohort. The decline is sharper for the franchise in the 1920s and 1940s but by 1980 both events are very closely linked to national independence. Note, however, that we have a more comprehensive picture of the relationship between country age and women's suffrage, since we are dealing with virtually all cases (124 nations) while our definition of liberalization includes only about half of the countries in our data set (60 nations) from this assessment.[8]

To summarize, Figure 1 shows the worldwide triumph of suffrage rights for women and the worldwide increase in the liberalization of abortion laws. Figure 1 also reveals that the abortion rights are less institutionalized than the right to vote and seek office. What happens to women and their bodies is a domain characterized by more contestation. Figure 2 offers support for the prediction that more recent cohorts of nation-states are more attuned to the models of progress and justice promulgated by world culture through organizational carriers and expert discourse. This cohort effect holds up for both the franchise and the liberalization processes.

Prior Cross-national Studies

Both the acquisition of the franchise and the liberalization of abortion laws may be fruitfully conceptualized as events and subjected to event history analysis (Tuma and Hannan, 1984). That is, one can cross-nationally analyze the rate of transition form origin state (no enactment of franchise or absence of liberalized abortion policy) to the destination state (enactment or liberalization). More concretely one can identify and assess the influence of a set of independent variables on the likelihood of an event taking place in a country "at risk." As indicated earlier we have undertaken even-history analyses of both the acquisition of the franchise and the liberalization of abortion laws. Throughout these analyses the "at-risk" set for any time period consists in those countries where the event has yet to take place. Our independent variables consist in measures of national or societal characteristics and in indicators of international linkage and world influence (Banks, 1986; Gurr, 1990). That is, we ascertain national and transnational influences on the dependent variables of interest. Much macrosociological theory emphasizes the importance of societal variation. World culture theory adds the idea that transnational influences of a cultural and geopolitical character are also consequential.

In what follows we highlight key findings from the cross-national analysis of both women's acquisition of the franchise and the liberalization of abortion laws. These key findings involve the influence of the following independent variables: independence era, international linkages, modernization, state activism, and, lastly, status of women. These variables are operationalized using different indicators in the different analyses. To compare across analyses we make the assumption that these indicators tap different dimensions of the same underlying conceptual domain. Confidence in any given set of findings is greater to the extent that the findings hold up even when different measures are used.[9]

The first finding of interest is the positive influence of what we call the independence era. This is a dummy variable measured at five-year intervals. The variable equals "1" if the country becomes independent in the five-year period prior to or following the enactment of women's suffrage. In this instance the same indicator is used in the analysis of the liberalization event. Here the idea is that national independence constitutes an opportunity for adhering to world models of progress and justice. In both sets of analyses, net of other effects, becoming or having just attained independence increases the likehood of affirming women's political (franchise) or civil rights (liberalization of abortion law).[10] This finding is consistent with the overall argument and its emphasis on the constructed character of the constitution and activity of nation-states.

World culture impacts nation-states through international linkages and influences; these constitute the carriers through which world models are articulated and transmitted. The more a nation-state is embedded in a web of such carriers and the more such carriers proliferate, the greater the likelihood of a nation-state enacting world culture scripts for progressive and just nation-statehood. In these analyses we find consistent support for this proposition. Women's suffrage rights enactment is positively influenced by both regional and world patterns of enactment. That is, a country is more likely to enact women's suffrage if its regional neighbors did so five years earlier. This effect captures the idea that geographical proximity may constitute a form of "peer pressure" through which preferred policy is effectively communicated. These analyses also show a world suffrage count effect. The probability of acquiring the franchise is positively influenced by the cumulative number of countries that have already done so. Both of these influences are consistent with the world-culture perspective.

In analyzing the liberalization of abortion law we examine the influence of variation in memberships in international nongovernmental organizations. The latter have been conceptualized and discussed as an example of world culture organizational carriers (Boli and Thomas, forthcoming). Countries vary in their tendencies to be "joiners" and "joiners" are more likely to have been more exposed to the world models that favor liberalization. The results of this analysis show positive effects, net of all other influences. A similar finding is obtained in the women's suffrage analysis: Membership in the international women's suffrage alliance increases the likelihood of acquiring the franchise. Here one sees how outcomes within nation-states are influenced by international linkages.

Taken as a whole these findings suggest the importance of international linkages and influences on two dimensions of the transformation of the status of women.

These findings are consistent with the insight that "the constitutions of women's position in society ... and in the home owes much to changes that are international and transnational. At the cost of some exaggeration, it is possible to assert that the personal is international" (Halliday, 1988).

By way of contrast there is little support in these analyses for standard modernization arguments. The liberalization of abortion is not affected by the level of economic development. Nor was liberalization a modernizing rational strategy adopted by countries with higher crude birth rates. Such countries were, in fact, less likely to liberalize early. Lastly, an attempt to estimate the effect of a Protestant West dummy variable yielded inconsistent results across different specifications. Much of the earlier liberalization impetus may have started in the Protestant West but as the models gain worldwide ascendancy and influence non-Protestant and non-Western countries are just as likely to enact the appropriate scripts. A similar pattern of results is found in the analyses of the women's franchise acquisition. Measures of economic development or political democracy do not work as modernization theory would lead one to expect.

A different picture emerges when we examine the influence of state activism. In these analyses, measures of state activism include the percent of the gross domestic product spent on social security and the number of key welfare state initiatives. We find that these indicators positively influence the liberalization of abortion and the acquisitions of women's suffrage. All other things being equal, an activist state is more likely to be a favorable climate for transformations in the status of women. This pattern of findings is consistent with previous cross-national studies of income inequality (Rubinson, 1976), suggesting that the redistributing or leveling effects of the activist state are not limited to class-based inequalities. The results are also in line with the second core assumption of world culture theory, that over time the state becomes responsible for the attainment of "progress" and "justice."

Lastly, in both analyses we estimate the effects of several measures of the status of women. It is reasonable to assume that other variations in the status of women may be consequential. These variations themselves may be driven by transnational or societal factors. That is, above and beyond their direct effects on the franchise and liberalizing of abortion, transnational and societal variables may have indirect effects through their influence on other status of women indicators. We highlight two findings and a third "nonfinding." The analyses show that the rate of franchise adoption is positively influenced by the number of women's political organizations, an indicator of the political clout of women. Employing another indicator of women's status, the proportion of women in the paid labor force, we also find that this measure positively influences the rate of liberalized abortion policy. Both of these results are relatively straightforward: When women attain either a greater level of political or economic leverage in society (as variously measured), the higher the rate of acquisition of the franchise or liberalization of abortion policy becomes.

These findings suggest that various aspects or dimensions of the status of women are closely related to each other. But that generalization is in fact inaccurate. Whether relying on cross-cultural data from mostly stateless societies (e.g., Sanday, 1981) or on data for nation-states (e.g., Ramirez, 1987), then burden of evidence contradicts this generalization. To further examine this issue we estimate the effects of years of female suffrage on the liberalization outcome. At issue is whether the accumulation of experience as voters and potential office holders increases the probability of a liberalized abortion law. We find a positive but small and statistically insignificant effect.[11]

Up to this point we have compared the results of two event history analyses covering roughly the same historical period. However, one implication of world culture theory is that international influences should become more consequential in the more recent period while societal factors should weigh more in the earlier period. That is, we assume an increase in the authority and influence of world models of progress and justice over time. This assumption is directly evaluated for the women's suffrage acquisition variable. Event history models are estimated for an earlier (1890-1930) and a later period (1930-1990). The results of these analyses strongly support the assumption: The effects of national-level factors decline over time while the international effects increase. To cite but one example, women's internal political organizational strength is more influential in the earlier period while linkages to the international women's movement show stronger effects in the later period.

To summarize, the results of prior cross-national studies indicate that both transformations in the status of women are positively affected by the era of national independence, international organizational linkages and the activities of other nation-states in the region and throughout the world, levels of state activism, and, finally, indicators of the enhanced political and economic status of women. Conventional measures of modernization fail to show effects. The liberalization of abortion policy is only weakly related to the length of time women have been enfranchised. Lastly, the import of transnational influences is greater in the more recent era.

These results are consistent with the expectations of world culture theory: Transnational influences and international linkages matter, and they matter more when the models are more institutionalized. Both dependent variables are strongly linked to the period of attaining nation-statehood. Neither is much affected by the level of economic development or, in the case of abortion policy, the societal need for fewer children. State activism is also consequential; state activism is an internal dynamic that enjoys much external legitimacy. The acquisition of women's suffrage and the liberalization of abortion policy are influenced by some common factors but there are also some differences in the development of these rights.

Concluding Thoughts

Why did so many otherwise different nation-states follow a similar trajectory regarding the political incorporation of women via the franchise? World culture theory postulates the rise, development, and spread of a standard of more inclusive political citizenship. This standard is anchored in world models of progress and justice and these models are diffused throughout the world via international organizations and social movements. Certified experts play an active role in these movements and consult for these organizations. It is through these experts, movements, and organizations that world culture unfolds as a series of blueprints for attaining authentic nation-statehood and these blueprints are especially influential in constructing the constitution and activity of nation-states. It is difficult to otherwise explain so universal a triumph of what was once so controversial a proposal. It is easy enough to understand why no sociological theory attempts to make sense of what is now experienced as a commonsensical and taken-for-granted reality.

A similar trajectory characterizes the worldwide liberalization of abortion policy. However, this process started later, is incremental in nature, and has undergone reversals following regime changes, and its present state is that of an incomplete project. In the United States the abortion debates are plentiful and heated. Throughout the world there is a growing literature on the subject. The liberalization of abortion in post-Franco Spain has been thoroughly contested, but no one seemed to notice that women acquired suffrage rights together with men in the same post-Franco Spain.

Why is one set of rights more institutionalized and the other still an object of contestation? One obvious answer centers on the issue of fetal rights. The latter are frequently invoked by antiabortion movements. It is indeed the case that the same more inclusive standards of political citizenship have been extended not only to women but also to children, and arguably, to fetuses. A clash of rights, though, is not unique to the abortion debates. At an earlier time, the right of the male estate to monopolize the public sphere clashed with demands for inclusion and some of these clashes involved violent confrontations.

We suggest that the difference lies in the nature and locus of the rights claimed. The earlier issue was whether women could be included under the category abstract individual and thus become voting citizens. The current debate is over whether the status of citizen can be expanded to include rights not earlier demanded by or extended to men. The right to choose or not to choose motherhood more directly impacts upon women than men. Furthermore the assumption that motherhood is a personal choice and a civil right undermines the association between women and nature in Western and some other cosmologies, an assumption that may implicitly justify the subordination of women to men (Ortner, 1974). The earlier triumph in the public sphere could coexist, however uneasily, with all sorts of asymmetries and inequalities in the familial sphere. Motherhood as a choice is a demand located in the familial sphere and strikes directly at the foundation of many of its inequalities.

The wall between the public and the familial spheres, however, is clearly crumbling. Abuse and violence in the family is the subject of transnational concern; note the more recent U.N. declarations on the rights of women to be free from violence within and outside their homes. Many governments are taking an increasingly activist stand in assuring the payment of child support rather than assume that parents will "do the right thing." Finally, issues of sexual identity (including control over one's fertility), whose discussion was previously confined to the bedroom if it occurred at all, are now topics for debate and activism in the international sphere.

These developments suggest that the reach of world culture will not be turned back on the front steps of private households. Models of progress and justice will foster expanded models of political citizenship and these in turn will provide more compelling rationales for further women's rights. Paradoxically, however, the expansion of the egalitarian yardstick generates the discovery of further inequalities culturally coded as inequities.

NOTES

1   The authors would like to thank Gili Drori, David John Frank, John W. Meyer, Mary Rauner, and the members of the Stanford Workshop on Comparative Political and Economic Systems for their thoughtful comments on this work.
2   Reproduction rights become social rights if public funding is guaranteed to all women or to at least those who cannot afford it. Unfortunately, data constraints do not allow us to consider the public funding issue in this paper.
3   In this paper, we take the liberalization of abortion laws to be one indicator of reproduction rights. Reproduction rights can be violated through compulsory motherhood or compulsory prevention of motherhood. In the area of abortion, the violation is most frequently in the direction of mandating a full-term pregnancy. Ceaucescu's Romania was an extreme example, with severe prohibitions on abortion, as well as dramatic surveillance techniques of potential mothers. All women in their childbearing years were required to have a monthly gynecological examination at her workplace. Pregnant women were monitored regularly until the time of delivery. Choosing to be childless was expensive: A special tax was levied on married childless couples without a medical excuse and unmarried persons over 25. In contrast, China has extremely liberal access to abortion services at government expense, often accompanied by up to two months paid medical leave. Hence, psychological pressure, physical coercion, and economic disincentive can be used to curtail reproductive rights in either direction.
4   Among countries that achieved independence prior to 1890, for example, the average gap between the granting of male suffrage and the extension of suffrage rights to women was about 50 years. For countries gaining their independence after World War II, this gap virtually disappears.
5   Australia followed New Zealand in extending suffrage rights to women in 1902. Great Britain, Australia, and New Zealand followed Papua-New Guinea and Russia by adopting liberal abortion laws in 1938 following the British decision *Rex v. Bourne*.
6   There is also an early, post-World War I upswing in the expansion of female suffrage. At that time, traces of emerging global models of progress may have been carried by the nascent international organizational structure beginning with the League of Nations.

7 Countries gaining independence at any time before 1895 are included in the 1890 cohort, countries becoming independent between 1896 and 1905 are included in the 1900 cohort, and so forth.

8 A similar analysis with a less strict definition of "liberalization," e.g., not completely prohibited, shows a similar pattern though with a somewhat steeper decline. However, there is a left censoring problem that makes this approach more problematic than the one we describe above. To reiterate a previous point, in the very early historical stages of the process, abortion was not a subject for official state intervention. The de facto prohibitions were so thoroughly secure that most states did not have laws specifically prohibiting the practice.

9 Data constraints prevent us from using the same set of multiple indicators in both analyses. Further exploratory data gathering and assessment is needed to move in this direction in future studies.

10 In our summary report of these event history analyses, we only report statistifically significant effects (i.e., $p < .05$, two-tailed test).

11 In future studies, we will investigate a more intricate relationship between franchise acquisition and abortion liberalization. Though this direct count of years of experience with female suffrage does not have an effect on the rate of liberalization, a suffrage-acquisition cohort coding may show effects. One variation of this is a "window of opportunity" effect: Recent adoptions of the franchise lead to higher rates of liberalization.

REFERENCES

ANDERSON, Benedict
  1991 *Imagined Communities*. 2nd ed. London: Verso.
BANKS, Arthur S.
  1986 *Cross-national Time Series Data Archive*. Binghamton, N.Y.: Center for Comparative Political Research, State University of New York.
BARRETT, Deborah
  1995 "Reproducing Persons as a Global Concern: The Making of an Institution." Ph.D. diss., Department of Sociology, Stanford University.
BENDIX, Reinhardt
  1964 *Nation-building and Citizenship*. New York: J. Wiley.
BERKOWITZ, Nitza
  1994 "From Motherhood to Citizenship: The Worldwide Incorporation of Women into the Public Sphere in the Twentieth Century." Ph.D. diss., Department of Sociology, Stanford University.
BOLI, John and George M. THOMAS
  Forthcoming "World Culture in the World Polity: A Century of International Nongovernmental Organization." *American Sociological Review*.
BOULDING, Elsie
  1976 *Handbook of International Data on Women*. New York: Sage.
BRADLEY, Karen, and Francisco O. RAMIREZ
  1996 "Women's Share of Higher Education: Cross-national Trends and Antecedents." *Research in Sociology of Education and Socialization* 11: 63-91.
CHABBOTT, Colette
  1996 "Constructing Educational Development: International Development Organizations and the World Conference on Education for All." Ph.D. diss., School of Education, Stanford University.

CHAFE, William H.
   1972 *The American Woman: Her Changing Social, Economic, and Political Roles, 1920-1970.* New York: Oxford University Press.
CONNELL, R.W.
   1990 "The State, Gender, and Sexual Politics: Theory and Appraisal." *Theory and Society* 19 (5): 507-544.
DALEY, Caroline, and Melanie NOLAN, eds
   1994 *Suffrage and Beyond: International Feminist Perspectives.* New York: New York University Press.
DUBOIS, Ellen Carol
   1994 "Women's Suffrage Around the World: Three Phases of Suffragist Internationalism." Pp. 252-276 in: *Suffrage and Beyond: International Feminist Perspectives*, edited by Caroline Daley and Melanie Nolan. New York: New York University Press.
GALEY, Margaret
   1984 "International Enforcement of Women's Rights." *Human Rights Quarterly* 6: 463-490.
GURR, Ted Robert
   1990 *Polity II Computer File.* Ann Arbor, Mich.: Inter-University Consortium for Political and Social Research.
HALLIDAY, Fred
   1988 "Hidden from International Relations: Women and the International Arena." *Millennium: Journal of International Studies* 17 (3): 419-428.
HEVENER, Natalie
   1986 "An Analysis of Gender-based Treaty Law: Contemporary Developments in Historical Perspective." *Human Rights Quarterly* 8: 70-78.
KATZENSTEIN, Mary F.
   1984 "Feminism and the Meaning of the Vote." *Signs* 10: 4-26.
LIPSET, Seymour M.
   1963 *The First New Nation.* New York: Basic Books.
MACKINNON, Catherine
   1983 "Feminism, Marxism, Method, and the Feminist Jurisprudence." *Signs* 8: 635-658.
MARSHALL, T.H.
   1964 *Class, Citizenship, and Social Development.* Garden City, N.Y.: Doubleday.
McENEANEY, Elizabeth H., and Francisco O. RAMIREZ
   1996 "Enactment of Liberalized Abortion Laws: An Event History Analysis." Paper presented at the annual meetings of the American Sociological Association, August, New York.
MEYER, John W., John BOLI, George M. THOMAS, and Francisco O. RAMIREZ
   1996 "World Society and the Nation-State." Unpublished paper, Department of Sociology, Stanford University.
OFFEN, Karen
   1994 "Women, Citizenship, and Suffrage with a French Twist, 1789-1993." Pp. 151-170 in: *Suffrage and Beyond: International Feminist Perspectives*, edited by Caroline Daley and Melanie Nolan. New York: New York University Press.
ORLOFF, Ann Shola
   1993 "Gender and the Social Rights of Citizenship: The Comparative Analysis of Gender Relations and Welfare States." *American Sociological Review* 58: 303-328.
ORTNER, Sherry
   1974 "Is Female to Male as Nature is to Culture?" Pp. 67-88 in: *Woman, Culture and Society*, edited by Michelle Rosaldo and Louise Lamphere. Stanford: Stanford University Press.

PIVEN, Frances Fox
1985 "Women and the State: Ideology, Power, and the Welfare State." Pp. 265-290 in: *Gender and the Life Course*, edited by Alice Rossi. New York: Aldine.
RAMIREZ, Francisco O.
1987 "Global Changes, World Myths, and the Demise of Cultural Gender: Implication for the U.S.A." Pp. 257-274 in: *America's Changing Role in the World System*, edited by Terry Boswell and Albert Bergesen. New York: Praeger.
RAMIREZ, Francisco O., Yasemin SOYSAL, and Suzanne SHANAHAN
Forthcoming "The Changing Logic of Political Citizenship: Cross-national Acquisition of Women's Suffrage Rights: 1890-1990." *American Sociological Review.*
REANDA, Laura
1984 "Human Rights and Women's Rights: The United Nations Approach." *Human Rights Quarterly* 3: 11-31.
ROKKAN, Stein
1970 *Citizens, Elections, Parties.* New York: McKay.
RUBINSON, Richard
1976 "The World Economy and the Distribution of Income Within States: A Cross-national Study." *American Sociological Review* 41 (4): 638-659.
SACHDEV, Paul, ed.
1988 *International Handbook on Abortion.* New York: Greenwood Press.
SANDAY, Peggy
1981 *Female Power and Male Dominance.* Cambridge: Cambridge University Press.
SAPIRO, Virginia
1983 *The Political Integration of Women: Roles, Socialization and Politics.* Chicago: University of Illinois Press.
SIVARD, Ruth L.
1985 *Women: A World Survey.* Washington, D.C.: World Priorities.
SKOCPOL, Theda
1992 *Protecting Soldiers and Mothers.* Cambridge: Harvard University Press.
SMITH, Jackie
1994 "The Globalization of Social Movements: The Transnational Social Movement Sector, 1983-1993." Paper presented at the annual meetings of the American Sociological Association, August, Los Angeles.
STINCHCOMBE, Arthur
1965 "Organizations and Social Structure." Pp. 142-193 in: *Handbook of Organizations*, edited by James March. Chicago: Rand McNally.
STRANG, David
1990 "From Dependency to Sovereignty: An Event History Analysis of Decolonization 1870-1987." *American Sociological Review* 55: 846-860.
THOMAS, George M., John W. MEYER, Francisco O. RAMIREZ, and John BOLI, eds
1987 *Institutional Structure: Constituting State, Society and the Individual.* Newbury Park, Calif.: Sage.
TUMA, Nancy B., and Michael T. HANNAN
1984 *Social Dynamic: Models and Mehtods.* New York: Academic Press.
TURNER, Bryan
1990 "Outline of a Theory of Citizenship." *Sociology* 24: 189-217.
UNITED NATIONS
1995 *Abortion Policies: A Global Review.* 3 vols. New York: United Nations.

UNITED NATIONS FUND FOR POPULATIONS ACTIVITIES
    1979 *Survey of Laws on Fertility Control.* New York: United Nations.
WALBY, Sylvia
    1994 "Is Citizenship Gendered?" *Sociology* 28: 379-395.

Political Assassination Events as a Cross-cultural Form of Alternative Justice[1]

NACHMAN BEN-YEHUDA*

ABSTRACT

Criminals or deviants can be viewed as trying to exercise some form of social control via being involved in deviance and crime. Interpreted somewhat differently, the implication is that those deviating from the law or norms are involved in practicing an interesting form of doing justice. This paper explores the meaning of a specific form of a political deviant act—that of political assassinations—and conceptualized it as a particular form of social control within an alternative system of informal justice. The nature, characterization, type, and mode of operation of this form of informal and alternative justice are examined.

IN THIS PAPER I shall examine the concepts of justice and injustice vis-à-vis social control. I will argue that these concepts can be useful when applied, historically and comparatively, to political assassination events. We shall see how the rhetorical device "political assassination" is utilized within an alternative system of justice, in social systems that use this lethal act in a struggle of legitimacy and social control and in setting moral boundaries. This paper thus provides a meaningful analytical and cross-cultural agenda within which political assassinations can be interpreted and understood.

Political Assassinations—Background

With some few notable exceptions, very little research has been done on political assassinations by either criminologists or sociologists (e.g., see Turk, 1983; Wagner-Pacifici, 1986; Wilkinson, 1976). Previous works on political assassination events either focus on one particular case (e.g., the assassination of John F. Kennedy, Abraham Lincoln, Aldo Moro etc.) or give very brief and telegraphic information about many such cases from different cultures (e.g., Ford, 1985; Kirkham, Levy,

* Department of Sociology and Anthropology, Hebrew University, Jerusalem 91905, Israel.

© Koninklijke Brill, Leiden, 1997

and Crotty, 1970, pp. 301-325). Some report a good deal of information about a few cases (e.g., Havens, Leiden, and Schmitt, 1970). All these approaches are often confusing and unsatisfactory because they do not provide a firm basis for generalizations.

The study on which this report is based (Ben-Yehuda, 1993) was aimed at developing a meaningful and comparative sociological, analytical framework within which political assassinations can be interpreted and understood. The way I approached this problem was to make an in-depth inquiry into the nature of political assassinations within what may be considered a more or less integrated (albeit complex), cultural matrix and to compare the results of this study with what we know about similar phenomena in other cultures.

The specific research focused on political assassinations by Jews in Palestine-Israel between 1882 through 1988; that is, from the days of renewed Jewish national life in the Middle East. This is an interesting culture and period to focus on because during this time period, in Palestine and Israel, an attempt was made to rebuild a new Jewish culture and society. This attempt involved some profound social and political changes for Jewish collective life, as well as profound changes in the personal identity and consciousness of Jewish individuals. The main reasons for limiting the scope of this study in this way were: (a) accessibility to data; (b) an opportunity to examine *in depth* a particular form of deviance within what may be considered as one culture, and thus provide a firm base for both cross-cultural comparisons and a framework for future research agendas.

The nature of this research was sociohistorical, from a sociology of deviance perspective. It employed a methodology that relied on both primary and secondary sources (see Ben-Yehuda, 1990d).

Killing and Political Assassinations

Taking people's life against their wish—killing—is referred to by a variety of rhetorical devices, the most famous of which is probably "murder." Much criminological and sociological literature was written on such forms of killings as homicide, suicide, genocide as well as a few others. This paper views political assassinations as a form of deviance and, more particularly, as another form of killing.

Forms of Killing

The biblical injunction *"Thou Shall Not Murder"* could be interpreted to mean that taking another human being's life is a universal crime. It is not. Such an act is defined differentially in different times and/or cultures (Nettler, 1982; Lester, 1986). Killing other people is not always interpreted as a negative and stigmatized act that is criminalized—it can certainly be interpreted as positive deviance (Ben-Yehuda, 1990b).

The type of rhetorical device that will be used to describe the death of an individual will, first of all, depend on whether we view that death as natural. A natural death would usually be taken to mean that the individual has finished what we may consider his/her natural life span and dies, without any intentional (e.g., suicidal, criminal) or unintentional (e.g., accidental) help from him/herself or another person. Such typical rhetorical devices as "deceased," "passed away," "died in an accident," or simply "died," would be employed in this case.

When death is not defined as "natural," other rhetorical devices are invoked. One very basic distinction in this case is whether the potential victim agreed, or even willed and wished, to die. If the answer to this question is positive, then a small pool of rhetorical devices becomes available. For example, the rhetorical device called "suicide" and its variations (e.g., hara-kiri, kamikaze, *kaitan*), euthanasia (with consent), and the like.

The other possibility is that the potential victim does not agree, or wish, to die. The act of taking the victim's life against his/her wish thus becomes a typically forceful and violent act. Some of the possible rhetorical devices that have been developed and are employed to interpret the act of taking another person's life against his/her will include homicide, infanticide, child homicide, self-defense, blood revenge, genocide, lynching, vendettas, human sacrifices, and duels.

When a situation is defined by using the rhetorical device "war," then taking other humans' life is not only excusable, it is mandatory for so-called "combat soldiers." It is even rewarded by powerful symbols and can be defined as "positive deviance." Hence, under normal combat circumstances, we do not say that a soldier murdered his enemy, or vice versa. Wars, however, do have some rules, and some acts of taking other peoples' life—even in a war situation—may in fact be regarded as murder (e.g., killing prisoners of war).

Characterization of Political Assassinations

There are numerous definitions of political assassinations, and it is evident that defining/characterizing the concept has become a Sisyphian task. Different definitions focus on a range that goes from a specific target to a collective target and from a "prominent" political target to any target. Such an analytical mix is not very useful.[2]

Kirkham, Levy, and Crotty suggest the use of an important and useful term: *assassination events*. The term *event* is useful for two reasons. First, it helps to demarcate the *act* from its *cultural interpretation*, that is, from the rhetorical device used to make a culturally meaningful interpretation of the act. Second, it helps reveal the important distinction between executions and assassinations (see also Ben-Yehuda, 1990c). The concept refers to:

an act that consists of a plotted, attempted or actual, murder of a prominent political figure (elite) by an individual (assassin) who performs this act in other than a governmental role. This definition draws a distinction between political execution and assassination. An execution may be regarded as a political killing, but it is initiated by the organs of the state, while an assassination can always be characterized as an illegal act. (Kirkham, Levy, and Crotty, 1970, Appendix A.)

The next question obviously is what makes a political assassination event a unique form of killing? How is such an event interpreted socially in a way that makes sense to members of particular and relevant cultural symbolic—moral universes? The working definition that I used was:

The characterization of a homicidal event as a political assassination or execution (a state-sponsored and legitimized assassination) is a social construction. It is a rhetorical device that is used to socially construct and interpret (that is, to make a culturally meaningful account) the discriminate, deliberate, intentionally planned, and serious attempt(s), whether successful or not, to kill a specific social actor for political reasons having something to do with the political position (or role) of the victim, his symbolic-moral universe, and with the symbolic-moral universe out of which the assassin(s) act(s). This universe generates the legitimacy and justifications required for the act, which are usually presented in quasi-legal terms. However, decisions to assassinate are typically *not* the result of a fair legal procedure, based on a "due process."

There are some important aspects to this definition. First, it emphasizes the social construction of a particular form of killing. This definition makes political assassination a claim-making activity (Best, 1995). The importance of this approach is that a major claim of the assassins can be interpreted as indicating the existence of an alternative system of justice.

Second, a major and typical problem in this area has been the analytic tendency to blur between the concept of *political assassination* with that of *terrorism* (e.g., see the deliberations of Wardlaw, 1982; Hyams, 1974, pp. 15-17, 166-167; Clutterbuck, 1977, pp. 31, 96). The distinction made here between an act of terrorism and political assassination and execution is very clear: The target of a political assassination plot *is a very specific individual*; the target of terrorism is not. In this way, a magnified (and more sensitive) perspective of this particular phenomenon emerges. It is the death of a particular social actor that the assassin(s) desire(s), and it is that particular person toward whom the gun/bomb/knife is aimed. The assassin would not search for a substitute for that target.

Following the part of the definition of political assassinations that emphasized "whether successful or not," a new typology was developed. The typology focused on the *modus operandi* and on the *political assassination event* itself, regardless of the motivation of the assassin(s). This typology is close to an older typology[3] that suggested that assassinations have two stages: preparation and execution. The typology classifies the cases into *four* different categories. The first two are closer to the preparation stage; the last two are closer to the execution stage.

The first is *"preplanning."* This category includes cases of serious deliberations and discussions of whether to assassinate a specific social actor. The second category is *"planning,"* that is, when the assassination plot passes the preplanning stage, and a decision and commitment to assassinate are made. However, "planning" means that for some reason, the plan was not executed. The third category is *"unsuccessful."* This category includes cases that passed the first two stages but where no assassination, or even physical injury to the victim, was made. The usual reason is technical—e.g., a gun that malfunctioned at the critical moment. The fourth category is *"successful."* This category includes cases that passed the first two stages and culminated in an execution that was either fully successful (victim died) or partially successful (victim wounded).

The degree to which the cases we eventually ended up with in each of the categories above is closer to a "representative sample," or to the "entire universe" of cases varies. The methodology used and the available information in the "preplanning" category makes this category closer to a sample. Not every preplanning is reported, and one may safely assume that this category was probably underreported. The category of "planning" is probably better in terms of reporting, and the one of "unsuccessful" better than "planning," even in the sense that reports of public "unsuccessful" attempts typically appeared in a few independent sources. The category of "successful" is probably closest to represent the entire universe of political assassinations in that category.

Main Findings

Ninety-one cases of political assassination events were found, but only 87 cases were taken into the analysis. Four cases could not be established as bona fide political assassinations (and not mistakes, or terror acts). From these 87 cases, six cases (7%) were in each of the "preplanning" and "planning" categories, 24 cases (28%) in the "unsuccessful" category, and a majority of 51 cases (58%) in the "successful" category. Unless specified otherwise, my use of the label "political assassinations" refers to all subcategories.

In the 1882-1988 period I looked at, the overwhelming majority of political assassination events (close to 90%) took place between 1939 to 1948 and then leveled off again. In only the minority of cases (6%) we have a *single* assassin. In the overwhelming majority of cases (94%) we have an *organized group* behind the assassination event (this conclusion is most certainly valid for cases of political executions as well). The salient groups involved in the assassination events were the main three pre-1948 underground Jewish groups (Hagana, Etzel, and Lehi). The typical case was a premeditated and planned act, committed by a member in a group. It was usually the group that planned the assassination, gave the assassin(s) much-needed moral support and the vocabularies of motives needed to justify and perform the task, and provided the means needed to execute the plan of assassination as well as shelter. In many cases the victim was warned, sometimes more than once.

The Prestate Underground Jewish Groups and Political Assassination Events

The fact that most cases occurred between 1939 and 1948 and that *organizations* were involved in them raises some interesting questions such as *who* were the victims in *symbolic* terms and what was the nature of the process leading to a political assassination event? Exactly who committed the acts? (Table 1).

Table 1
Ethnicity of Victim and Category of Political Assassination Events

Victim's Ethnicity	Category of Political Assassination Event						
	Preplanning	Planning	Unsuccessful	Successful (victim) died	Successful wounded	Total	% of total
Jewish	4	1	10	35	2	52	60%
British	2	2	12	6		22	25%
Arab		3		3	1	7	8%
Other			2	4		6	7%
Total	6	6	24	48	3	87	100%

The fact that *most* victims were Jewish is surprising, especially when we realize that most "successful" cases (in the two categories) involve Jewish victims (73%). The British victim group is also over represented in the "unsuccessful" category (50%). Since most assassinations were committed by the three prestate (1948) Jewish underground groups who boasted of using such tactics as political assassination to help end the British occupation of Palestine (1917-1948), how is one to explain the fact that there were only about 25 percent British victims vis-à-vis 60 percent Jewish victims? Before answering this important question we have to examine more data.

The Reasons Given for Political Assassinations Events—Squealers, Traitors, and Revenge

The claims made by the assassins (the "claim makers," see Best, 1995) ranged from specific and detailed accusations to instances where no specific charges were made, and the "reasons" given were phrased in very broad terms. I tried to divide the "reasons" by the order of frequency in which they were presented. The category "traitor/squealer" was used most frequently (91.2%) in association with Jewish targets. The category "revenge" was used most frequently (63.2%) in association with British targets and 20.4 percent of the time in association with Arab targets.

Thus, the structure and content of the claims made by the groups that were involved in assassinations, implies that these groups justified their assassinations on the ground that they were involved in a struggle for national independence. That struggle necessitated the use of various forms of killings, of non-Jews (as "enemies") and of Jews, too, in an attempt to purify the inner group and redefine its moral boundaries (Ben-Yehuda, 1985). Why were such claims made? What type of a sociological interpretation can we offer for this behavior?

The Main Feature of Claim-making: Treason and Vengeance

The rhetorical devices "traitor," "squealer," "collaborator," and "spy" received special and understandable meaning by the claim makers (see Best, 1995), particularly between 1939 and 1948. The painful slow realization of the Yishuv (Jewish community in Palestine) of what was happening to Jews in Nazi-occupied Europe forced the issue of cooperation with occupation forces to surface in the most powerful way (Palestine, until 1948, was under British occupation). Hence, targeting specific action for assassinations because of "squealing" or of being defined as a "traitor," "collaborator," or "spy" made sense to many contemporaries.

Revenge and vengeance were other very important and central issues. "Revenge is a universal pattern of behavior. It is also an ineradicable feature of our emotional lives ..." (Bar-Elli and Heyd, 1986, p. 68). Revenge and vengeance provide an emotional outlet, and, in situations where it assumes the form of an assassination (or a blood revenge), the potential assassin(s) must think that he/they have indeed suffered a very serious and grave injury and injustice. Here, vengeance becomes a quest for justice in a social ecology that is perceived to be unjust by the potential assassins (see Marongiu and Newman, 1987).

One need not be mislead by the false impression that vengeance and revenge can be reduced to primarily *psychological* issues. As this study and Rieder's discussion (1984) point out, they are, in fact, *systemic* characteristics of many cultures. Underlying vengeance is a very strong moral character, guided by a simple principle of justice that stipulates that symmetry must be restored to what is perceived as an unbalanced situation. Therefore, it is not surprising to find that revenge and vengeance operate according to socially constructed and defined values and norms (and not as a result of some "irrational" psychological and individual motivation). This is a rational, nonemotional reaction, equal in logic to other forms of punishment and social control. As Rieder points our, the wish to retaliate against a perceived injustice points to its logical nature. Thus, the "rationality of vengeance as a method of social control, not its unreasoning ravaging, emerges as one of its striking signatures" (1984, p. 134).

An Integrative Sociological Interpretation: Justice, Vilification, Deviantization, and Strangerization

Alternative System of Justice

Most cases of political assassination events occurred between 1939 and 1948. There were very few cases prior to 1939 and after 1948. Those 1939-1948 fateful years certainly marked a significant intensification of the Jewish efforts (mostly by the three prestate Jewish underground groups) toward political independence. Between 1896 and 1938, a period of 42 years, we have eight cases. Between 1939 and 1948, a period of nine years, we have 73 cases. Between 1949 and 1987, a period of 38 years, we have six cases.

In general terms, between 1930 and 1948 there were three underground Jewish groups with an ideology of direct action. These groups saw themselves as deeply involved in an actual *struggle* with the British and the Arabs for the creation of a new and independent Jewish state. From what we know about other works on underground prestate movements, this particular aspect of political assassinations is universalistic and not culture specific (Kirkham, Levy, and Crotty, 1970).

Taking into consideration the fact that the major "reasons" for the assassinations were that the victim was defined as a traitor/squealer, that revenge and vengeance were involved, the collective nature of the cases and the fact that most victims were Jewish leaves us with almost no choice but to conclude that what we have here is the operation of an interesting system of alternative and popular "justice" (Abel, 1982).

Jacoby (1983) points out that "justice is a legitimate concept in the modern code of civilized behavior. Vengeance is not" (p. 1). Consequently, demanding revenge in our culture must be rephrased in rhetorical devices that will not be understood as simple vengeance. Rather, rhetorical devices that emphasize justice and proneness to future crimes (prevention) are used instead of "vengeance" and "revenge." However, vengeance *has* been a major part of Western civilization and *can* become a chief component in an alternative system of popular justice.

The concept of justice that emerges from this study can be applied to two domains. One domain is focused on conflicts within the Yishuv, the other is focused on conflicts between members and groups in the Yishuv to external groups (e.g., Arabs, British).

The idea of justice and vengeance was also explored by Kirkham, Levy, and Crotty's landmark study (1970). There, among other things, they tried to examine the feelings of injustice on the individual level, as well as the potential rage experienced by different individuals and groups that is produced by living in a politically unjust society (pp. 241-295). "High assassination ... scores are related to political vengeance and that political vengeance is closely tied to the concept of political trust" (pp. 257-258).

Political assassination, as a particular rhetorical device, is invoked as a claim to explain and justify acts that the assassins want to project as a case of "justice" in situations where they felt that they could not get a fair justice because the opportunities for such "justice" were felt to be blocked (see R. Cohen, 1986).

The idea that political assassination events, in the context of this study, can be conceptualized as constituting a tool in an "alternative system of justice," both for insiders and outsiders, is related to other works. The most salient of which are those by Hobsbawm (1959) and others (e.g., Wilson, 1988) and by some British scholars (see S. Cohen, 1986, for a short review) and Crummey (1986). These works, from a different point of view, focus on popular justice and on what Hobsbawm called "Primitive Rebels." In these perspectives, a hard and long look is made at societies with very problematic (and typically biased) formal mechanisms of justice. In such cultures, the rise of various mechanisms to enforce a different type of popular and alternative "justice" can be observed (Robin Hood being *the* example, but there are numerous other examples of banditry and similar forms of "justice," see Kooistra, 1989). On of the central ideas that emerges from this tradition is that "crime under certain conditions serves equivalent functions to such recognized political forms as protest and resistance" (S. Cohen, 1986, p. 470).

Another group of scholars developed a conceptualization that is most definitely related to the above interpretation. These scholars rely on Black's works (1983, 1984a) in the area of social control. Here is how one of them presents the approach (Weisburd, 1989, pp. 5, 10):

> Focusing upon the concept of self-help criminal justice, Black argues that: "There is a sense in which conduct regarded as criminal is often quite the opposite. Far from being an intentional violation of a prohibition, much crime is moralistic and involves the pursuit of justice. It is a mode of conflict management, possibly a form of punishment, even capital punishment. Viewed in relation to law, it is self-help. To the degree that it defines or responds to the conduct of someone else—the victim—as deviant, crime is social control." (1984b, p. 1.)

In a very real sense, all the organizations that are mentioned in this study created a system of social control, in most cases a self-help type of justice followed, and this justice was focused on monitoring the moral boundaries of what these groups considered as the "collective." To some limited extent this conceptualization will apply to cases of political executions as well.

Justice, Collaboration, and Treason

What we have here is an interesting and generalizable, sociological observation, extending beyond the specific claim making activity. We can observe an alternative, popular system of justice that operates on principles of *political* and popular justice and as a powerful system of social control as well. The emergence of this system is within the framework of a struggle for national independence and, hence, within a process of nation building, against what the relevant social actors see as an occupying and alien force. We can most certainly expect to find a similar pattern of political assassinations under similar social conditions.

This is the main reason why the rhetorical devices that were used by the different prestate Jewish underground groups to describe the acts of political assassinations are so meaningful and revealing. The assassins made claims that focused on "individual terror," *hisulim* (eliminations), or "justice to collaborators," expressions that testify that those who utilized them saw themselves as participating in processes of political and popular justice and social control. These processes are obviously aimed at delineating the boundaries of symbolic—moral universes that are perceived to be crucial in a struggle for national independence.

Nettler's perception of this issue was indeed illuminating: "Killing for justice translates homicide as "execution" rather than as "murder." This is a translation that appeals to groups that regard themselves as legitimate possessors of moral authority. Thus both governments in power and revolutionary challengers of that power refer to their killing of enemies as homicides rationalized by their sense of justice, a sense that fluctuates between demands for revenge, retribution, deterrence, and submission" (1982, p. 201).

The "justice" that was operating here was based on some information, sometimes on "confessions," and on command/administrative decisions. In such a system, the potential victim did not stand much of a chance to "prove his innocence." This is a system of justice that is based on negotiated claims, hearsay, partial information, and on social constructions of "guilt," "collaboration," "treason," and "vengeance."

The issue of the "collaborators" ("Shtinkers" in the prevailing intelligence slang) is interesting and important. The subject that hides behind this issue is that of treason. Treason implies betraying one's commitment and loyalty to a particular symbolic—moral universe and violating the trust relationships that emerge from such a commitment. This is conceptualized as an almost universal "crime" by most cultures and punished very severely (e.g., see Ploscowe, 1935; Hurst, 1983).

A relevant question here relates to the position of Judaism regarding "collaborators" and political assassination. Squealers and collaborators are called in the Jewish tradition *Moser* ("giver" in Hebrew), or *Masor*. Living for many years in the *Galut* (diaspora), squealers could become very dangerous for the well-being and survival of a persecuted minority. Such an expression as "there shall be no hope for the squealers" became very relevant. It seems that the consensus was that, if someone was known as a squealer, that person had to be killed *before* he/she actually squealed (there is an argument whether a warning was to be delivered or not). It must be emphasized that a *suspicion* of squealing was not enough. Proof had to be presented. Assassinating a squealer was justified on the ground that this act was meant as saving many others who were in danger because of the squealing.

As can be inferred, deciding who exactly was a dangerous squealer and why was not a simple matter. However, this was perceived as a preventive measure. Once a damaging squealing *was* in fact committed, a punishment was called for. That was a totally different issue because to do that a legitimate court had to be established, with an authority to pass a death sentence. The Jewish tradition is characterized by a very strong reluctance to pass death sentences, and there are very severe limitations on passing such a sentence. Furthermore, in only some very rare occasions Jewish courts *had* the authority to pass a death sentence. However, there were a few cases of squealers who were executed (see, e.g., Eisenstein, 1951).[4]

While Jewish planners of political assassination events could use the above justifications to defend decisions to assassinate those that they felt were squealers—they typically did not. With the exception of the 30 June 1924 assassination of Dr. Ya'acov De Hahn in Jerusalem,[5] we did not find any serious or meaningful references to the Jewish *Halacha* (Jewish legal codes on law and customs) in justifications of political assassinations. This could be due to four reasons. One, that those involved in the assassinations did not know the relevant *Halacha*. Second, that they knew the relevant *Halacha* but since they also knew that they were not acting according to the *Halacha*, they did not rely on it. Third, it is also possible that the early attempt to rely on the *Halacha* in the De Hahn case in 1924 and the criticisms that followed, indicated that reliance on the *Halacha* could not be used to justify the assassinations of suspected "squealers." Finally, the three prestate underground organizations and the ones that were involved in assassinations and executions after 1948 (with one possible exception) viewed themselves primarily as secular—political, not religious, organizations. As such, it would not be reasonable or logical for them to justify acts of political assassinations on *Halachic* grounds.

Vilification, Deviantization, and Strangerization

Most pre-1948 assassinations were committed by the three main prestate underground Jewish groups, and most victims were Jews. This result is quite surprising. These groups, especially Lehi, boast of fighting the Arabs and of helping (and even causing) to drive the British occupation forces out of Palestine by their acts. How could so much lethal aggression and deadly force that was directed against members of the "in" group accomplish that?

There are two superficial, and one more profound, answers for the above puzzle. One key to solve this puzzle lies with the fact that political assassinations are *discriminate*. The three prestate underground Jewish groups assassinated *many* more Arabs and British by indiscriminatory terrorism acts than Jews. Hence, the narrow focus on the rather specific and discriminate political assassination events should not cloud the overall picture. Another, and most evident, answer is that it was much easier, technically, to gather information about and assassinative unprotected members of the "in group."

A third symbolic reason requires a prior discussion about political assassination events generally. The real puzzle here is why was political assassination chosen as a route to begin with, as Cullen's (1983) work put it. The answer to this question is, necessarily, a functional one. It is that, from the point of view of those involved, they simply *had no other choice*. As we could see, the overwhelming majority of political assassination events revolved around very bitter arguments regarding the nature of the boundaries of symbolic-moral universes. The nature of the arguments was such that a physical liquidation and annihilation of the adversary seemed to the relevant actors as the only route possible. Furthermore, for Lehi, the group that was *most* active and involved in political assassination events, that was a major *modus operandi*. In this context one may even reverse the question—why were there so *few* political assassination events? The answer is that the Etzel and Hagana simply restrained their members, and Lehi *was* a rather small group. The decision to be involved in political assassination events was a deliberate, intentional, and planned course of action. Interpreting the choice of the more specific target—Jews, can now be attempted.

Indiscriminate terrorism is aimed at the "stranger" à la Simmel (1971, pp. 143-150): the one who is physically close but mentally and socially very far away. The British and the Arabs could be easily defined as strangers. No discrimination was required against those who were perceived as alien strangers because "they," the strangers, could and were defined as "enemies." Thus, with some reservations and exceptions, aggression and deadly force could be unleashed against them virtually indiscriminately.

However, one could not simply define all of the "in group" as enemies, hence, discriminate political assassinations became a major way of dealing with what was regarded and perceived as severe threats to the symbolic-moral boundaries of those in the "in group." Once treason was suspected, the rhetorical devices, "traitor," "squealers," "cooperator," were all invoked and served to mark the boundaries of what was permitted and acceptable and what not, in a degrading and stigmatizing process of vilification, focused on reputation making. This process made loyalties, commitments, and the nature of trust very clear. Those from the "in group" that were defined as deviant in this social context were obviously portrayed as presenting a grave and a most serious threat for the integrity of the symbolic-moral universe of those in it.

The process that works here, if we are to adhere to the Simmelian terminology, may perhaps be called "strangerization," that is, turning someone in the near and "in" group into a stranger. When this process is accompanied by parallel processes of stigmatization and deviantization (Schur, 1980), then the end product may be a "stranger," deviantized, stigmatized, and despised. Not being part of the "in" group any more, perhaps a different (and dangerous) human being (sometimes to the point of being totally dehumanized), makes killing such a person easier. This process gains importance in a culture that is in a struggle to assert itself in a revolutionary process and where the different and individual members of that culture may not be sure where their loyalty lies.

The vocabularies of motives and the rhetorical devices that were frequently used in the "strangerization" process were words such as "squealer," "spy," "traitor," "cooperator with the enemy." Such devices, regardless of their validity, could open the way to take the life of the actors against which the expressions were used. These rhetorical devices structured the deviantization process and helped to construct the social reality in which these deviants became defined as outsiders, pariahs—in short, aliens like the British and the Arabs only morally worse.[6]

The Pattern Before and After 1948

The most salient feature of assassinations before and after 1948 is the dramatic decline in the frequency of cases after 1948, when the state of Israel was formally established. Only eight cases (9.2% of all the cases) took place after 1948. Three of the cases occurred in the 1950s, and the rest are dispersed from 1967 to 1980. It is evident, therefore, that once the state of Israel was established in 1948, there was a significant drop in the frequency and vigor of political assassination events. This is also the period when we have three cases of lone attackers and potential assassins. In the rest of the cases, we had again a group involved.

How are we to explain the dramatic fact that after the state of Israel was formally established in 1948 the incidence of political assassination events declined very sharply and significantly? With the establishment of the state of Israel in 1948 the establishment and institutionalization of two very important national systems took place: the system of justice and the political system. Through these two systems the different groups, representing different symbolic-moral universes could, after a relatively short period of adjustment, find a fair, open outlet—within formal and public new "rules of the game," for their views, wishes, and values. Thus, the "need" for an alternative system of justice vanished to a very large degree, causing the sharp decline in the prevalence of the cases. This obviously did not just happen in one day. The 1950s witnessed this stormy and problematic passage. Furthermore, when, in the late 1970s and early 1980s, a group of young and militant actors felt that they were not getting the type of justice they expected to get from the state of Israel, they organized a direct action group—the "Jewish underground" (see Segal, 1987; and Weisburd, 1981; see also endnote #6 discussing Rabin's assassination).

In ordinary situations and states, we may have two types of alternative systems. One type consists of systems that claim the state has *failed* to do something and so a pretense to complement, or rectify, the failure is presented as the "reason" for the existence of the alternative system (e.g., the "Jewish underground"). Another possible alternative system may emerge as *antagonistic* to the state. These systems would emerge more rapidly in situations where the authority of the state itself is unclear. The Hagana, Etzel, and Lehi could not claim that the British authorities did not help, or that their authority was not clear. They created antagonistic systems to the British colonial rule.

While, in general terms, the pattern of political assassination events (and executions) throughout the period from 1882 to 1988 is quite consistent, there is one important difference between the pre-1948 period and the post-1948 period. To the extent that after 1948 there were cases of political assassination events committed by *groups*, in most cases these were groups whose description was closer to groups of *vigilantes*, that is, groups who resorted to the use of violence in order to preserve the order that they felt should have prevailed. The pre-1948 groups in Palestine were *revolutionary* groups whose use of violence was aimed to overthrow the British occupation forces. In both cases, however, a system of popular justice and control was in operation (see Karmen, 1983).

The one new development that took place after 1948 was that of state-sponsored political executions (most of them probably outside of Israel) of which we have very little and scarce information. This development, however, had a fertile seed bed from which it grew. As far as we know, state-sponsored political executions were *not* aimed at members of the "in group," an observation that sets the pattern of state-sponsored political execution in a different category than political assassination. The fact that most political executions about which we know were primarily committed as acts of revenge and vengeance fits the pattern of political assassinations that we found.

Some Comparisons: Prevalence and Generalizability

The *prevalence* of political assassinations by Jews in Palestine and Israel is not very high compared to some other cultures (e.g., in some South American societies, where there were so-called "assassination squads;" or in some Muslim Mediterranean societies). This conclusion is not changed much by what we know about state-sponsored political executions.

Ninety-one cases of political assassination events were recorded in a time span of almost a century, from the 1890s until 1988. If we take into consideration only the "successful" cases, then the figure drops to 51. We were able to locate about ten probable cases of state-sponsored political executions, but there can be no doubt that there were probably quite a few more cases. The cases of state-sponsored political executions do not really change the conclusions.

Making meaningful comparisons requires a glimpse at three clusters of relevant events. First, it was estimated that during the so called "Arab Revolt" in Palestine between 1936 and 1939 the number of Arab casualties was around 6,000. Only 1,500 died as a result of British or Jewish activities, and the major bulk of about 4,500 victims died as a result of the internal terror among different Arab groups (Arnon-Ochana, 1982, pp. 139-140; Eshed, 1988, pp. 55-56). Second, between 1980 and 1986, a period of seven years there were about 23 cases of Arabs assassinating other Arabs, in the same political, target specific, context, in the Israeli-occupied West Bank and Gaza Strip (see *Ha'aretz*, 3 March 1986, front page). The Arab *Intifada* (uprising) began in the Israeli-occupied West Bank and the Gaza strip in December 1987. Between this time and 1990, around 200 Arabs were assassinated by other Arabs.

The second cluster of relevant events must be searched outside the local area. Unfortunately, it is very difficult to find a study like this one in other cultures, hence finding empirical information for a meaningful comparative perspective is not an easy undertaking. However, the available information indicates that similar systems of "justice" against collaborators were utilized by other underground groups under similar conditions. Hence, this type of system was utilized by the French resistance during World War II (the Maquis) and by the Kenyan Kikuyu Mau Mau. One conservative appraisal estimates that the Mau Mau killed about 11,500 Kikuyu and only about 95 Europeans, showing again that most of the lethal aggression was directed toward members of the in—group (Rosberg and Nottingham, 1966, p. 303). Political assassinations of those who were defined by such rhetorical devices as "traitors," "squealers," "politically and ideologically dangerous opponents" characterized the activities of *Catechism* in the second half of the 19th century Russia (including a secret student organization that called itself *Narodnaya Rasprova*, meaning "The People's Revenge") (Gaucher, 1968, pp. 3-27); the struggle in Macedonia (and the involvement of the I.M.R.O.) at the beginning of the 20th century (Gaucher, 1968, pp. 155-173; Ford, 1985, pp. 259-260); the infamous Iron Guard (the military section of the Rumanian fascist movement called the Legion of St Michael) in Bucharest (Gaucher, 1968, pp. 140-152; Ford, 1985, p. 268); some of the unrest in Germany during the 1920s (Gaucher, 1968, pp. 128-130); and the activities of the F.L.N. and O.A.S. in Algiers in the 1950s and 1960s (Guacher, 1968, pp. 238-239, 260-264). Obviously, the underground groups in Northern Ireland utilized a similar system of justice as well (e.g., see Clutterbuck, 1977, pp. 62-65; Corfe, 1984; and Alexander and O'Day, 1984, pp. 21-22 who imply that the IRA even "occasionally obtained the services of professional assassins"). Similarly, Ford reports that: "by February 1972 ... a group of die-hards [from the Japanese Red Army] were surrounded in an abandoned hotel at Karuizawa ... When the Karuizawa 'fortress' was stormed by police, the bodies of fourteen defenders were found already dead, killed as deviationists by the survivors in what one writer has described as 'an orgy of self-purification'" (1985, p. 310; quote is from Dobson and Payne, 1977, pp. 187-191).

Clark (1986) points out that out of 696 attacks that were carried out by the Basque ETA (Euzkadi Ta Askatasuna) between 1968 and 1980, 49.8 percent were aimed at an individual target (1986, p. 132). Furthermore, Clark also notes that out of 287 dead victims as a result of ETA assaults, 5.6 percent were killed as "spies" or "informers" (that is, about 2.3% out of *all* of ETA assaults for the above years) (1986, pp. 136, 138). Interestingly enough, the term Clark uses for these killings is "executions," and only about 16 members (at least three of which were ETA members) were killed in this way. The typical charge against them was that they gave information to the police. As in my study, Clark notes that the *only* source that these 16 people were "traitors" comes from ETA sources. In almost *all* the cases, families of the victims denied the allegations and demanded open and public evidence (1986, p. 138). The type of work done by Clark is quite rare, and, despite our efforts, we could not locate other and similar works on this particular issue.

Other, more impressionistic, sources also tend to corroborate the above observations. This pattern exists in some South American countries; as noted, it also existed during the Arab revolt in Palestine between 1936 and 1939 when thousands of Arabs were killed by other Arabs (e.g., see *Davar*, 21 November 1938; Arnon-Ochana, 1982, pp. 139-140), and this pattern emerged again when, from December 1987, Arabs in the Israeli-occupied West Bank and Gaza strip began their *Intifada* (uprising) and continued to assassinate other Arabs (see also *The New York Times*, 12 November 1989, p. 1, on a similar phenomenon within Abu Nidal terror group).[7] In all these cases we can observe the unleashing of lethal forces mostly against actors from the "in group."

It also seems that even in a somewhat different context the idea of "justice" is brought by assassins to justify their act—from their point of view. For example, John Wilkins Booth, assassin of President Abraham Lincoln (14 April 1865), thought of himself as the hand of justice eliminating a "tyrant" (Ford, 1985, p. 353). Evidently, Nathuram V. Godse, the Hindu newspaper editor and the assassin of Mohandas K. Gandhi (30 January 1948), and the group with him, also felt that they were involved in some sort of a process of justice against Gandhi (Ford, 1985, p. 296; Lentz, 1988, p. 120).

Clearly, the two clusters of relevant events mentioned above indicate that a universal pattern exists here. Assassinations mark, in an unequivocal way, the symbolic-moral boundaries of the group as well as cleanse and purify the group from what it evidently views as dirt (see Douglas, 1966, and Scott, 1972), that is, from those that are defined as internal enemies. Thus, the pattern of political assassination events we observed, in depth, in this study is generalizable to other cultures as well.

Before concluding this section, there is a third set of relevant information that should be taken to support this conclusion. This set is focused on state-sponsored political assassinations. That countries send assassins to kill specific persons is a well-established fact. These assassins can be part of a secret intelligence unit, or be part of a military unit. The first of two famous cases was the assassination attempt of Leon Trotsky on 20 August 1940 (he died the next day) by a Stalinist agent in Mexico. The assassin—Ramon Mercader (using the name Frank Jackson)—was caught and served 20 years in a Mexican prison. He was later designated as a hero of the Soviet Union (Lentz, 1988, pp. 78-79). Second, the killing of fleet admiral Isoruku Yamamoto, planner of the Japanese attack on Pearl Harbor (7 December 1941). Yamamoto's flight plan was intercepted by U.S. intelligence, and, while he was flying over the Solomon Islands in a Betty bomber, he was ambushed by a squadron of P-38 Lightning flighters (led by Maj. John W. Mitchell), shot down, and killed (18 April 1943). One of the reasons Glines gives for this assassination is: "The opportunity to shoot down Yamamoto in retaliation for Japanese cruelty was a rare one that could not be lost" (1993, p. 10). Ford (1985, ch. 12) mentions a few more cases. After the establishment of the state of Israel 1948, there is little doubt that its secret service was involved in assassinations outside of Israel (see Ben-Yehuda, 1993, ch. 9). Some of the more famous cases involve planning to assassinate former Egyptian president, Gamal Abdul Nasser (in 1956); attempts to kill German missile technicians working for Egypt during 1962 to 1965; various assassination plots against Palestinian terrorists/guerrillas, the most famous of which is the systematic pursuit of those believed to be involved in the massacre of members of the Israeli Olympic team during the Munich Olympic games in September 1972. All governments seek to conceal their political execution plots. Certainly, information regarding political executions constitutes hidden, dark, and discrediting information. Thus, it is virtually impossible to gather inclusive and reliable information about this particular form of killing. From the scare publications available, it is clear that Israel's external secret service ("Mossad") must have had an assassination unit, and, clearly, the Israeli army had units who where involved in killings of specific figures. From the cases we have, both for Israel and other countries, the conclusion that these killings indicate an alternative system of justice (certainly from the point of view of those ordering the killings) is reinforced. Those ordering and justifying the acts felt as if they were "settling a score" with victims that could not have been brought to trial otherwise.

Summary

This paper suggests that political assassination events (including state-sponsored assassinations) can be interpreted sociologically as an alternative and popular system of justice. We can easily view this form of killing within the conceptual context of conflict resolution.

It is argued that political assassinations are a specified social construction of a homicide event. Examining all the cases that could be counted as such between 1882 and 1988 in Palestine and Israel by Jews yielded a list of 87 confirmed cases within the cultural matrix that was studied. The findings indicate that most assassination events involved organized groups as initiators. These groups were characterized by particular symbolic-moral universes. Hence, one of the hallmarks of the pattern of political assassination events that emerges from this analysis is the fact that they are organized, collective, political assassination events. An obvious majority of the cases were committed by the three main prestate Jewish underground groups—Hagana, Etzel, and Lehi.

Most political assassination events were directed against other Jews who were characterized by the assassins as "traitors" or "squealers." Another typical "reason" for assassination events was "revenge." Going beyond the subjective claims, we concluded that political assassination events, as particular rhetorical devices within the context of a claim making activity, were invoked to explain and justify acts that seemed like "justice" to the assassins, in situations where they felt that they could not get a fair justice because the opportunities for such "justice" were felt to be blocked. It is as if an alternative system of "justice" was put into operation. Once a formal system of "justice"—political and legal—was established when the state of Israel was created in 1948, the frequency of political assassination events dropped dramatically.

The fact that a majority of the targets were Jews was explained by interpreting these events as markers of boundaries of symbolic-moral universes in a period of a deep and severe crisis and struggle over the very nature of the emerging and crystallizing Jewish state and, hence, of a new and secular culture as well as of forming new collective and personal identities. We used Simmel's concept of the "stranger" and Schur's concept of deviantization to argue that a political assassination event directed against another Jew involved a process of "strangerization" and "deviantization" of that Jew. A group provided the social context in which such a process could take place, as well as its legitimization.

This study focuses on the meaning of political assassinations in one culture within the comparative context of other cultures and similar conditions. The data presented in this study bring us to conclude that such alternative systems of justice as the one described here have a strong cross-cultural existence. Conceptualizing political assassinations by individuals, groups or governments, within an interesting system of alternative justice is a fruitful and promising way of looking at such events. The potential research agenda that is implied by this conceptualization lies in three main directions. The first is to look at such events in cultures not studied so far using this conceptualization. Second, an expansion of the concept of "justice" to include such violent acts as assassinations, within informal and alternative systems of justice. Third, the importance of understanding the rhetorical devices and justifications used by such a system (as contrasted by the facts) is a major factor to take into consideration when analyzing assassinations through the analytical prism suggested here.

NOTES

1 This paper is based on, and continues, some of my previous works, and particularly 1985, 1990a. It is mostly based on my 1993 book. I am grateful to the Israeli Foundations Trustees, whose research contract no. 86-01-007 funded the research on which this paper is based, and to the helpful comments offered by Gideon Aran, Zali Gurevitz, Cyril Levitt, Dennis L. Peck, Hagit Rosenfeld, and Ehud Shprinzak. Gratitude is to Einat Usant and Vered Vinitzky-Seroussi whose assistance made this effort possible.

2 For some of the prevalent definitions see Lerner (1930, p. 27); Kirkham, Levy, and Crotty (1970, p. 1); Padover (1943, p. 680); Havens, Leiden, and Schmitt (1970, pp. 2-6); Hurwood (1970, p. 1); Crotty (1971, p. 8); Lester (1986, p. 216); Ford (1985, p. 2); Ivianski (1977, p. 50; 1981, p. 409); Turk (1983, p. 83); Rapoport (1971, p. 4). See also Ben-Yehuda (1990c).

3 Probably developed originally by Machiavelli. For a discussion of this issue see Rapoport (1971, pp. 12-22).

4 I am deeply grateful for the help and guidance of Dr. Berachyahu Lifshitz, from the faculty of law, Hebrew University, whose assistance in this particular issue was indispensable.

5 Where some reference was made to Jewish sources on what to do to squealers, see Nakdimon and Mayzlish (1985, pp. 194-195) and Meshi-Zahav and Meshi-Zahav (1985, pp. 242-243).

6 Although Prime Minister Rabin's November 4, 1995 assassination by Yigal Amir clearly falls outside the time limits of the study reported here, it is virtually impossible to ignore it. Briefly, let me only state that in almost all the important aspects, the assassination of Yitzhak Rabin does not deviate from the pattern of political assassination events discussed in this paper. As in the other cases, the killing of Rabin had a strong political-ideological background—Rabin was hit because of his political position, power and acts. This assassination was committed from a distinct, planned and carefully premeditated intention, and not from any momentary rage. Assassinating Rabin was the end product of a long process that Amir was going through. This process did not only provide the context within which Amir was persuaded that Rabin was to be killed, but it was also the context which provided Amir with the rhetoric of justification that he, Amir, was to do it. As in other cases, this assassination was committed by an individual belonging to the same ethnic, or cultural, group as that of the victim, that is a Jew killing another Jew. As in the other cases, the assassin was a member of a group. In this context we must make a distinction between two groups. The first one is the small and immediate group within which Amir interacted intensely. This rather small group was immersed in the subculture of a much larger political, religious and ideological group from which this small group drew its legitimation, inspiration, ideas, and the powerful rhetorical and psychological devices with which it interpreted and shaped its world view in a very specific way. However, the assassination of Rabin constitutes one very important and significant deviation from the other assassinations found in the study and that is, the nature of the target. In the history of political assassinations by Jews in Palestine and Israel, from at least the end of the last century till the late years of the twentieth century, no Jewish target on the magnitude of Yitzhak Rabin was hit. Would this assassination serve as a warning signal, not to be repeated, or will it pave the way for other such killings is a question which cannot be answered at the moment. Suffice it to state that the political, social, and ideological potential for additional such cases most certainly exists.

7 As noted, the estimation is that since the "Intifada" began in 1987 and until November 1993, 771 to 942 Palestinians were assassinated by either Palestinians on "charges" of "collaboration" or "cooperation" (some of the victims were interrogated and tortured before they were killed). At least around 573 others were severely beaten and/or targeted for unsuccessful assassinations, and there may have been a few cases of brutal group rape (Shalev, 1990; Amnesty International, 1989; Schiff and Ya'ari, 1990; Shaked, Broida, and Regev, 1990; B'Tselem, 1994).

REFERENCES

ABEL, Richard L., ed.

1982 *The Politics of Informal Justice.* 2 vols. New York: Academic Press.

ALEXANDER, Yonah, and Alan O'DAY, eds

1984 *Terrorism in Ireland.* London: Croom Helm.

AMNESTY INTERNATIONAL

1989 Amnesty International Report (November). London: Amnesty International.

ARNON-OCHANA, Yuval

1982 *Falachs in the Arab Revolt in Eretz Israel 1936-1939.* Tel Aviv: Tel Aviv University, Papirus (Hebrew).

BAR-ELLI, Gilead, and David HEYD

1986 "Can Renvenge Be Just or Otherwise not Justified?" *Theoria* 21 (1-2): 68-86.

BEN-YEHUDA, Nachman

1985 *Deviance and Moral Boundaries.* Chicago: University of Chicago Press.

1990a *The Politics and Morality of Deviance.* Albany: State University of New York Press.

1990b "Positive and Negative Deviance: More Fuel for a Controversy." *Deviant Behavior* 11: 221-243.

1990c "Political Assassinations as Rhetorical Devices: Events and Interpretations." *Journal of Terrorism and Political Violence* 2 (3): 324-350.

1990d "Gathering Dark Secrets, Hidden and Dirty Information: Some Methodological Notes on Studying Political Assassinations." *Qualitative Sociology* 13 (4): 345-372.

1993 *Political Assassinations by Jew.* Albany: State University of New York Press.

BEST, Joel, ed.

1995 *Images of Issues: Typifying Contemporary Social Problems.* 2d ed. New York: Aldine de Gruyter.

BLACK, Donald

1983 "Crime as Social Control." *American Sociological Review* 43: 34-45.

1984a *Toward a General Theory of Social Control.* 2 vols. New York: Academic Press.

1984b "Crime as Social Control." Pp. 1-27 in: *Toward a General Theory of Social Control*, vol. 2, edited by Donald Black. New York: Academic Press.

B'TSELEM

1994 Collaborators in the Territories During the Intifada: Violations of Human Rights (January). Jerusalem: B'Tselem (Hebrew).

CLARK, Robert P.

1986 "Patterns of ETA Violence: 1968-1980." Pp. 123-141 in: *Political Violence and Terror. Motifs and Motivation*, edited by Peter H. Merkl. Berkeley and Los Angeles: University of California Press.

CLUTTERBUCK, Richard

1977 *Guerrillas and Terrorists.* London: Faber and Faber.

COHEN, Ronald, ed.

1986 *Justice: Views from the Social Sciences.* New York: Plenum Press.

COHEN, Stanley

1986 "Bandits, Rebels or Criminals: African History and Western Criminology (Review Article)." *Africa* 56 (4): 468-483.

CORFE, Tom

1984 "Political Assassination in the Irish Tradition." Pp. 106-120 in: *Terrorism in Ireland*, edited by Y. Alexander and A. O'Day. London: Croom Helm.

CROTTY, William J., ed.
  1971 *Assassinations and the Political Order.* New York: Harper and Row.
CRUMMEY, Donald, ed.
  1986 *Banditry, Rebellion and Social Protest in Africa.* London: James Currey.
CULLEN, Francis T.
  1983 *Rethinking Crime and Deviance Theory.* Totowa, N.J.: Rowman and Allanheld.
DOBSON, C., and Ronald PAYNE
  1977 *The Carlos Complex: A Study in Terror.* London: Coronet Books/Hodder and Stoughton.
DOUGLAS, Mary
  1966 *Purity and Danger.* London and Henley: Routledge and Kegan Paul.
EISENSTEIN, Yehuda David
  1951 *Ozar Israel: An Encyclopedia of all Matters Concerning Jews and Judaism.* New York: Pardes Publishing (Hebrew).
ESHED, Haggai
  1988 *One Man "Mossad." Reuven Shiloach: Father of Israeli Intelligence.* Jerusalem: Edanim Publishers, Yediot Aharonot Edition (Hebrew).
FORD, Franklin L.
  1985 *Political Murder from Tyrannicide to Terrorism.* Cambridge: Harvard University Press.
GAUCHER, Roland
  1968 *The Terrorists from Tsarist Russia to the O.A.S.* London: Secker and Warburg.
GLINES, Carroll V.
  1993 *Attack on Yamamoto.* Atglen, Penn.: Schiffer Military History.
HAVENS, Murray C., Carl LEIDEN, and Karl M. SCHMITT
  1970 *The Politics of Assassination.* Englewood Cliffs, N.J.: Prentice-Hall.
HOBSBAWM, E.J.
  1959 *Primitive Rebels.* Manchester: Manchester University Press.
HURST, James Willard
  1983 "Treason." Pp. 1559-1562 in: *Encyclopedia of Crime and Jsutice,* edited by Sanford H. Kadish. New York: Free Press.
HURWOOD, Bernhardt J.
  1970 *Society and the Assassin.* New YOrk: Parents' Magazine Press.
HYAMS, Edward
  1974 *Terrorists and Terrorism.* New York: St. Martin's Press.
IVIANSKI, Ze'ev
  1977 "Individual Terror: Concept and Typology." *Journal of Contemporary History* 12: 43-63.
  1981 "Individual Terror." Pp. 409-414 in: *Encyclopedia of Social Sciences*, vol. 6, edited by David Kna'ni. Tel Aviv: Al Hamishmar (Hebrew).
JACOBY, Susan
  1983 *Wild Justice: The Evolution of Revenge.* New York: Harper and Row.
KARMEN, Andrew A.
  1983 "Vigilantism." Pp. 1616-1618 in: *Encyclopedia of Crime and Justice*, edited by Sanford H. Kadish. New York: Free Press.
KIRKHAM, James F., Sheldon G. LEVY, and William J. CROTTY, eds
  1970 *Assassination and Political Violence.* New York: Praeger Publishers.
KOOISTRA, Paul
  1989 *Criminals as Heroes: Structure, Power and Identity.* Bowling Green, Ohio: Bowling Green State University Popular Press.

LENTZ, Harris M.
 1988 *Assassinations and Executions.* Jefferson, N.C.: McFarland and Company.
LERNER, Max
 1930 "Assassination." P. 27 in: *Encyclopedia of the Social Sciences,* vol. 2, edited by Edwin
  Seligman. New York: MacMillan Company.
LESTER, David
 1986 *The Murderer and His Murder.* New York: AMS Press.
MARONGIU, Pietro, and Graeme NEWMAN
 1987 *Vengeance: The Fight Against Injustice.* Totowa, N.J.: Rowman and Littlefield.
MESHI-ZAHAV, Zvi, and Yehuda MESHI-ZAHAV
 1985 *De Hahn: The First Zionist Murder in Eretz Israel.* Jerusalem: Institute of the Jewish
  Haredim (Hebrew).
NAKDIMON, Shlomo, and Shaul MAYZLISH
 1985 *De Haan: The First Political Assassination in Palestine.* Tel Aviv: Modan (Hebrew).
NETTLER, Gwynn
 1982 *Killing One Another: Criminal Careers.* Vol. 2. Cincinnati, Ohio: Anderson Publishing
  Company.
PADOVER, Saul K.
 1943 "Patterns of Assassination in Occupied Territory." *Public Opinion Quarterly* 7: 680-693.
PLOSCOWE, Morris
 1935 "Treason." Pp. 93-96 in: *Encyclopedia of the Social Sciences,* edited by Edwin R.A. Selig-
  man and Alvin Johnson. New York: Macmillan.
RAPOPORT, David C.
 1971 *Assassination and Terrorism.* Toronto: Canadian Publishing Corporation.
RIEDER, Jonathan
 1984 "The Social Organization of Vengeance." Pp. 131-162 in: *Toward A General Theory of
  Social Control,* edited by Donald Black. New York: Academic Press.
ROSBERG, Carl, and John NOTTINGHAM
 1966 *The Myth of "Mau Mau": Nationalism in Kenya.* New York: Praeger.
SCHIFF, Ze'ev, and Ehud YA'ARI
 1990 Tel Aviv: Schocken Publishing House, Ltd. (Hebrew).
SCHUR, Edwin M.
 1980 *The Politics of Deviance.* Englewood Cliffs, N.J.: Prentice-Hall.
SCOTT, Robert A.
 1972 "A Proposed Framework for Analyzing Deviance as a Property of Social Order." Pp. 9-36
  in: *Theoretical Perspectives on Deviance,* edited by R.A. Scott and J.D. Douglas. New York:
  Basic Books.
SEGAL, Haggai
 1987 *Dear Brothers.* Jerusalem: Keter (Hebrew).
SHAKED, Roni, Haim BROIDA, and David REGEV
 1990 "Yesterday the 200th Victim from the Beginning of the Intifada Was Murdered by Reulei
  Panim." *Yediot Aharonot* (March 22) (Hebrew).
SHALEV, Aryeh
 1990 *The Intifada Causes and Effects.* Tel Aviv: Papirus and the Institute for Strategic Studies,
  University of Tel Aviv (Hebrew).
SIMMEL, Georg
 1971 *On Individuality and Social Form.* Edited by Donald Levine. Chicago: University of Chicago
  Press.

TURK, Austin
  1983 "Assassination." Pp. 82-88 in: *Encyclopedia of Crime and Justice*, Sanford H. Kadish. New York: Free Press.
WAGNER-PACIFICI, Robin Erica
  1986 *The Moro Morality Play: Terrorism as Social Drama.* Chicago: University of Chicago Press.
WARDLAW, Grant
  1982 *Political Terrorism.* New York: Cambridge University Press.
WEISBURD, David
  1981 "Vigilantism as Rational Social Control: The Case of Gush Emunim Settlers." Pp. 69-87 in: *Cross-currents in Israeli Culture and Politics*, edited by M.J. Aronoff. New Brunswick: Transaction Books.
  1989 *Jewish Settler Violence: Deviance as Social Reaction.* University Park: Pennsylvania State University Press.
WILKINSON, Doris Y., ed.
  1976 *Social Structure and Assassination Behavior.* Cambridge, Mass.: Schenkman Publishing Company.
WILSON, Stephen
  1988 *Feuding, Conflict and Banditry in Nineteenth-century Corsica.* New York: Cambridge University Press.

The State of Injustice

The Politics of Terrorism and the Production of Order[1]

ANNAMARIE OLIVERIO*

ABSTRACT

The construct of terrorism, as it is used in contemporary research and media texts, emerges from 18th- and 19th-century orthodox assumptions of man, nation-state, and political sovereignty. In this paper, terrorism is examined as a discursive process in the art of statecraft from a sociological, comparative perspective. The discursive processes of two ostensible cultures of terrorism are compared: the United States and Italy. The analysis reveals the inextricable link between terrorism, statecraft, and the production of domination, injustice, and social order. It is a practice that privileges rhetorical language over direct experience. The value of analyzing terrorism as the product of a historically produced political discourse rather than as an essential human expression is that it has the potential to be replaced by a more heuristic construct.

Introduction

THE MODERN STATE appears to be indispensable to economic development, social security, and liberty as well as life and death through its creation and control of violence via increasingly sophisticated forms of weaponry and surveillance. Yet, relatively little scholarly attention has been devoted to the relationship between the politics of the state, the politics of terrorism, and the production of injustice in the world (Durkheim, 1948; Weber, 1958; Marx, 1967; Gramsci, 1971; Foucault, 1972, 1979; Tilly, 1985). Terrorism is currently defined and widely understood as a particular type of politically motivated violence challenging the authority of the state and spreading fear among innocent victims. Terrorism is blamed for the senseless killing of humans, the wasting of energy and money, and the destabilizing of economies and governments. Terrorism is often considered to be the "cause" of worldwide instability (Wilkinson, 1990; Eitzen and Zinn, 1994). The media bombard our senses and sensibilities with daily reports on various forms of violent

*   Department of Sociology, Stanford University, Stanford, CA 94305, U.S.A.

crime threatening society's sense of morality and justice; yet, violence defined as terrorism is viewed as particularly horrific.

The contemporary conceptual understanding of terrorism emerged during the late 18th and 19th century. It therefore includes the historical and philosophical referents of that time such as orthodox assumptions of "man," nation-state, and political sovereignty (Stehr, 1994). Despite the obvious anachronism of the late 18th- and 19th-century intellectual thought about the state, these views continue to dominate in contemporary knowledge and politics related to terrorism. Carnoy (1984, p. 4) notes that: "the issue of the State has become much more complex, and with this increased complexity, we need theories that deal with it adequately and accurately." Some sociologists have attempted to more precisely define and overcome some of the conceptual problems as well as ideological biases related to research on terrorism. In his theoretical conceptualization of terrorism, for example, Gibbs (1989, p. 333) suggests that terrorism should not be equated or misunderstood with "terror" that he defines as the state's use of this tactic and conceptually distinct from terrorism. While Gibbs (1989) presents a compelling argument for the development of a theory of terrorism in terms of control, his analysis does not consider the rhetorical component of terrorism inextricably related to the state, the art of statecraft and the production of injustice.

The purpose of this paper is to suggest a broader, comparative sociological interpretation of terrorism and the production of injustice by integrating specific definitions and discursive understandings of terrorism within larger political processes of statecraft, hegemony, and social order. Terrorism needs to be examined theoretically as a form of complex social control that occurs as a result of the relations of domination produced in societies whose structures, institutions, and organizations privilege hierarchy, stratification, and control. Terrorism can therefore be analyzed as a political construct; one that is most relevant to social theory as a discursive or theoretical practice, a substantive component in the art of statecraft (compare Ben-Yehuda, 1990, 1992). Viewed in this way, the central question to be examined in this paper regarding terrorism and the production of injustice is: Under what conditions is terrorism and index of a deeper hegemonic crisis, rather than the cause of it? The first part provides a theoretical background and approach examining terrorism as a historical, rhetorical, and politically produced phenomenon. The second part compares the discursive processes of two states, the United States and Italy, their ostensible cultures of terrorism, and how the above theoretical approach can be used to develop a comparative, sociological interpretation of injustice and hegemonic crises.

While the United States is currently struggling to enforce an orthodox definition and perception of terrorism, Italy has been viewed by the United States as notorious for negotiating the meaning of terrorist action. The discursive process of each state represents the state at (1) different historical moments of discursive struggle over the definition of terrorism, and (2) different geographical contexts affecting the role of each state in national and international politics. In each site, the discourse of terrorism has allowed for the specific construction of ideological and political boundaries and has facilitated the production of hegemony, order, and injustice.

Theoretical Framework

Terrorism as a Historically Produced Discourse

The intellectual descendancy of contemporary conceptual understandings of terrorism is based on 18th- and 19th-century orthodox assumptions of social relations. The construct of terrorism includes the paradigms and conceptual referents from the age out of which it emerged. "Man" as the center and author of the universe, the process of civilizing nations vis-à-vis the development of the modern state and protecting the political sovereignty of these states was central to their social and political agendas (Stehr, 1994). Aristocratic man, though divinely ordained, replaced God, and logic, reason, or science replaced religion. Social order and relations were authored by man, and the state represented them to the rest of society (Ebenstein, 1969). One of the most important referents of the social realities and theories of the 19th century with respect to the conceptualization of terrorism is the territorial demarcation and sovereign survival of the nation-state.

Terrorism, therefore, can be viewed as a historically produced phenomenon, the product of a particular political discourse rather than the expression of certain underlying and fixed human capacities. As a particular political discourse, terrorism emphasizes and privileges language and polemical interpretations over direct experience (Foucault, 1972, 1979).

Edmund Burke's *Reflections on the Revolution in France*, written in 1790, provides a classic example of the intellectual descendancy, discursive nature, and symbiotic relationship between terrorism, statecraft, and the production of injustice. This symbiotic relationship includes the production of hegemony as a natural, taken-for-granted, fixed reality, or "truth" (Augelli and Murphy, 1988). In this work, Burke refers to the revolutionary spirit of the French democratic movements as terrorism. The struggles of the masses to obtain human and civil rights was seen as treasonous and barbaric. The discourse of terrorism in Burke's work reflects the references of aristocratic man and, by extension, man as a unit of analysis in the production of knowledge and hegemony at this time.[2]

Thus, the conception of aristocratic man as subject and author of the universe was being threatened by the "terrorist" movements of the day, i.e., the ideas of working class men as being allowed to vote, ideals of democracy as the rule of the masses. The ideal of the nation-state and its sovereign survival was also under increasing threat. Numerous states, such as the United States, sought freedom from colonial rule. In defining terrorism, threats to sovereignty are not acknowledged as being the result of deep-seated historical injustice and conflict, but the incorrect doctrines of philosophers who were animated by fanatical atheism and vile ambitions of politicians who were driven by opportunist lust for power. French philosophers, such as Rousseau and Voltaire, for example, were defined as robbers, assassins, bandits, treasonous, mentally disordered, and, of course, terrorists, for inspiring feelings of discontent among the masses.

Burke failed to see that the terrorism of which he spoke was not necessarily the result of some metaphysical fanaticism but rather the result of experience—the experience of protracted injustice and suffering. Yet, the underlying transformations of social and political institutions, whether it was their breakdown and failure or their growth and development, were overlooked in exchange for the demonization of "terrorist" violence in the state's neurotic attempt to reestablish control and order.

Terrorism as a State Produced Discourse

Two hundred years later, little has changed with the conceptualization of terrorism in many nation-states. It still refers to a "warfare from below," one challenging state authority and spreading fear (Colvard and Wallman, 1995, p. 15; compare Stehr, 1994). States that are defined as "terrorist" are viewed as essentially unstable and insecure for having to resort to an overt "reign or terror" in maintaining control (compare Gibbs, 1989). The U.S. State Department recently named Syria, Iraq, Libya, Algeria, and North Korea to be among the major supporters of terrorism in the world today (National Advisory Committee, 1991, pp. 102-106). In examining terrorism, however, Former Attorney General Ramsey Clark (1993, p. 71) concedes that "the things that we call terrorism, horrible in human terms as they are, are overwhelmingly the acts of powerless people." There is little difference and a great deal of irony between the way terrorism is invoked in the political discourse of the contemporary U.S. state and the discourse of classic, intellectual, 19th-century thought. It should not be surprising, therefore, that contemporary knowledge and policies relating to "terrorism" have been ineffective at either resolving the problem or providing useful approaches to this issue in over two hundred years.

From the late 1960s to the present, considerable research has emerged on terrorism. During this time, nearly 4,000 acts of terrorism were cited as occurring in the United States alone. By 1986 official statistics declined sharply, reporting only 25 deaths as a result of terrorism (Clark, 1993). The decline of ostensible terrorist incidents in the 1980s simultaneously produced a decline in scholarly interest but paradoxically produced an increase in formal social control: luggage searches, radar detection, baggage checks, immigration laws, surveillance experts, and "central intelligence" agencies. Some writers concluded that the implementation of such repressive measures was effective at countering terrorism (Jenkins, 1985; Bell, 1994).

But in the 1990s the bombings of the New York World Trade Center, the Oklahoma City Federal Building, the Atlanta Olympic Park, and explosions of the Waco Compound, Ruby Ridge, and TWA flight 800 cracked the hegemonic facade of the U.S.A. And, while many scholars and policymakers alike are looking to redefine, reconceptualize, or simply refine previous knowledge about terrorism, it is time to question its validity. Indeed, most previous research on terrorism, similar to the writings of Burke and his contemporaries provide little more than a demonization of terrorism. This demonization is explained (and justified) according to ethnocentric versions of reductionist psychology supporting simple motivational generalizations despite the obvious heterogeneity among ostensible terrorist groups. While the imperative for historical and cultural analyses is frequently acknowledged, most research on terrorism provides sweeping individual-oriented conclusions, generalizations, and reductionist historical chronologies (see, for example, Ascher, 1986; Laqueur, 1977; Wilkinson, 1986, 1990).

The concept of terrorism is inextricably associated with the formation and expansion of modern nation-states, including control of territory, moral boundaries, human resources, and the construction of political identities (Oliverio, 1997). This symbiotic relationship between the state and terrorism provides two essential features: First, the state reinforces the use of violence as a viable, effective, mitigating force for managing conflict; second, such a view is reinforced by culturally constructed and socially organized processes, expressed through symbolic forms, and related in complex ways to present social interests. Within increasing economic and environmental globalization, gender politics, and the resurgence of nationalities within territorial boundaries, the discourse of terrorism, as a practice of statecraft, is crucial to the construction of political boundaries. As such, terrorism is invoked in the art of statecraft when multiple, often conflicting versions of the past are produced and, at particular historical moments, become sites of intense struggle. This would appear to be one such moment for many nation-states around the globe and, in particular, the United States.

In this light, it is easy to understand the subjective nature of terrorism (compare Crenshaw, 1995). Even though terrorism has been defined as a type of political violence undermining the legitimacy of the state, not all such acts have been defined as terrorism. In the United States, for example, George Washington is remembered as a revolutionary hero for illegally challenging, defeating, and purging the English state. Yet, Gerry Adams, leader of Sinn Fein, a party related to the Irish Republican Army (IRA), is viewed as a terrorist by the United States for similar actions. Less than a decade ago, Yasir Arafat was defined as a terrorist par excellence. Today, he is viewed as a man of peace and condemns "terrorist" action. Examples such as these which utilize terrorist rhetoric differently are common and obvious. What is less obvious, however, are the cultural narratives that have changed and have been manipulated throughout history by different states.

Narratives and stories sometimes become transformed into exemplary modes of behavior, especially when the narratives become part of collective memory (Pfohl, 1985). For example, the Boston Tea Party, the 47 masterless Japanese samurai, Robin Hood, Columbus sailing the ocean blue, or the Spirit of Crazy Horse are not simple political events of "facts." They all share an authentically popular base and historical complexity; yet, in the rush to make disciplinary generalizations that justify the enactment of repressive policies, the history of various cultures in the United States and around the world are seen as little more than a chronology of political events, devoid of social context, that together or in isolation may "cause" another event (Colella, 1989).

Comparing Cultures of Terrorism

In this section, the proposed theoretical approach is used to examine the ostensible cultures of terrorism in both Italy and the United States. In the former country, ostensible terrorist action reached its climax in 1978 with the kidnapping of prime minister Aldo Moro. Since then, violent incidents, such as bombings, hijacking, and kidnappings directed against the state have occurred, but use of the term "terrorism" to define these incidents has declined dramatically. In the United States, on the other hand, ostensible terrorist action and discourse has gained momentum in recent years. Currently, in the United States, the term terrorism is persistently invoked by the media, politicians, and many experts to define incidents of violence.

Italian Culture of Terror

The collective remembering or forgetting of events and the production of meaning emerges from a complex process. One of these processes involves what Gramsci (1971) refers to as the historical contradiction or paradoxical relationship in Italy between the *paese legale* (legal country) and the *paese reale* (real country); that is, the antagonism between the state and the people (compare Lumley and Schlesinger, 1982). Since the *Risorgimento* (Resistance) in 1860, when Italy's different regions became unified as a nation-state, several national disasters, (viewed internationally as embarrassments) occurred. Among them, the three defeats most referred to in historical texts are the defeat at Adowa in 1896 by the Ethiopians, the defeat in 1917 at Caporetto by the Austrians and, of course, the defeat of Mussolini's fascist regime in 1943. Paradoxically, after each of these political failures, the Italian state (as well as the people) redeemed its pride and sense of national mission with the exception of the defeat in 1943. Italy's unprecedented social and economic repair and eventual prosperity in the 1950s and 1960s after the fascist debacle, proved to Italians that "the obsessions of Italian nationalists were entirely unfounded, that moral and national issues were not, as they thought, intimately linked. That is how Italians came to think that Italy could exist without being national, that a national pride, far from being necessary, could damage its survival, development, and prosperity" (Romano, 1984, p. 25).

The dominant political parties of the post-World War II era, however, namely the Christian Democrats and the Communists, attempted once again to mobilize a sense of Italian nationality and common destiny. Both the Christian Democrats and the Communists rhetorically referred to the ideals of the Resistance and to Italy's contributions to the plan of a unified Europe. And, while the Christian Democrats strove to represent spiritual renewal, the Communist party invoked the rhetorical promise of a great "proletarian revolution." By the mid-1960s, it was clear they had made empty promises, fueling the historical antagonism between the people and the state. While the Christian Democrats became defined as a party of opportunistic, immoral, and manipulative politicians, the Communists were viewed as cowards and as dependent on foreign, Soviet interests. As Romano (1984, p. 26) notes, compared with such concrete revolutionary prospects, the Communist party's revolution became an empty and ludicrous slogan, a mere trick. . ." Also, by the 1970s, the process of attempting to decentralize the federal government into regional governments exposed glaring disparities between the economically affluent areas and the poorer regions (Putnam, 1993).

During this time, the Italian state and its representative institutions experienced hundreds of violent confrontations. Among them the Piazza Fontana bombing in Milan, the kidnapping of public prosecutor Mario Sossi, and the killing of Chief Magistrate Francesco Coco received the most official and public attention. Despite the attention, however, these events were not defined as "terrorism." It was not until the mid-1970s that repressive legislation in the form of emergency laws were enacted. Upon the introduction of the new laws, the rate of such violent activity rose. Between 1974 and 1977, the repressive innovations introduced such as preventive detention, interrogation of suspects, restriction of rights to bail, expansion of police powers for provisional arrests, searches without judges' orders, recourse to physical coercion, and the use of an external security service "threw the penal system into a condition which can be considered as worse than the fascist heritage" (Ferrari, 1981, p. 23; Lumley and Schlesinger, 1982). Yet, despite these repressive measures, no explicit definition for terrorism was (or has been) ever introduced (Pisano, 1987).

There were a number of politically active groups that threatened the use of violence against the state. But, by 1974 one group, the *Brigate Rosse* (Red Brigades, referred to as BR herein) emerged as the dominant threat. Yet even during this time the Italian state generally had a very agnostic attitude toward this sort of violence. Until 1978, terms such as "extremism, subversivism, *squadrismo* [gangs], and *stragismo* [slaughterings]" were most commonly used to define and describe this sort of violent activity (della Porta, 1995, p. 106, brackets mine). Such activity was viewed as part of the unending Italian "crisis," a code word used by Italians to refer to the country's high unemployment, inflation, overpopulation, government instability, depleting natural resources, and, of course, increasing violence (compare Wagner-Pacifici, 1986). But, when the President of the Christian Democratic party, Aldo Moro, was kidnapped, held hostage for 55 days, and then killed by the BR, for the first time the term "terrorismo" was virulently invoked by the state in the political discussions and moral interpretations of the incident. Indeed, this event represented a very important turning point with reference to the process of defining terrorism (Drake, 1995; Wagner-Pacifici, 1986).

A competitive practice of political discussion and moral interpretation of the Moro affair ensued among state, media, Moro, Moro's family, and the BR. This practice reflected a fundamental social precedent regarding public understandings of high-profile events and state responses to them. The process of socially negotiating the meaning and the actors of the event became a matter of overt public, political participation. The interpretations presented during the unfolding and aftermath of the event actually gave the event its shape and meaning. The media, in particular, took on a strong interest in defending the forces of order. They managed to suppress the "'unacceptable face' of the Italian state" while at the same time transform it "into an ideal form" (Lumley and Schlesinger, 1982, p. 609). By giving overt credit to certain interpretations while pronouncing others as faulty, the political, moral, and aesthetic meaning, or quality, of the interpretation was changed (Wagner-Pacifici, 1986).[3] Politics and power, for a brief historical moment, was socially recognized in the way Foucault (1979) recognized them—as involved in the production of truth (compare Di Palma, 1977). As a result, the actors in the Moro affair, while receiving an enormous amount of media attention, contributed to their own systematic demise as their interpretation of events were publicly falsified denying any one interpretation popular support.

While no clear entity or groups of persons emerged as the winner in the Moro affair, what has become clear years later is the ability of the Italian state to, in a sense, absorb the so-called problem of terrorism and to go on defining other social problems as the "real" cause of the unending Italian crisis (Grundle and Parker, 1996). Despite numerous emergency laws, "special security," and couterterrorist formations, repressive government action was, for the most part, ineffective. Such measures were deemed by the government itself as depraving civil rights and, ultimately, as unconstitutional (della Porta, 1995). Wagner-Pacifici (1986) analogously compares the ending of the Moro affair to a "mass suicide." The BR did not deliver on its promised proletarian revolution despite such a dramatic, systematic operation; rather they provided a catharsis, an anticlimax for any such operations thereafter. Despite the Communist party's attempts to dissociate from the BR, they were in the end viewed as a radical faction of the party. As Ben-Yehuda (1990, p. 15) notes "a successful and enforceable social construction of a particular label of deviance depends on the ability of one or more groups to use or generate enough power so as to enforce their definition and version of morality on others." Neither the BR nor the Communist party were successful at popularizing their interpretation of reality.

Since the Moro kidnapping, a number of other incidents for which the BR have taken credit occurred, such as the kidnappings of Giovanni D'Urso (a prominent functionary in the Ministry of Justice) and American diplomat Leamon Hunt and the killings of Lando Conti (a mayor from Florence) and General Galvaligi. But none of these events had the same political impact or fervor of the Moro kidnapping despite their definition as "terrorist" acts. Groups from other countries with ethnic ties to various Italian communities were also active during this time for their own national interests. Yet their violent activity did not become an issue for the media or government until the early eighties and, by then, Italy was represented more as a third-party battleground rather than a directly threatened national entity (Pisano, 1987). So-called terrorist action was viewed as anticlimactic.

When the Achille Lauro seizure occurred in 1985, despite the fact that an Italian luxury liner was the target of attack, the Italian state was unwilling to utilize force as a means for resolution as instructed by the United States. Furthermore, the Italian state was reluctant to define the incident as an occurrence of "terrorism" as well as arrest Abul Abbas (the suspected leader of the group who seized the ship, but who was not himself present). Instead, the state showed compassion toward the Palestinians and contempt toward the demands of the United States to use force (Cassese, 1989, especially p. 118). Italian magistrates refused to define the actors as terrorists, referring to them as victims of oppression and injustice and sent them back to their homeland.

It would appear that the construct of terrorism, rather than the action so defined, has been central to the reorganization of the Italian state and the redrawing of boundaries for political activity. Some Italian writers have provocatively argued that the state benefitted from the spectacle of terrorism to its logical extreme, as a form of indirect defensive terror orchestrated to strengthen its power and image (Sanguinetti, 1979).[4] In the Italian case, however, the process of competition and compromise among different interpretations led to the desuetude of the construct of terrorism. The state reemerged naming other entites, such as the mafia, as the "real" source of Italy's unending social problems. Indeed, since the Moro affair, even though numerous political bombings, killings, and hostage takings have occurred in Italy, fewer and fewer have been officially defined as terrorism, nor have the BR been credited for such action despite their continuing existence (compare della Porta, 1995; Pisano, 1987). Terrorism as a category of deviance, as a way of knowing, as a social problem, and as a perceived threat against the stability of the nation-state transcended all political boundaries of knowing, unravelled itself, and sealed its own doom.

The U.S. Culture of Terrorism

At present the United States may be viewed as a site of intense discursive struggle over the construction and interpretation of its national past. Groups defined as subordinate, including racial, gender, religious, and issue-interest groups are challenging dominant representations of history. These include ongoing challenges posed by American Indians resurrected during the Columbus Day historical rendition and recent race riots in Los Angeles reminding the public that 30 years after the resurrected Civil Rights movement, African Americans are still not treated equally or fairly by government social control agents and agencies (Inverarity, Lauderdale, and Feld, 1983). As a complex society, the United States is rich with different social groupings and diverse people. Maintaining the production of the past as a monolith is becoming increasingly difficult in a society where multiple and, oftentimes, conflicting versions of the past exist simultaneously in place and space. And, while these larger struggles provide an index of hegemonic crisis in the United States, terrorism once again is pictured as the real crisis, the ostensible real threat to the stability of the nation-state, the real enemy of national peace and security.

Events of the recent past at the New York World Trade Center, the Waco Compound, the Oklahoma City Federal building, Ruby Ridge, Atlanta Olympic Park, the Unabomber attacks, the Amtrak derailing near Phoenix, and the TWA explosions are events deserving of indignant responses; yet their definition and interpretation by the media and the state as homogeneous "terrorist" events are misleading. These "waves" of social unrest and instability in the United States are not without historical precedent. As Erikson (1966) notes, for example, in the comparatively smaller, more homogeneous world of the Puritans in colonial America, the encroaching heterogeneity (including different ethnicities, religious worldviews, and gender roles) led to increasing threats and challenges to the dominant order. These and related external crises led to the witch hunts, which in the end were unsuccessful at arresting the social turmoil and preventing larger underlying processes of change from occurring. Relatively recently a period famous for social unrest was the 1960s. This era of struggle saw the emergence of the counterculture movement: the hippies, yippies, black panthers within the social milieu of the Vietnam War. When the war ended, the United States paid a price in economic and political terms, much of which was blamed on the remnant "flower children" for questioning traditional structures and institutions such as gender roles, family relations, racism, and sexual preferences (compare Inverarity, Lauderdale, and Feld, 1983). And, in 1995, we observed the reemergence of this national scapegoating or "which hunt" in the form of "terrorism" as U.S. President Clinton outlined his systematic, aggressive stance which included executing the "terrorists." He stated on national television that "If this is not a crime for which capital punishment is called, I don't know what is." As the United States is involved in larger social struggles challenging hegemonic ideas concerning its national past, pride, and action, events defined as "terrorist" appear to recur. The state turns to creating policies which expand its means of formal social control to name and justify its eradication of what it defines as the "real" destabilizing influence, the terrorists, in the name of restoring peace and stability (compare Erikson, 1966; Durkheim, 1948).

At present, in the United States, most texts discussing or explaining the nature of terrorism consider it to be a fixed, uniform phenomenon. Models of the individual "terrorist" personality as alienated from society are common in scholarly and popular representations. Timothy McVeigh and Terry Nichols, for example, originally were depicted by the U.S. media as solitary men who did not appear to bear the hatred for such a heinous act. It has also been publicly suggested that their personalities were shaped by an abandoning mother and a dominant wife. David Koresh, the Unabomber, Islamic suicidalists, and the initial suspect in the Atlanta bombing have also been defined as disgruntled and alienated. Simple motivational generalizations based on ethnocentric versions of reductionist psychology are predominantly used to explain such action despite the obvious heterogeneity among ostensible terrorist groups.

Models explaining "why" certain action occurs assume a nondiverse order in society much as in Burke's 18th-century writings. They play a crucial role in the process of establishing a socially acceptable definition of terrorist action that is devoid of any political appeal (Lauderdale, 1980). Representations of terrorism in the United States are dominated by an ostensible scientific discourse. This discourse shaping contemporary knowledge and meaning on terrorism is also a legacy of 18th- and 19th-century discourse of logic and reason. Scientific discourse is considered to best contain and reflect objective truth. Other discourse usually is relegated to the realm of fiction or polemics. Without the development of detached reason and logical arguments (often accompanied by facts and figures), contemporary analysis of social reality is not viewed as serious research. Thus, most contemporary knowledge on terrorism, in form, attempts to offer conceptualizations and theoretical parameters for empirical analyses (Stohl, 1988).[5] It is crucial, however, to explicate the form of the explanations as the form of the discourse represents and shapes dominant political values, relations, and references of the historical period (see Gusfield, 1976; Foucault, 1979; Stehr, 1994).

Even melodramatic representations by the U.S. media—where dualisms such as the "evil" terrorists versus the "righteous" state abound—use the language of science. But "the facts" do not guarantee that the "form" of their presentation is innocent or apolitical, any more than the language used to represent them (Wagner-Pacifici, 1986; White, 1987).

In addition to conceptual problems and sweeping generalizations, definitions of terrorism that deviate from the state's position are often viewed as controversial, politically biased or dangerous (Rubenstein, 1987; Gibbs, 1989). Small wonder the study of terrorism in the United States has eluded most comparative sociological research concerned with providing systematic analyses or tests of a theory or even critiques of the many writings that are largely polemical. Especially in the area of terrorism, where it appears that our knowledge and use of this construct does not differ considerably from its use in 18th- and 19th-century discourse on social reality, a reexamination of relevant contemporary social referents with the production of discourse on terrorism is needed.

Conclusion

> Massive campaigns of political terrorism, ranging from centuries of genocide against the American Indians to the continuing campaigns of violence, torture, disappearance, and mass extermination of peoples in Indonesia, Cambodia, Latin America, South Africa, Palestine, our own inner-city streets, and within our families and workplaces have been met with a range of responses. Depending upon our particular quota of ignorance, racism, xenophobia or homophobia, we may claim that these histories are "political propaganda," "exaggerations," "maybe true but don't have anything to do with us," or "just the way things are" (Brown and Merrill, 1993, p. 208).

The process by which the definition of terrorism is shaped and enforced involves a theoretical approach that recognizes "terrorism" as a historically and contextually produced discourse. Because of its 18th- and 19th-century intellectual descendancy, terrorism as it is defined and understood in contemporary U.S. society is the by-product of an androcentric discourse in which relations of domination are central to an understanding of identity.

But if we attempt to understand terrorism itself as a discursive construction in the art of statecraft, an art predicated on dominant references of man, nation-state, and sovereignty emerging from 18th- and 19th-century reality, it inspires the creation of new questions to old categories of knowledge and suggests research agendas focusing on difference and diversity. As Laclau (1990, pp. 244-245) has noted with respect to the understanding of "humanism," a by-product of 17th- and 18th-century discourse, it is more useful and valuable if it is seen as a historically produced phenomenon that can disappear rather than as an essential human expression. By analyzing terrorism as a discursive practice, it too can be seen as the product of a particular political discourse that can disappear. Such an approach to the analysis of terrorism, while threatening to disciplinary discourses of knowledge and power, is more committed to eradicating terrorism and injustice as a political project, than our current pseudoscientific practices which appear to reproduce or amplify them.

This is not to suggest that the practice of positing boundaries, definitions, and identity is useless. On the contrary, what this paper suggests is that there is an inherent problem in positing an essence or definition to terrorism as though it is timeless. It dooms states to repeat the mistakes and injustices of the past (compare Lauderdale and Cruit, 1993). Herein lies the value of a discursive analysis: it examines the incompleteness of analyses which impose themselves as complete for all time and space (Nash, 1994).

In the context of current research on terrorism reproducing understandings of society that are from centuries past, based on a dominating/territorial notion of man and society, it appears timely to suggest an alternative theoretical approach and comparative analysis of the construct of terrorism.

Just as discursive analyses recognize no boundaries and categories of knowing by exposing, questioning and blurring distinct demarcations, so too contemporary notions of time and space whether in economic activities or environmental ones, know no boundaries.[6] This is the most persuasive argument for reformulating discourse on terrorism—opening the door to the production of new questions and research agendas and ceasing the production of further state-sponsored answers informed by archaic, inadequate social references of reality.

NOTES

1   Parts of this paper are reprinted from *The State of Terror* by Annamarie Oliverio by permission of the State University of New York Press, ©1997. I am grateful for the technical support of the Department of Sociology at Stanford University and the Onati International Institute for the Sociology of Law. I also appreciate the constructive comments of Henry Walker, Morris Zelditch Jr., Nachman Ben-Yehuda, Andre Gunder Frank, Ray Corrado, Randall Amster, and Pat Lauderdale.

2   Burke writes about the sufferings of Marie Antoinette, for example, with shock and fury in a "nation of men of honor, and of cavaliers" (Ebenstein, 1969, p. 482). Yet, he completely denies and ignores the oppression and suffering of the French masses before the revolution. Pro-revolutionaries such as American Thomas Paine wrote scathing responses: "Burke pities the plumage, but forgets the dying bird." Paine defended the development of French democracy, and his works became inspirations (and influences) for the U.S. Declaration of Independence.

3   State officials were very concerned that Moro might leak out state secrets to the BR. Moro's writings from captivity were subjected to an elaborate competition of meaning. Prime Minister Andreotti declared that Moro's letters could not be "morally ascribable to him," and the media further generated this perspective. Moro's interpretation of the event itself was therefore, often falsified (Lumley and Schlesinger, 1982, p. 609).

4   Sanguinetti's book was banned in Italy. The French edition was published one year later.

5   Yet, there is little systematic theory with clear distinctions among definitions, assumptions, and hypotheses. And, the interpretations of the empirical data typically claim their theory is correct, rather than in a state of confirmation or disconfirmation.

6   When the Chernobyl incident occurred, the world learned that contaminated air, water, and soil pays no attention to the political boundaries and definitions constructed and privileged by humans. This incident terrorized millions; yet, it was neither defined nor perceived as terrorist violence.

REFERENCES

ASCHER, W.
    1986 "The Moralism of Attitudes Supporting Intergroup Violence." *Political Psychology* 7(3): 403-425.
AUGELLI, Enrico, and Craig MURPHY
    1988 *America's Quest for Supremacy and the Third World.* London: Pinter.
BELL, Bowyer J.
    1994 "The Armed Struggle and Underground Intelligence: An Overview." *Studies in Conflict and Terrorism* 17: 115-150.
BEN-YEHUDA, Nachman
    1990 *The Politics and Morality of Deviance.* Albany: SUNY Press.
    1992 "Criminalization and Deviantization as Properties of the Social Order." *Sociological Review* 40 (1): 73-108.
BROWN, David J., and Robert MERRILL, eds.
    1993 *Violent Persuasions: The Politics and Imagery of Terrorism.* Seattle: Bay Press.
BURKE, Edmund
    1969 [1970] *Reflections on the Revolution in France.* Edited by C.C. O'Brien. London: Penguin.
CARNOY, Martin
    1984 *The State and Political Theory.* Princeton: Princeton University Press.
CASSESE, Antonio
    1989 *Terrorism, Politics and the Law: The Achille Lauro Affair.* Cambridge: Basil Blackwell.
CLARK, Ramsey
    1993 "Beyond Terrorism." Pp. 67-86 in: *Violent Persuasions: The Politics and Imagery of Terrorism,* edited by David Brown and Robert Merrill. Seattle: Bay Press.
COLELLA, Ugo
    1989 *Alienation and the Story of the Story.* Stanford University. Typescript.
COLVARD, Karen, and Joel WALLMAN
    1995 *1995 Report of the Harry Frank Guggenheim Foundation: Research for Understanding and Reducing Violence, Aggression, and Dominance.* New York: Guggenheim Foundation.
CRENSHAW, Martha
    1995 *Terrorism in Context.* University Park: Pennsylvania State Univ. Press.
DELLA PORTA, Donatella
    1995 "Left-Wing Terrorism in Italy." Pp. 105-159 in: *Terrorism in Context,* edited by Martha Crenshaw. University Park: Pennsylvania State Univ. Press.
DI PALMA, Giuseppe
    1977 *Surviving Without Governing: The Italian Parties in Parliament.* Berkeley: University of California Press.
DRAKE, Robert
    1995 *The Aldo Moro Murder Case.* Cambridge: Harvard University Press.
DURKHEIM, Emile
    1948 *The Elementary Forms of the Religious Life.* Glencoe, Ill: Free Press.
EBENSTEIN, William
    1969 *Great Political Thinkers.* New York: W. W. Norton.
EITZEN, D. Stanley, and Maxine BACA ZINN
    1994 *Social Problems.* Boston: Allyn and Bacon.
ERIKSON, Kai
    1966 *Wayward Puritans: A Study in the Sociology of Deviance.* New York: Wiley.

FERRARI, Vincenzo
  1981 "The Policy of Law and Order in Italy: The Voice of the Power and Its Impact." *International Journal of the Sociology of Law* 9: 23-39.
FOUCAULT, Michel
  1972 *The Archeology of Knowledge*, translated by A.M. Smith. New York: Harper and Row.
  1979 *Discipline and Punish: The Birth of the Prison*. New York: Vintage Books.
GIBBS, Jack
  1989 "Conceptualization of Terrorism." *American Sociological Review* 54 (June): 329-340.
GRAMSCI, Antonio
  1971 *Selections from the Prison Notebooks*. New York: International Publishers.
GRUNDLE, Stephen, and Simon PARKER
  1996 *The New Italian Republic*. New York: Free Press.
GUSFIELD, Joseph
  1976 "The Literary Rhetoric of Science: Comedy and Pathos in Drinking Driver Research." *American Sociological Review* 41 (February): 16-34.
INVERARITY, James M., Pat LAUDERDALE, and Barry C. FELD
  1983 *Law and Society*. Boston: Little, Brown and Co.
JENKINS, Brian
  1985 *The Future Course of International Terrorism*. Santa Monica, Calif.: Rand.
LACLAU, Ernesto
  1990 *New Reflections on the Revolution of Our Time*. London: Verso.
LAQUEUR, William
  1977 *Terrorism*. Boston: Little, Brown.
LAUDERDALE, Pat, ed.
  1980 *A Political Analysis of Deviance*. Minnesota: University of Minnesota Press.
LAUDERDALE, Pat, and Michael CRUIT
  1993 *The Struggle for Control*. New York: SUNY Press.
LUMLEY, Bob, and Philip SCHLESINGER
  1982 "The Press, the State, and Its Enemies, the Italian Case." *Sociological Review* 30 (4): 603-626.
MARX, Karl
  1967 [1867] *Capital*. Vol. 1. New York: International.
NASH, Kate
  1994 "The Feminist Production of Knowledge: Is Deconstruction a Practice for Women." *Feminist Review* 47: 65-77.
NATIONAL ADVISORY COMMITTEE ON CRIMINAL JUSTICE STANDARDS AND GOALS
  1991 *Disorders and Terrorism: Report of the Task Force on Disorders and Terrorism*. Washington, D.C.: Government Printing Office.
OLIVERIO, Annamarie
  1997 *The State of Terror*. New York: SUNY Press.
PFOHL, Stephen
  1985 *Images of Deviance and Social Control*. New York: McGraw-Hill Ryerson.
PISANO, Vittorfanco S.
  1987 *The Dynamics of Subversion and Violence in Contemporary Italy*. Stanford University: Hoover Institution Press.
PUTNAM, Robert D.
  1993 *Making Democracy Work: Civic Traditions in Modern Italy*. Princeton: Princeton University Press.

ROMANO, Sergio
    1984 "The Roots of Italian Terrorism." *Policy Review* 25: 25-27.
RUBENSTEIN, Richard E.
    1987 *Alchemists of Revolution*. London: I. B. Tauris.
SANGUINETTI, Gianfranco
    1979 *Del Terrorismo e Dello Stato: La Teoria e la Pratica del Terrorismo per la Prima Volta Divulgate*. Translated into French, *Du Terrorisme et de L'Etat*, 1980, Le fin mot de L'histoire.
STEHR, Nico
    1994 *Knowledge Societies*. Thousand Oaks: Sage.
STOHL, Michael
    1988 *The Politics of Terrorism*. New York: Marcel Dekker.
TILLY, Charles
    1985 "War Making and State Making as Organized Crime." Pp. 169-191 in: *Bringing the State Back In*, edited by Peter B. Evans, Dietrich Rueschemeyer, and Theda Skocpol. Cambridge: Cambridge University Press.
WAGNER-PACIFICI, Robin E.
    1986 *The Moro Morality Play: Terrorism as Social Drama*. Chicago: University of Chicago Press.
WEBER, Max
    1958 "Politics as a Vocation." Pp. 77-128 in: *From Max Weber: Essays in Sociology*, edited and translated by Hans Heinrich Gerth and C. Wright Mills. New York: Oxford University Press.
WHITE, Hayden
    1987 *The Content of the Form: Narrative Discourse and Historical Representation*. Baltimore: Johns Hopkins University Press.
WILKINSON, Paul
    1986 *Terrorism and the Liberal State*. London: MacMillan.
    1990 *Conflict Studies, 236: Terrorist Targets and Tactics: New Risks to World Order*. Washington, D.C.: RISCT and the Center for Security Studies.

State Disintegration and Human Rights in Africa

JULIA MAXTED and ABEBE ZEGEYE*

ABSTRACT

This article discusses external and internal disintegrative pressures at work on contemporary African states and examines the consequences of the failure of ideologies of nationalism and nation-statism for human rights. In particular, this paper examines the causes of state disintegration in Liberia and Somalia, suggesting that the effect is to exacerbate the already vulnerable position of marginalized groups.

IN THIS ARTICLE we discuss some disintegrative pressures on African nation-states, in particular Liberia and Somalia, and the implications of the failure of nation-statism for human rights. The destruction of the legitimacy and accountability of many states results, in part, from their territorial awkwardness. Formed by the colonial partition and "transferred" to African hands, overlapping ethnicity is sometimes more a source of suspicion rather than unity between states. In the past two decades more than two million people have died from conflict and many hundreds of thousands have been displaced. The geographical mobility of Africans remains enormous; hundreds of thousands of people have emigrated to escape from dictatorship or war. This desertion of the space of the state reflects an extreme degree of alienation from the state.

The economic sovereignty of African states is being undermined by pressure to join regional blocs at the same time as banditry and unofficial cross-border trading networks are growing at the expense of the state. A further threat to state autonomy and civilian populations arises from the growing militarization of conflicts. As the functionings of the state begin to deteriorate, as evident in Sierra Leone, Togo, Southern Sudan, Zaire, Rwanda and Burundi, low-level warfare, famine, deprivation, and political crisis overlap. Those nominally in control of the state cannot provide security for their citizens, are not in full control of its territory, cannot lay the basis for economic improvement and are unable to either co-opt or to defeat their opponents. In Liberia and Somalia there has been total state disintegration. In

* University of California, Santa Barbara, Santa Barbara, CA 93106, U.S.A.

these circumstances historically vulnerable groups including women, children and minorities are receiving little or no state protection. In other states, those holding the reins of power flout the rules of international law on human rights in the absence of civil society.

A further factor undermining the legitimacy of the state is environmental degradation. A fragile ecological inheritance has been further degraded during the course of civil war. Populations in the pastoralist cultures have been subjected to an almost criminal scourge of natural and man made impoverishment. The uneven development of states, as well as the socioeconomic systems anchored on those exploitative relations, create a fertile base for recourse to ethnicity as the area for struggle for the control of economic and political power. Ethnic identities, while having a "beneficial" spillover for the ethnic groups or groups in power, are primarily utilized to consolidate and serve the interests of the ruling classes of the dominant ethnic groups. The failure to resolve intrastate social tension is weakening central government from within in many cases. Economic pauperization and an ideological vacuum arising from the uglier face of nationalism, its capacity to erode freedom, are fueling a contemporary boom of religious cults and extremism, forcing a redefinition of social cohesion, of civil space even.

"Democratization" and the Mobilization of Ethnic Identities

Since 1989 many countries in Africa have experienced unprecedented waves of demands for democracy which have succeeded in bringing about the downfall of several authoritarian regimes and forced others to accept multiparty politics. Amongst the external factors contributing to a revival of democracy, specifically African dynamics were perhaps the most decisive, including the introduction of multiparty politics in Algeria, Nelson Mandela walking free in South Africa and the strongly contagious effect of the Beninois prototype of the National Conference (Bayart, 1993, p. xi). However these external events did no more than precipitate internal dynamics. Democratic forces had been smoldering a long time and had only been smothered by the combined efforts of African actors of the 'passive revolution' together with their foreign partners.

As Bayart (1993) notes, it remains to be seen if events however turn out in democracy's favor. Authoritarian regimes have managed to retain control over security forces which have enabled them to maintain a covert harassment of opposition forces, control over economic rents (with which they have bought off dissident politicians and financed the creation of a multitude of smaller parties which have fragmented the opposition), and control over the funding and support of western powers and the multilateral institutions of Bretton Woods. Having waved the flag of democracy and respect for human rights these institutions have not dared pursue such sentiments to their logical conclusion.

Economic austerity programs, made inescapable in the 1980s by worsening balance of payments and pressure from creditors, have been used to advantage by the ruling class. The dismantling of the public sector, which the international institutions demand, need not condemn the regimes in power. By drying up the principal channels of autonomous accumulation without creating a true market, the center can regain control from a political class and a bureaucracy which had finally cut loose (Bayart, 1993, p. 225). The politics of structural adjustment are thus not so very different from the politics of nationalization during the previous two decades and by different means have pursued the same end. With the end of the Cold War, economic and military support from the West or East has fallen, and aid is now increasingly tied to western notions of "democratization" and improved implementation of human rights. Democratic discourse has become a new form of economic rent; aid to pay for democratization is very welcome, and democratization gives the base the task of carrying out purges which would have been difficult to undertake from the top.

The experience of the past five years, which has led to unprecedented numbers of elections, has not ushered in an era of popular and effective government. Many countries are precariously balanced between the authority of an increasingly compromised state, both politically and economically, and a political periphery formed from an alliance of dissidents marginalized by the state, but as yet unable to force the center to devolve power. The change in climate has emboldened opposition organizations, journalists, human rights activists and others to take on political authorities and often the result has been heightened social tensions, articulated through a proliferation of ethnically or regionally based parties.

Ethnicity itself cannot provide the basic reference point for the postcolonial political arena. It is constantly being formed and is largely mingled within the phenomena of the state for which it is supposed to provide the explanatory key (Bayart, 1993, p. 49). Even as a scheme of identification it is contextual. Ethnic identities do not exclude other lines of identification; family, age, gender, religious, and economic. Far from the problematic intangibility of tradition, ethnic consciousness reveals social change, of which it is a matrix. It cannot be divorced from other changes of this century—urbanization, the construction of a new communications network, the introduction of new relationships of production, and the increase in migratory and commercial movements. Most situations where the structuring of the contemporary political arena seems to be enunciated in terms of ethnicity relate to identities which did not exist a century ago, or at least were not then so clearly defined (Bayart, 1993, p. 51). Although it is too much to maintain that all contemporary ethnic groups are the products of the colonial period, the precipitation of ethnic identities becomes incomprehensible if it is divorced from colonial rule. The colonizers conceptualized indistinct human landscapes which they had occupied, as specific identities constructed in their imagination on the model of a bargain-basement nation-state. Europeans believed Africans belonged to tribes and so Africans built tribes to belong to—genuine products of African diversity—but also invented weapons of self-defense.

Thus the function of a chief was swiftly taken up by the elders of the lineage who then drew an administrative salary and became entitled to levy a so-called customary "tribute." These payments were proportional to the number of people and sub-chiefs which the chieftain could boast and led the title bearers to appeal to ethnicity in order to invent historical and genealogical arguments in their own support. Interactions of identity became tied between important structures of power and of allocation of resources on the one hand, and on the other the population over whom power was exercised. Since the notion of an ethnic group was one of the ideological premises of the colonial administration, it became the "means of affirming one's own existence," and hence the language of relationship between the subject peoples themselves. The colonial powers quickly lost their grip on the process they had unleashed. It became a system and literally produced particularities (tribe/ethnic group). Fighting rivalries, a scramble for land and the formation of land reserves later made this even more necessary. Ethnic representations were crucial in the flow of goods and services established by the functionaries of the colonial bureaucracy. What we sometimes call ethnicity, implying the intervention of regional chains of political and economic transactions equivalent to the articulation of internal and external networks of exchange, circulation of power and wealth, followed similar modalities in former times. The colonial situation did not suspend the historicity of African societies; rather it was a new development, albeit one in which the cards were radically reshuffled.

As the possibility of independence loomed the colonial powers turned to building nation-states. This crystallized the division of African's many hundreds of peoples and cultures into a few dozen nation-states, each claiming sovereignty against each other. Nationalism that became nation-statism looked like a liberation and really began as one, but did not continue. Like Janus, nationalism had two faces: a capacity for enlarging freedom and a potential for destroying it (Davidson, 1992, p. 52). The ideology of nation-statism in Africa, as in Europe, was appallingly reductive, rather as though a wealth of cultures was really an impoverishment. Striving to transform colonial territories into national territories they found this wealth both distracting and hard to fit in with their schemas.

In Africa, ethnicity is almost never absent from politics yet at the same time it does not provide its basic fabric. Manifestations of ethnicity inevitably involve other social dimensions, and in the context of the contemporary state, ethnicity exists mainly as an agent of accumulation both of wealth and political power. "Tribalism" is thus perceived as less of a political force in itself than as a channel through which competition for the acquisition of wealth, status, or power is expressed (Bayart, 1993, p. 55). The contemporary force of ethnic consciousness comes more from its reappropriation by local people circumscribing the allocation of the state's resources.

The postcolonial state functions as a rhizome of personal networks and assures the centralization of power through the agencies of family, alliance and friendship. The majority of phenomena, such as tribalism or instability seen as indicative of the exogenous nature of the postcolonial state are indicative, on the contrary, of the reappropriation of institutions of foreign origin by indigenous societies. The use of kinship in a political context acts as compensation against the weakness or the incapacity of state institutions to protect citizens and advance their interests. Family bonds and ethnicity are instrumental arguments and idioms at the service of actors. However, the intimate character of African societies is in no sense the opposite or even necessarily the reduction of domination and inequality; the expression of personal strategies is not incompatible with the creation of a system of social stratification.

The salient feature of the last three centuries is not the growing integration of Africa into the western world economy but, on the contrary, the latter's inability to pull the continent into its magnetic field. Class relations are in no way the primary source of conflict despite the acuteness of social inequality; for example, in Ghana, factional or local struggles have dominated over class politics in the decades following the proclamation of independence. Actors organize themselves in factions in order to win or conserve power at the various echelons of the social pyramid. This competition is the very stuff of political life; conflicts appearing to feed off tribalism, ambivalent couplings of official political hierarchies and discrete local hierarchies. Factional struggle is a mode of political production not of disintegration. Competing entrepreneurs and political cliques succeed each other in power. In the absence of almost any revolutionary threat south of the Sahara, these factional struggles represent the principle genesis of change in government.

State Disintegration

The social foundations of any state are socially, geographically and culturally heterogeneous. The most spectacular manifestation of this characteristic is the extreme complexity of political identification from one context to another in Africa. Coexisting within the heart of any given power are several time-spaces whose adjustment is problematic and always precarious. Consequently the state in Africa is not an integral state but a state of variable polarization. The development of an "integral state" from a "soft state" has not taken place despite advances in the technology of social control.

The autonomy of the nation-state in Africa is increasingly under pressure; internal social tensions joining with the pressure for large groupings more able to respond to current economic demands. Technological innovation, which made the nation-state possible, is now helping to undermine it as capital and information flows are unaffected by national boundaries. As a result, supranational units such as the Economic Community of West African States and the Common Market of Eastern and Southern Africa are encroaching upon the national sovereignty from above, while the failure to resolve intrastate social tension is weakening central government from within. Economic sovereignty is being undermined by pressures to join regional blocs at the same time as unofficial cross-border trading networks are growing at the expense of the state.

Another factor undermining the legitimacy of the state is environmental degradation, affecting in particular, pastoral communities. Through the combination of the ecological inheritance of the 1970s, cyclical drought, commercial devastation of tropical hardwoods, and raging civil wars, populations in the pastoralist culture have been subjected to an almost criminal scourge of natural and manmade improverishment. While desertification and drought result in the displacement of large numbers of people, environmental degradation and the competition for resources are promoting massive migrations of people and putting new pressures on state boundaries. Interlocking with the political and economic centrifugal forces on the state, the threats are specific and measurable. They include deforestation and soil erosion, adding to existing problems deriving from the scarcity of good soil in Africa; widespread water shortages particularly in the hinterland, and probable rising water levels in overpopulated places such as the Nile Delta. As people move southward and northward through the Sahelian zone in search of resources they exacerbate the pattern of deforestation; migration towards the coastal cities highlights the already poor urban provision of housing, health and education.

Frontiers are more fluid than at any time since Independence. Hundreds of thousands of economic and political refugees have emigrated to escape from dictatorship or war, often placing their host communities under considerable stress. "Escape" in the old sense of the word—the action of escaping from place—is still one of the constituent strategies of the production of politics and social relations. "It has remained as a major mode of historicity south of the Sahara. It persists in eroding the civil space, constraining the processes of accumulation of power and wealth and in making predacity easier than exploitation" (Bayart, 1993, p. 259).

The contours of the postcolonial state are not fully stabilized, and the idea that sometime in the future the colonial boundaries may either be altered or abolished is not absurd, notwithstanding the solid vested interests that would resist such a move. History is full of examples of such territorial adjustment. In these circumstances it is hardly surprising that the spatial hold of the state is incomplete. There are some capitals which enjoy effective domination of territory but some states, though stable, do not meet these criteria. The exit option as a viable strategy remains persistent in the political arena. At its most extreme it is exemplified by territorial secession. It is more commonly found at a microlevel, for example in the cohabitation of religious minorities with the state. The state cannot officially agree to the existence of movements which refuse all civil obligations, but contemporary sects ignore rather than contest the state. For example in Touba, a holy town in Senegal (which is also the headquarters of smuggling with the Gambia), Mouride groups have rejected taxation. The frontiers of the state are transgressed in many ways: "the informal sector is a canker on the official economy, taxes are not collected, poaching and undisciplined exploitation of mineral resources becomes endemic, weapons circulate, resettled villages split up, the people appropriate the legitimate use of force to themselves and deliver summary justice, delinquency spreads" (Bayart, 1993, p. 258).

The contemporary boom of religious cults and extremism may provoke a redefinition of social cohesion, of civil space even. The Islamic *umma* is already creating problems for western models of the state. The reconstruction of identity may become systemic especially if combined with economic/military reordering. Islamic extremism is affecting the precarious status of non-Muslim minorities in Egypt and Sudan, including the Copts and ethnic groups of Southern Sudan. The present Islamization policy in Sudan and the ongoing civil war could lead to secession which could precipitate interethnic conflicts in Southern Sudan on the one hand, and disputes over water and grazing resources between the two Sudanese states on the other. Eritrea is now being seen as a potential ally of Israel in the region by the Arab media and the Sudanese government, possibly triggering Arab nationalist and conservative states alike to support the Muslim community in Eritrea and in the wider Horn of Africa. This could in turn lead to conflict between the highlanders and lowlanders inside Eritrea. The most likely beneficiaries are the Eritrean Liberation Front and the Jihad movement in Eritrea whose presence in Sudan has led to the current rift between Sudan and Eritrea, which has apparently provided support for the ethnic Beja and other groups opposed to the present government in Sudan.

The territorial division of Africa into nation-states based on colonial partition with borders sanctified by the OAU as inviolable, is under its greatest pressure since Independence. African states have placed great emphasis on the principle of territorial integrity, in part to counter their weakness and artificiality. The demise of the one-party state in many countries, together with the cessation of much foreign sponsorship has exposed the worst dictatorships to new political forces. However diverse the origins of social conflict, some predate colonization while others derive from colonial manipulation, it is increasingly difficult to contain them within present state frameworks.

The postcolonial (and colonial) economic substructure under which commodity producers had much of their surplus extracted to support the state machine has been overturned. The disbanding of commodity marketing boards, the sale of most state assets in shock treatment privatization programs, and the growth of "illegal" or informal trade have combined to deprive the state of its key levers of economic control and patronage. In most countries the system of regional and continental tariffs makes no sense. Money and goods cross borders regardless of export incentives, import bans or tariff walls. Just as governments are powerless to control trade in commodities and manufactures they also appear powerless to control the much more threatening smuggling of drugs and weapons and the multiplying money laundering operations. The involvement of several government officials in these activities, as for example in Nigeria, further violates economic and political sovereignty ("Unmaking and Remaking," 1995).

There are few foreign support systems for Africa's unwieldy states; for the most part western countries are involved in reactive measures. Only a serious restriction on the arms sales which have been used to dismember nation-states and the provision of alternative sources of income to soldiers would have much effect (Luckham, 1980). The differences between war and crime are being eroded. Liberia's conflict was firstly a looting operation providing both personal enrichment and a route to power. For many of the unemployed and poverty stricken followers of African warlords, membership in an armed militia is a step up, not down. Facing the armed bandits, Africa's professional armies are, like their state paymasters, under great pressure. Budgets are smaller, equipment more dilapidated, salaries late or not even paid, and morale sinking. War's great advantage over simple delinquency is that it legitimizes, in the name of "justice" and the "revolution," the use of arms to get access to the resources of the state. It can mobilize the "youth" where the single party has failed and besides giving them bread it can provide them with an ideology including the exaltation of martial values (Bayart, 1993, p. xiii). The reduction of war to a mode of political production, a source of accumulation through the collection of international aid and seizure of the resources of the modern economy enables adaptation to the growing criminalization of the economy.

As the functionings of the state begin to deteriorate as evident in Sierra Leone, Togo, Zaire, Burundi, Rwanda and as emergent in Nigeria, low-level warfare, famine, deprivation, and political crisis overlap. Regional structures of conflict present for a long time in the Horn of Africa are now emerging in West Africa. Charles Taylor in Liberia (with support from Cote d'Ivoire, Burkina Faso and Libya) has enlisted the support of militant separatists in Casamance, Gambians involved in an unsuccessful putch, and members of Guinean and Sierra Leonean opposition movements. Taylor has been confronted by the forces of Economic Community of West African States under General Babangida of Nigeria who had strong links with Samuel Doe. A further threat to state autonomy arises from the larger number of trained soldiers, many of whom feel no sense of loyalty to the nation-state and whose presence is destabilizing. Military organizations, or rather segments of them, sometimes harbor disintegrative objections about the very state they have formally sworn to serve and in support of particular ethnic claims and identities. What is striking is the ease with which regular armies and regimes of increasing numbers of African states have been defeated and replaced by insurgent guerrilla forces organized from among their own citizens. The latter used to be considered and identified with revolutionary warfare strategy employed by a colonial people for fighting against and wresting independence from a foreign imperial power. But as with cases such as Ethiopia and Eritrea, armed liberation has succeeded through donning the mantle of a variety of national liberation movements, or "fronts."

One major problem is how to disarm and demobilize the plethora of ethnically based guerrilla forces even as these new regimes embark on creating new armies. Another is the recruitment, training and organization of new armies in newly emergent political orders, most of which are still badly divided ethnically. After three decades of proxy cold-war battles being fought in Africa such as in Angola, Ethiopia, Mozambique, and Somalia, the militarization of superpower allies such as Liberia and Zaire, and guerrilla struggles in Sudan, Uganda, Zimbabwe and South Africa, there is an abundance of trained soldiers (and untrained "volunteers") and weaponry available to any would-be warlord.

The colonial practice of ethnic juggling in the army has created one of the major sources of instability that came to plague army/state relations in postcolonial Africa. In Ghana at independence the army was dominated by minority groups from the north, Grunshi and Dagomba. In Nigeria, Tiv and other middle-belt minorities groups were groomed for military service; Lugard tried to keep the military participation of Fulani to a minimum because of their *Jihadist* antecedents. The major concern for the French was how to avoid recruiting soldiers among African historic groups or precolonial kingdoms that had initially proved difficult to conquer. Their strategy was to make the politically strong militarily weak and the politically weak militarily strong.

The colonizing process was invariably presented by its promoters and explained by its propagandists as a "modernizing process." In fact it induced in practice one after another form of moral and political disintegration (Davidson, 1992, p. 251). The decolonization process has repeated this downward slide. Once the force of the "social struggle" of the colonized was spent, the drive against social inequalities and perceived injustices was supplanted by a "national struggle" within the institutional "containers" of an imported nation-statism. At this stage there ensued a dogfight scramble for state power by would-be ruling groups acting outside and against the rules and restraints of historical cultures and their compromises.

The result became the reverse of whatever may be meant by nation building. Rather it promoted the destructive spread of kinship "tribalism" or "clannism":

> By the middle of the 1980s this generalized collapse of the nation-statist project was widely perceived whether inside or outside Africa. But what now became scarcely less obvious were the incapacities of the "developed world" to act on any self-critical analysis or even refrain from purely negative interventions. Of these interventions there were various and many. Some were of an economic nature designed to project the industrialized countries' advantageous terms of trade with primary producers. Others were political measures aimed at overtaking government blunders or comparable disruptions. Others again were simple acts of militarized violence adding to the

legions of licensed or merely criminal gun toters. More and more of the latter were the often murderous puppets of aims and forces they could neither have understood nor even have known a way of understanding. (Davidson, 1992, p. 252.)

In the contemporary period the structure of military and state relations have become unhinged: the geoethnic make-up of the group which still wields military power may be disassociated from and no longer articulate with that of the group whose members now claim the mandate to rule (Adekanye, 1996). This process is open to cynical manipulation of old prejudices by elites on both sides.

Descent into Statelessness: Liberia and Somalia

Liberia

Under exacerbating conditions of economic crisis, debt, and adjustment, the postcolonial state has come under increasing pressure and threat from ethnically induced disintegrative sources. Conflicts increasingly have come to assume the dimension of bloody combat or even total war, unrestrained by any norms and aiming at the total annihilation of opponents on both sides. Liberia was a black American republic launched in 1847 for the benefit of former slaves and their dependents in north America, a black republic conceived so as to exercise "the genius of free government" over this "seat of ancient despotism and bloody superstition" as its founders claimed. The settlers saw as their mission the introduction of the elements of civilization in Liberia to a "vast population of degraded subjects" (Davidson, 1992, p. 245). They knew almost nothing about this indigenous African population, consisting of sixteen groups, each with its own language. Generations of Americo-Liberians proceeded to rule their "degraded subjects" by a contemptuous tyranny presented to the outside world as the forerunner to universal suffrage and representative democracy. But democracy never arrived.

Liberia was able to maintain its independence only with U.S. support. In order to restore a languishing economy, a 99-year rubber plantation concession was granted to the Firestone Company in 1926 in exchange for a large long-term loan from the U.S. government. Americo-Liberians, constituting five percent of the population, dominated Liberian society until the military coup of 1980. The indigenous people were not given citizenship until 1904 and were not granted the right to vote until 1944. However this right was restricted to property owners or those who paid a "hut tax." The non-Americo-Liberian peoples generally received little economic benefit from developments such as agricultural improvement and foreign investments. The remote hinterland, home to the Gio, Mano, Loma, and Krahn, was not penetrated by road or rail until after the Second World War.

One area where the indigenous population was dominant through sheer weight of numbers, was in the armed forces. However for many years any signs of unrest amongst its ranks were effectively controlled by imprisonment. Americo-Liberians pursued ethnic stereotyping in maintaining control over the army. The Krahn were held in low prestige and Loma from Lofa County, who formed the single largest grouping in the army were pejoratively called, Buzi ("wild person"). The ruling True Whig party maintained a kind of feudal oligarchy, monopolizing political power and subjugating the largely peasant population with the help of the Liberian Frontier Force, an army of non-Americo-Liberians deployed to collect taxes and forcibly recruit laborers for public works projects. While the settlers along the coast developed an elaborate lifestyle reminiscent of the antebellum southern United States of America, the indigenous people in the hinterland endured poverty and neglect. Reports of floggings and forced labor were so common that a League of Nations report in 1931 recommended that Liberia be deprived of its independence and colonized. Five percent of the population owned more than half of the country's wealth (Liebenow, 1969).

The combination of repression and mounting corruption was especially acute during the prolonged regime of President V.S. Tubman who ruled from 1944 to 1971. Tubman attempted reform but heightened expectations that could not be satisfied within the existing political structures. The country began to experience more frequent labor disputes and political unrest. Rice riots broke out on April 14, 1979 as an increase in the price of rice was announced intensifying economic hardship for most in the face of increasingly ostentatious displays of wealth by the elite. When police opened fire on unarmed demonstrators, forty were killed and hundreds injured. A coup in 1980 organized by a master sergeant, Samuel Doe, was initially greeted with enthusiasm. Doe promised to liberate the indigenous masses from the corrupt and oppressive domination of Americo-Liberians, pledging a more equitable distribution of the nation's wealth.

This did not happen. The soldiers of the Liberian Armed Forces proved a law unto themselves and there were persistent reports of looting, arson, floggings, arbitrary arrests, rape, summary executions and brutality. In 1984 voters approved a new, U.S.-style constitution. Doe remained head of a civilian government and installed elections in 1985 from which the main opposition parties were barred. Doe was widely believed to have stolen an election in October 1985 that was to have brought about a return to civilian power. Persons such as Doe, Amin, Bokassa, and Macias-Ngeuma have demonstrated "time and again just why it was that leaders of an entirely different mold and mentality, men strong in their wisdom such as Cabral in Guinea Bissau, so clearly warned that armed violence was a road to be entered with austere reluctance and traveled with an ever-present fear of its infections" (Davidson, 1992, pp. 246-247).

This pathology is explicable but only in terms of alienation. "The ancestral culture of the peoples of Liberia as with those of their neighbors near and far, knew plenty of abusive violence. But they possessed rules and regulations for the containments and repression of abusive violence; and these were the rules and regulations, before the scourge of the slave trade and the colonialism that followed it, that enabled them to evolve their sense and value of community" (Davidson, 1992, p. 247). In Liberia the perversion of community can be rationally explained as arising from the consequences of the slave trade (Rodney, 1970). But alienation from ancestral community was then carried further and systematized by imposition of the culture of an imported oligarchy, an oligarchy whose ignorance of local realities was easily encouraged by the corruption of power into a contempt for the people who lived in these realities. And Doe, with others, was the eventual product of this systemic alienation.

Since the 1980 coup, relations between the country's distinct 16 groups (and particularly between the Krahn and almost all others) were increasingly strained. Since the 1980s, members of a tiny clan faction within the Krahn community, many of them from Doe's home village of Tuzon in Grand Gedeh County, appeared to emerge with a disproportionate share of the fruits of indigenous rule. At the time of a coup attempt in November 1985, five of the 16 government ministries and the armed forces were headed by Krahns who comprise barely four percent of the total population. The Krahn historically were maligned by other larger groups who considered the Krahn to be relatively backward and uncivilized. The abortive coup unleashed a firestorm of arbitrary reprisals that left scores of soldiers and civilians dead, opposition figures detained without charge and a trail of beatings and floggings (Lawyers Committee, 1986). A constitution was set in place in 1986 but many of the decrees curtailing free speech and limited popular participation under martial law remained in effect.

The government failed to control or acknowledge human rights abuses. Krahn soldiers meted out brutal summary justice against members of rival tribes presumed to have supported the coup attempt. Ethnic divisions, largely dormant before 1980, had been percolating towards the surface of Liberian life during the 1980s. The violence following the coup attempt brought these to a boil. University students and faculty were some of the most frequent targets of repression. After 1985 the Krahn controlled all key divisions within the Liberian Armed Forces. After the 1980 coup failed, Gios and linguistically related Manos were the main targets of reprisals as discipline was eroded. Hundreds of Gio and Mano soldiers and civilians were herded into the grounds of the Executive Mansion and Barclay Training Center, were stripped, and then killed. The non-Krahn inhabitants of Grand Gedeh and Nimba counties, Grebos, Gios and Manos, were subjected to arrests, beatings, extortion and killings carried out by Krahn soldiers and civilians, including high school students wielding machetes and whips made from radial tires. High ranking government officials took the view that the government could not be held responsible for abuses committed even by those acting on government authority. The Executive Mansion guard served as personal militia composed of Krahn not from Liberia, but from neighboring Cote d'Ivoire across the border from Grand Gedeh, well armed with American guns (Lawyers Committee, 1986).

On December 24, 1989, Charles Taylor and his National Patriotic Front of Liberia (NPFL) launched an incursion from Cote d'Ivoire into Nimba County. The Armed Forces of Liberia (AFL) responded with a ruthless counter insurgency campaign indiscriminately killing civilians burning villages raping women and looting. The brutality served to swell the ranks of NPFL recruits, many of whom were Gio and Mano boys orphaned by the fighting. Within weeks over 160,000 fled into neighboring Guinea and Ivory Coast beginning a refugee exodus that escalated to 700,000 by late 1990—one-third of the population.

In 1990 the outcome of this long experiment in civilizing Africa by denying Africa's own history and achievements was to reach its ultimate degradation as a video was shown to a journalist of the violent death on September 9, 1990, of Doe. Doe was equally the victim of another typical pathology of the times that formed him—the pathology of a colonial or neocolonial "tribalism," or clientalism, which itself was a product not of Africa's precolonial development, but a desperate mode of self-defence by citizens whose state could not or would not protect them.

The NPFL targeted supporters of the Doe regime, particularly members of the Krahn and Mandingo ethnic groups, slaughtering civilians and destroying villages along the way. The Mandingos, for the most part traders and businessmen, were considered by the rebels to have collaborated with the Doe government. By late June the NPFL had reached Grand Gedeh country which is populated largely by the Krahns. The NPFL fighters attacked civilians and devastated the area prompting a huge influx of Krahns to seek sanctuary in neighboring Cote d'Ivoire. Krahn refugees described indiscriminate rebel attacks with houses rocketed or burned and civilians tortured and killed. Other targets included those who were mistaken for Krahn or Mandingo—particularly the Grebo and Vai—and anyone who served or cooperated with the Doe government. The indiscriminate killing increased as more territory fell into NPFL hands.

In the 1992 round of fighting the ethnic character of the killing was less apparent than in 1990. Murder was incidental to robbing. The civilian population in NPFL territory, especially around Buchanan and Gbinta on the border with Cote d'Ivoire, has been terrorized by bombing by ECOMOG (the West African peace-keeping force, mostly Nigerian) planes. The United Liberation Movement for Democracy in Liberia (ULIMO) was formed in 1991 by former AFL soldiers who fled to Sierra Leone, predominantly Krahn and Mandingo soldiers. One focus of concern with ULIMO, in addition to human rights abuses and the manipulation of humanitarian aid, involves the use of children as young as 12 as soldiers.

The multinational force installed an interim government headed by Dr. Amos Sawyer and gradually established control in Monrovia but Taylor's forces controlled most of the countryside, while former members of ex-President Doe's army con-trolled the two western provinces. By 1993 it was estimated that 150,000 had died in the civil war, many of them civilians killed as a result of tribal rivalries exacerbated by civil war, and that half of the population had fled the country or been displaced in their own country. In July 1993 the various factions signed a UN-brokered peace ac-cord calling for a cease fire, the disarming of the various factions by a reconstructed West African peace keeping force and the holding of new elections in 1994. These were held in 1995 and a new government inaugurated on September 1, 1995, as a transitional government intended to bring to an end nearly six years of war. This included rebel leaders Charles Taylor, George Boley, and Alhaji Kromah. Numerous violations of this fragile cease-fire have been recorded, including those widely re-ported in April 1996 of fighting between the Taylor-Kromah faction and the militias of the dissident Krahn leader, General Roosevelt Johnson.

Although the United Nations contributed significantly to the emergency relief and humanitarian aid that has gone to Liberia, the UN did not address the Liberian crisis in political terms until November 1992, almost three years after the crisis erupted. The UN's emphasis has been to shift responsibility to the ECOWAS. Little effort was taken to ensure that human rights issues figured prominently in the regional organization efforts and that the organization itself does not contribute to aggravating the war.

Somalia

Once under Italian and British colonial rule, Somalia became independent in 1960. Traditional rivalries among various clans including the Isaaqs of the North, Ogadenis of the South and the Hawiye of central Somalia were exacerbated by the divide and rule policies of Mohammed Said Barre whose regime (1969-1991) had one of the world's worst human rights records. When Barre fled in January 1991 as many as half a million Somalis starved to death as warring clans struggled for power. In December 1992, a UN-sponsored, U.S.-led military peace keeping operation was launched to attempt to restore order and to guarantee the delivery of relief supplies. It was the first time the UN had ever intervened without permission in the affairs of an independent nation. The last of the U.S. troops left Somalia in March 1994.

Somalia has an ethnic homogeneity unusual in Africa, with Somalis constituting 96 percent of the country's population. Various explanations have been proposed in seeking to explain why one of the few nations on the continent with predominantly one ethnic group, one culture, one language and religion should have become em-broiled in a devastating civil war. Some have focused on the autocratic nature of Said Barre's rule (Jackson and Rosberg, 1982); others see kinship as the pivotal and defining character of Somali culture and politics (Lewis, 1988). Despite a generally acknowledged fact of common traits, Somalis are divided into three major clan families, the Saab, the Irir and the Darood. Each in turn has its own subfamilies which further break down into numerous lineage segments all the way down to the homestead. This intricate system is delicately held together by two practices—a loosely accepted set of unwritten codes called xeer, and a collective blood-paying process, the diya. While the Irir and Darood are predominantly pastoral, the Saab who live in the riverside area of the south have long mixed herding with peasant farming. Traditionally this has been a small component of the population and economy of Somalia. Members of each group trace their descent from a single male ancestor independent from the ancestors of other clan families. Intermarriage is widespread among the groups but maternal blood does not count as far as clan identity is concerned.

The arguments of those who see kinship as pivotal are that pastoral Somalis, given communal access to the range and family ownership of the means of production (the herd) are highly egalitarian and democratic (for males), and that primordial affinities not withstanding, theirs is a highly anarchic society and subsequently susceptible to internicine feuds. Such observers suggest that the causal factors for the current crisis should be sought in these nomadic tendencies towards fragmentation. Long lasting pastoral clannism has invaded the fragile urban outposts. Pastoralism is seen as an original condition, immune to history and change; kinship and clannism are deployed interchangeably.

Alternatively, Samatar (1988) suggests that we focus on the clash of two different historical modes of livelihood as the underlying causes of the current crisis. The first of these is subsistence, which is kin ordered, the other is modern and commodity ordered, and the problems associated with the creation of a viable national polity or state. Within the subsistence based production system, ancient and reciprocal norms had strength in meeting the basic needs of the community (and still do where these survive intact) except in times of great drought or other natural calamity. Their weakness has been an inability to produce surplus to keep up with growing needs and wants of a rising population. The traditional pastoral Somali economy produced for consumption and was typically communitarian. Thus kin relations defined the political and cultural life. With the inception of the colonial state in the late 19th, this communal mode was hitched to the internationally expanding mode of commodity production and class forms began to emerge including pastoral producers, dilaals and merchants. The colonial state and merchants began to extract surplus from pastoral producers through unequal barter terms of trade in livestock and consumer items.

Livestock was the preeminent export of Somalia, accounting for 80 percent of earnings, but the returns to producers have been meager. Development expenditure for this was less than 14 percent in 1986-1987 (Samatar, 1992), much of which had been used to improve marketing facilities. A significant change in prices took place in the early 1980s as Somalia faced stiff competition for the Saudi market (which accounted for over 90 percent of Somali exports) from countries like Australia.

Declining oil prices, the internationalization of the market and the anxiety of the Somalia state at the possibility of losing this market precipitated a steep decline in export prices. This affected both state revenues and produced incomes. The volume of animals exported began to stagnate. Pastoral producers faced the gravest problems and environmental degradation of the Somali rangelands intensified during the 1980s. The north with its steeper topography and proximity to ports is severely eroded and the expansion of plantation cash crop production in the interriverine areas of the South has brought widespread deforestation and soil degradation. The ecological destruction of the range in Somalia rendered pastoral management systems defunct and incapable of reproducing this form of communal pastoral production.

The interaction of the demands of international financial institutions, the debilitating weight of Somali debt, a negative balance of payments, declining production and a high rate of population growth (3.1 percent) drove the Somali state to look for external transfusion. From 1980 to 1983, under a standby agreement with the IMF the government imposed fiscal and monetary restraints, cut public expenditure and privatized the banana export agency. With an ever increasing budget deficit and debt service arrears the government increased its borrowing and in 1984 repudiated the IMF program, reportedly over demands for cuts in military budget devaluation and in government personnel. In 1987 as the IMF and other donors withdrew support; expenditure, fiscal deficit and money supply all increased.

Somalia had attracted comparatively large amounts of aid both in per capita terms and as a percentage of GNP (aid to refugees alone was estimated at 25 percent of GNP in 1986) but had the highest debt to export ratio of any country. Debt service payments in 1989 on $2.53 billion were 127 percent of export earnings. The emphasis in the structural adjustment policies was on short term growth and strengthening the private sector. In their wake followed inflation, the decay or disappearance of social services (including education) and growing unemployment and immiseration, especially among rural women and children (Onimode, 1989). The intrusion of a commodity oriented social system (one that accents utilitarianism and private welfare) coupled with shrinking material circumstances have eroded the old linkage between kinship ties and xeer. Disconnected blood ties have been made the main prism to interpret the world, kinship supplanted with clannism and deprived of its civilizing (i.e., universalizing) and restraining moral code.

In the new government of 1960, politicians from the south took the presidency, prime ministership, two-thirds of the cabinet positions and the two top posts in the military and police. Almost immediately this southern domination was challenged. An attempted coup by junior army officers from the north was quickly put down in 1961. By 1969 there were no less than 60 political parties but no national issues were debated, but the cultivation of sublineage interests accentuated the demise of kinship and the rise of clannism. Somali parliamentary democracy had become a travesty; once elected, politicians ignored the needs of the majority of the population.

In October 1969 the President was killed by one of his own police. Six days later armed forces seized power in a bloodless and popular coup. Major General Said Barre dissolved the national assembly and suspended the 1960 constitution. Political parties and professional associations were abolished. Barre and the Supreme Revolutionary Council (SRC) received a tumultuous welcome. Corrupt politicians were put on trial but the 1970 Power to Detain Law, against which an individual had no safeguards, was increasingly being used against dissidents. In 1971 two senior coup leaders were executed as the SRC concentrated power with the help of an omnipresent secret police (Samatar, 1990).

Defeat in the war with Ethiopia in 1978 marked a major watershed. With defeat came acrimony and blame. Many were executed, mostly military leaders for challenging the conduct of the war. Internment was introduced amidst a climate of mutual suspicion and fright and fleeing dissidents turned into organized opposition. The Somali Salvation Democratic Front (SSDF) was founded in Addis Ababa composed primarily of ex-politicians, senior civil servants and traders from the Majerteen lineage who had lost standing in the SRC. The weakness of the military state became conspicuous with the disappearance of Soviet aid and technical assistance. The failing economy and political system reawakened long suppressed discontent over the regional neglect of the north. The various lineage groups in the north were not treated equally. The historically strong and wealthy Isaaqs had been systematically undermined in military and civil service posts and through the unequal development of resources and the siting of development projects. Barre constructed the inner core of his government from representatives of three clans belonging to the Darood clan family; his own (the Majerteen), that of his son-in-law (the Dulbahante) and that of his mother's brother (the Ogadeen). The head of the National Security Service belonged to the Dulbahante clan which occupied the strategically important border area between the former British and Italian Somalilands. More than 70 percent of high military and civil service posts were held by members of the Darood clan family (Panos Institute, 1991, p. 67). When Ethiopian refugees (predominantly Ogadenis) were settled in northern Isaaq pastoral lands, increasing the pressure on scarce resources, this was seen by the Isaaqs as a calculated policy to replace them, especially when the government illegally recruited refugees into the army and created paramilitary groups among them. Military and party officials in the North were southerners with close family links to Barre.

In 1981 the Somali National Movement (SNM) was formed in London with financial support from the Isaaq diaspora in Saudi Arabia and the Gulf states. They were granted operational space by Ethiopia. Before the summer of 1988 they presented little more than an occasional nuisance. The government, however, tried to undermine support by gearing spending towards areas not sympathetic to the SNM or SSDF and unleashing a regime of terror and pillage in those areas viewed as sympathetic to rebel groups, especially in the North. In the mid-1980s Somalia and Ethiopia had severe problems including continuing hostilities between them and growing insurgencies within each state. In 1987 Barre offered the Ethiopian government a peace treaty in which Somalia gave up its territorial claims on the Ogaden region in return for depriving the SNM of their Ethiopian bases. Ethiopia agreed and thus the SNM decided to attack Northern Somalia and "liberate their clan territory" the Hargeisa, Berbera and Burao Triangle. The result was a blood bath. To benefit from the element of surprise the SNM overran many villages until they captured Burao. The government responded by unleashing all northern military forces and reinforcements from the South. Burao was razed to the ground and under aerial bombardment and heavy artillery fire, seventy per cent of Hargeisa was destroyed. Tens of thousands of civilians fled to Ethiopia (Dowden, 1989).

By mid-1988 Somalia was embroiled in one of the worst civil wars in Africa, involving the government and five armed, but disunited, opposition groups. These included the United Somali Congress (USC; Hawiye), the SNM (Isaaq), and the Somali Patriotic Movement (SPM) composed of Ogadenis, who until recently were part of the Somali armed forces and bureaucracy. The spread to the south had several consequences. With livestock trading in the north severely disrupted the most fertile and productive part of the country, the middle and lower Juba Valley, began to slide into violent conflict. This was tantamount to the destruction of the fragile survival base of the country. Said Barre's regime deployed the same savagely punitive tactics applied in the north to cow the peasant population in the south where the SPM was suspected to operate. Africa Watch records that the government deliberately targeted the civilian population in an effort to make the countryside inhospitable to rebel movements by killing, looting and rape. More than a million people fled to Ethiopia and Kenya. Tens of thousands of civilians were displaced and many were killed (Africa Watch, 1989, p. 2).

As the discontent spread to Mogadishu, troops clashed with protesters and a curfew was imposed. Many arrests and some executions followed, especially of Isaaq residents of the Medina district (Amnesty International, 1990, pp. 4-5). However with the spread of discontent into the capital came defeat for Barre and in January 1991 he fled to Kenya. Since this time there has been a continued state of civil unrest throughout the country with a profusion of arms and large scale malnutrition. NGOs and the UNHCR withdrew totally at one stage. Hargeisa and four other towns as well as numerous rural settlements mostly in Northern Somalia have been reduced to rubble. At a conservative estimate 50-60,000 civilians were killed by government forces in the streets of Mogadishu prior to Barre's defeat.

Somalia was largely neglected during the 1980s by the international community. The basic civil institutions disappeared during the last years of Barre's rule. In 1991 Somalia was a nation without a government or central security force, where a collection of armed clan militia fought over spoils, and in a combination of political and ethnic conflict, ravaged the land and systematically killed and displaced the civilian population. As many as 500,000 Somalis are estimated to have died and another two million fled their homes to become displaced persons within their own country or unwelcome refugees in Kenya, Ethiopia, and Djibouti (Human Rights Watch, 1993, pp. 107-134).

By the time UNOSOM troops arrived in force two years after Said Barre's fall, the crisis was far advanced. The two years allowed the warleaders to fragment the country, to consolidate their use of force as a weapon and to deny resources to civilian communities as the source of their power. When UNISOM arrived the new aid and resources provided them with a new source of power (Human Rights Watch/Africa, 1995, p. 16). De facto authorities have worked with militias in the murder of their enemies, the deliberate killing of civilians from clans they designated as their enemies and measures intended to destroy whole communities through hunger and thirst. The deliberate destruction of wells, burning of crops and looting of food stores combined with drought to cause the death of hundreds of thousands. The warleaders' strength is based on the promise of protection, supremacy and spoils for their clans, and the domination of others in an order founded on social and economic division and discrimination (Human Rights Watch/Africa, 1995, p. 16). Ethnic minority groups face expulsion from their land or looting of the means of survival by the armed militias of more powerful groups. The victimization of women, particularly the displaced, is widespread. Others under threat are leaders of their own communities who are seen as problematic to the coalition led by rival warleaders. Although the relation to authority of most Somalis is through traditional clan structures, significant sectors of the population fall outside this multitiered system. Those who have no clan to stand behind them or who come from Somalia's Bantu ethnic minority populations may be marginalized by traditional and modern authority structures alike and so more vulnerable to abuse (Maxted and Zegeye, 1997).

Since independence, successive elites were preoccupied with restoring ethnic Somali territory and cultivating an assumed Arab identity. The international community has clearly failed Somalia. In the early 1990s the UN made no serious sustained effort to break the cycle of civil war, human rights abuses and famine even through international standards of human rights laws had been grossly violated. With UNOSOM gone, traditional clan leaders (and not faction leaders) have begun to meet to discuss free movement, grazing and water rights, and interclan family disputes. But within this process the clan identity of victim and accused may result in bias and impunity. With the clan protecting rights and security, justice too often ultimately depends on one's group and its relative power in a local community. Under this system, however, ethnic minorities and women possess few rights, either as groups or as individuals. The desire of these groups for the imposition of Islamic law through the shari'a courts represents a desperate attempt to gain some form of protection.

Conclusion

The contemporary situation reveals a crisis of institutions for decolonized Africans. Unfortunately the argument over institutions has been debased to the level of what is said to be "democracy" versus what is said to be "tribalism." Most conflicts in the past two years have been within states or former states. Modern tribalism is the opposite of civil society; it flourishes in disorder and flouting the rule of law. Banditry has become one of the principal modes of political action. The question is less whether the nation-state can be rescued than how long and painful this transition to new forms of federation and political community will be. The most viable states will be shored up and strengthened to provide a bridge to more effective regional arrangements. However, it is also clear that the territorial division of Africa into nation-states based on colonial partition with boundaries sanctified by the OAU as inviolable is under the greatest pressure since independence.

From independence African states have placed great emphasis on the principle of territorial integrity, in part to counter their weakness and artificiality. The demise of the one-party state in many countries, together with the ending of much foreign sponsorship has exposed the worst ethnic dictatorships in Africa to new political forces. However diverse these ethnic conflicts—some date back hundreds of years to warring kingdoms, while others derive from colonial meddling and manipulation—it is becoming increasingly difficult to contain them within present state frameworks. The space of the nation-state is increasingly fabricated with recourse to coercion through forced labor and slavery, police raids, authoritarian repatriation of unemployed town dwellers to the countryside as undesirables, floggings, extrajuridical imprisonment and a network of informers.

For the most part African nationalism has been official rather than popular, political rather than cultural. The mostly urban, westernized elites who formed the first political parties and campaigned for independence had little difficulty in forging interethnic alliances so long as the object was to get rid of colonial powers. Once independent they faced a crisis of legitimacy: by what right did they rule? The conventional solution favored by nationalists in many other parts of the world—that political and ethnic boundaries converge—was not available since Africans had inherited from the colonial period a set of frontiers drawn up in total disregard (and generally without the slightest knowledge) of local cultural or ethnic borders.

The OAU settlement (1963) reinforced the conventional interpretation of national self-determination. Its charter, as that of the UN, is based on the twin principles of territorial integrity and noninterference in the domestic affairs of other states. In the OAU's case these principles were strengthened in 1964, by the adoption in Cairo of a resolution binding African states to recognize the "tangible reality" of the borders they inherited on the day of independence. Taken together the charter and the Cairo resolution provide a powerful support for the territorial status quo.

Whenever an African state has been challenged by irredentist or secessionist forces it has successfully invoked the principle of *uti possidetis* to preserve its territorial integrity. The problems caused by rival national identities must be analyzed primarily in their own terms, as embedded in the histories and social structures of their people. They cannot however be properly understood without some attention to the role that nationalism has played in shaping the modern world. Since 1945 the two propositions that the state should be a national state and that sovereignty rests with the people have driven all contending principles of political legitimacy from the field. However many African countries contain deeply divided societies which constantly challenge the national pretensions of the state. Yet nationalism provides the political idiom in which many dissident movements justify and press their claims.

Under the League of Nations Covenant, minorities were theoretically provided with a measure of protection which was withdrawn in favor of an even more theoretical entrenchment of individual human rights within the UN system. While most African constitutions guarantee equal enjoyment of human rights some specifically provide that these rights should be enjoyed by all without any distinction as to ethnic origin. There is no reference to minorities in the African Charter of Human and Peoples Rights (Banjul Charter) of 1986. "People" are the people of the state considered as a whole and not minority groups or religions. Many constitutions adopt the Universal Declaration of Human Rights but the formal inclusion of human rights provision in the constitution is not enough to ensure that there are in fact recognized. African states participate widely in UN bodies: they have been particularly active in proposing and supporting international instruments condemning racial discrimination and apartheid. However, concentration on self-determination and independence have deflected attention from the postindependence human rights performance of states.

Self-determination is a continuing process and will endure as long as basic human rights are not effectively guaranteed and protected. This can occur as a result of colonial or minority racist imposition as well as oppression by apparently lawfully constituted governments of independent African states. Military regimes may also fundamentally negate human rights. What has originated as the right of nations to independence has been transformed into a concept with variable and varying contents. The right extends to nations as well as peoples, whether colonized or forming part of independent states, and has transcended the attributes of its external manifestation to a democratization process, that in some cases may justify the right to rebel against constituted authority. Ethnic and religious minorities, and most notably the women and children of these groups, have been shown to be most vulnerable in cases of state failure. It is by no means clear that the rights of minorities would be better served under more regional groupings. Proposals that failed states should be put under regional trusteeship (a type of benign recolonization) depend critically on effective regional organization. They also depend on regionally powerful states such as Nigeria, Egypt, South Africa, Kenya and Ethiopia being capable of sponsoring such diplomatic efforts. These pole states may make up the nucleus of an OAU security council, capable of decisive intervention in conflicts. These very states are also riven with divisions and have a poor record on the treatment of minorities.

The path to such regionalized state support will be difficult, as the Liberian crisis has shown. It is not enough, however, to consider exclusively the supranational. Addressing the need for effective devolved government and finding new structures to contain the regional, national, ethnic and class loyalties will be as exacting as establishing new regional authorities. Reformers seem to face a new paradox: If they are to reform the nation-state system, their first task may be to strengthen existing nation-states to bear the weight of the transition. Although African governments are basically opposed to the dismemberment of states emanating from colonial territorial demarcation, that process can only be arrested if certain social groups, whether large or small, feel that they are part of the instruments and machineries by which decisions affecting them are made.

REFERENCES

ADEKANYE, J.
    1996 "Rwanda/Burundi: 'Uni-ethnic' Dominance and the Cycle of Armed Ethnic Formations." *Social Identities* 2(1) (February): 37-72.

AFRICA WATCH
    1989 *Kenya: Forcible Return of Somali Refugees and Government Repression of Kenya Somalis.* London: Africa Watch.

AMNESTY INATERNATIONAL
    1990 *Somalia: Report on an Amnesty International Visit and Current Human Rights Concerns.* London: Amnesty International.

BAYART, Jean-Pierre
    1993 *The State in Africa: The Politics of the Belly.* London: Longman.

DAVIDSON, Basil
    1992 *The Black Man's Burden.* London: James Currey.

DOWDEN, R.
    1989 "Somalia Is Disintegrating into Anarchy." *Independent* (London), 10 October, p. 17.

HUMAN RIGHTS WATCH
    1993 *The Lost Agenda: Human Rights and UN Field Operations.* New York: Human Rights Watch.

HUMAN RIGHTS WATCH/AFRICA
    1995 *Somalia Faces the Future: Human Rights in a Fragmented Society.* New York: Human Rights Watch.

JACKSON, R.H., and Carl G. ROSBERG
    1982 *Personal Rule in Black Africa: Prince, Autocrat, Prophet, Tyrant.* Berkeley: University of California Press.

LAWYERS COMMITTEE FOR HUMAN RIGHTS
    1986 *Liberia: A Promise Betrayed.* New York: LCHR.

LEWIS, I.M.

 1988 *A Modern History of Somalia: From Nation to State.* Boulder: Westview Press.

LIEBENOW, J. Gus

 1969 *The Evolution of Privilege.* Ithaca, N.Y.: Cornell University Press.

LUCKHAM, R.

 1980 "Armaments, Underdevelopment, and Demilitarization in Africa." *Alternatives* 6: *179-245.*

MAXTED, J., and A. ZEGEYE

 1997 "North, West, and the Horn of Africa." In: *World Directory of Minorities.* 2d ed. London: Minority Rights Group International.

ONIMODE, Bade, ed.

 1989 *The IMF, World Bank, and the African Debt: The Economic Impact.* 2 vols. London: Zed Books.

PANOS INSTITUTE

 1991 *Greenwar: Environment and Conflict.* London: Panos Institute.

RODNEY, W.

 1970 *A History of the Upper Guinea Coast.* Oxford: Clarendon Press.

SAMATAR, Abdi

 1992 "Social Class and Economic Restructuring in Pastoral Africa: Notes from Somalia." *African Studies Review* 35: 101-119.

SAMATAR, Ahmed

 1988 *Socialist Somalia.* London: Zed Books.

 1990 "Internal Struggles in Somalia." Paper presented to Regional Security Conference, Cairo.

"UNMAKING AND REMAKING THE STATE"

 1995 *Africa Confidential* 36 (1) (January 6).

Capital, Inequality and Injustice in Latin America[1]

RICHARD L. HARRIS*

ABSTRACT

This article examines contemporary economic, political and social conditions in Latin America. A combination of three key analytical concepts are used to provide an integrated and global conceptualization of the predominant social structures, processes and relations in the societies located in this important region of the world. These three concepts are *capital*, *inequality*, and *injustice*. The application of these analytically powerful concepts to the analysis of the historical development and contemporary affairs of the Latin American societies reveals the fundamental social relations of contemporary capitalism that are primarily responsible for the pronounced extent of inequality and injustice that characterize the societies in this region.

MORE THAN TWO decades ago, two Latin American social scientists—Fernando Henrique Cardoso and Enzo Faletto—produced what soon became a classic analysis of the economic, political and social development of Latin America. In the preface to the English edition of this much-acclaimed book, they stated the fundamental basis of their perspective as follows:

> We seek a global and dynamic understanding of social structures instead of looking only at specific dimensions of the social process. We oppose the academic tradition which conceived of domination and sociocultural relations as "dimensions," analytically independent of one another, and together independent of the economy, as if each one of these dimensions corresponded to separate spheres of reality. In that sense, we stress the sociopolitical nature of the economic relations of production, thus following the nineteenth century tradition of treating economy as political economy. This methodological approach, which found its highest expression in Marx, assumes the hierarchy that exists in society is the result of established ways of organizing the production of material and spiritual life. (Cardoso and Faletto, 1979, p. ix.)

This article is based on the same perspective as that employed by Cardoso and Faletto.[2] Over the last three decades, many scholars have produced analyses of the prevailing conditions and historical development of the region based upon a similar perspective (see, for example, Marini, 1974; Bambirra, 1976; Vasconi, 1978;

*   Institute of Global Studies, California State University, Monterey Bay, CA 93955-8001, U.S.A.

Chilcote and Edelstein, 1986; Petras and Morley, 1992; and Halebsky and Harris, 1995).

To analyze and make sense of the complex and changing conditions that are shared in whole or in part by the societies that make up the Latin American region, I have chosen to select three key organizing concepts that permit an integrated and global conceptualization of the major structures, processes and relations that characterize and prevail across societies in the region. These three concepts are *capital*, *inequality*, and *injustice*. They share in common certain important analytical qualities: They permit a multidimensional, multilevel, and comparative analysis of the complex set of conditions that prevail in Latin America. They also facilitate an integrative and inclusive analysis of the interdependent societal structures, processes and relations underlying contemporary Latin American economic, political and social affairs. In addition, they are compatible with the intellectual tradition of comparative, structural, historical, and critical analyses mentioned above.

These concepts are employed in this article in full recognition of the postmodernist critique of metanarratives and metaconcepts. According to the conventional postmodernist perspective, the metaconcepts and theories developed by Western intellectuals in the nineteenth and twentieth centuries have created a false consciousness of reality based upon a belief in the myth of modernity and unilinear social progress. Thus, from a postmodernist perspective, these concepts and theories are regarded as invalid and outmoded images for understanding the complex nature of the "postmodern" societies of the late twentieth century (Schuurman, 1993, pp. 23-29).

According to the postmodernist critique of modernist thought, the events of the closing decades of the twentieth century have revealed the erroneous nature of the previously constructed "metatheories" or "grand historical narratives" that were developed on the basis of concepts such as social progress, modernization, capitalism, socialism, imperialism, development, underdevelopment, industrialization, human emancipation, and internationalism. For the proponents of this perspective, the incredibly complex, diverse and unpredictable nature of contemporary life cannot be explain by such metatheories and grand historical narratives, nor can contemporary reality be adequately perceived through the use of the universal concepts upon which these theories are based.

The main problem with this perspective insofar as its applicability to contemporary Latin America is concerned is that there is scarcely any evidence that the region consists of "postmodern societies" or that it has moved into a "postmodern era" (Schuurman, 1993, p. 27). Most of the problems and issues addressed by the so-called obsolete metatheories persist in contemporary Latin America. In fact, many of the inhabitants of the region live under conditions which can be more accurately described as "uneven modernity" rather than postmodernity (Beverley, Oveido, and Aronna, 1995, p. 4). The complex social reality of contemporary Latin

America is perhaps best thought of as a complex hybrid of "premodern," "modern," and "postmodern" ideologies, practices, and conditions.

The "globalization" or increasing integration of the region into the global capitalist system has not propelled the Latin American peoples into a new era of postmodernity. Many of the "old" problems and issues continue to be contemporary problems and issues. In fact, the contemporary effects of globalization (the expansion of "postmodern" or "late" capitalism) have aggravated the most chronic problems of the Latin American region. These problems include the pronounced degree of economic exploitation, social and economic inequality, and social and political injustice that have characterized the region since the first indigenous peoples of the Western Hemisphere were by force subjugated to European colonial domination in the sixteenth century.

The striking degree of extreme inequality that has existed for the last several centuries between the privileged minorities and the impoverished majority in Latin America cannot be adequately explained from a postmodernist perspective. However, viewed from a global perspective and through the conceptual lens provided by the three concepts employed in this article, it is clear that the nature of the region's contemporary integration into the global capitalist economy has reinforced, if not accentuated, this extreme inequality as well as the unjust relations of subordination and domination that maintain and complement this inequality.

Thus, the conceptual framework employed in this article is offered in a sense as a defense of the continued validity of such metaconcepts as capital, inequality, and injustice. However, I am well aware of the limitations of these concepts and the biased manner in which they have generally been employed in the past. For this reason, the mode in which they are employed in this article is tempered by the critique of such concepts by postmodernist intellectuals, who have correctly criticized the past use of such concepts as having been flawed by the Eurocentric, rationalistic, deterministic, and universalistic biases imbedded in the ideologies and analyses in which they were employed.[3]

In this regard, it is worth noting the justification that Cardoso and Faletto gave for their use of the concept of capital in their historical analysis of Latin America's social, economic, and political development. They argued that this concept was necessary because they needed a concept that was "able to explain trends of change ... [and] opposing forces" (Cardoso and Faletto, 1979, p. xiii). In addition, they argued that "it was necessary to relate these forces in a global way, characterizing the basic sources of their existence, continuity and change, by determining forms of domination and the forces opposed to them." Finally, they contended that "without the concept of capital as the result of the exploitation of one class by another it is not possible to explain the movement of capitalist society."

In this essay, I use the theoretical concept of capital to draw attention to the inequitable and unjust manner in which wealth has been, and continues to be, accumulated in Latin America through exploitative relations of capitalist production and exchange. As Catherine MacKinnon notes in her work *Toward a Feminist Theory of the State*, this theoretical tradition, despite its limitations:

> confronts organized social dominance, analyzes it in dynamic rather than static terms, identifies social forces that systematically shape social imperatives, and seeks to explain human freedom both within and against history. It confronts class, which is real. If offers both a critique of the inevitability and inner coherence of social injustice and a theory of the necessity and possibilities of change. (MacKinnon, 1989, p. ix.)

The application of the concept of capital to the analysis of the historical development and contemporary affairs of the Latin American societies reveals the fundamental social relations of exploitation and domination that are primarily responsible for the pronounced degree of inequality in material conditions that prevail among the contemporary human inhabitants of Latin America. It also permits a critical analysis of the unjust structures and practices of social domination, subordination and discrimination suffered by the impoverished majority of the inhabitants of the region.

Inequality and injustice have similar conceptual and analytical properties as the concept of capital. They are similar to the concept of capital in that they facilitate a critical analysis, both systematic as well as normative, of the dynamic relations, structures and processes that underlie the contemporary conditions of human existence in Latin America.

Applied broadly to the analysis of social reality in Latin America, the concept of inequality focuses our attention on the "unequal access to power, to resources, and to a humane existence" that prevails in the Latin American societies (Schuurman, 1993, p. 30). Thus, at the microlevel of social reality this concept can be applied to the inequality between men and women within the family unit, at the midlevel it encompasses the unequal access of different categories of the population to the basic necessities of human existence, and at the macro- or global level the concept encompasses phenomena such as the unequal economic relations between the Latin American economies and that of the United States. In fact, because social, economic, and political disparities are so ubiquitous and extreme in Latin America, it is possible to argue that inequality should be the main *explanandum* (i.e., focus of explanation) of any intellectual effort that seeks to explain the historical development and contemporary conditions of the Latin American societies (Schuurman, 1993, p. 31).

As for the concept of injustice, it focuses analysis on the numerous forms of unfair, discriminatory and injurious treatment suffered by the majority of human beings in Latin America. This concept directs analytical attention to all those structures, practices and relations that involve the subordination, domination, persecution and repression of human beings through the use of exploitation, acts of violence, and/or intimidation. In an earlier issue of this journal, Pat Lauderdale and Annamarie Oliverio have pointed out that the indigenous peoples in the Western Hemisphere and throughout the world continue to experience "the full presence of injustice in the form of poverty, landlessness, dispossession, political and religious oppression, and genocide" (Lauderdale and Oliverio, 1995, p. 141). They also point out that the prevailing conception of jurisprudence "claims that law and order creates justice, [but] ignores the inequitable use of punishment" in the same way neoliberal ideology claims capitalist economic development creates freedom while in fact it results in "the punishment of inequity in all areas of life."

The concept can be applied at all levels of social reality in Latin America. At the microlevel, the concept can be applied to the paternalistic subordination and domination of women within the family unit (Larguia, 1995); at the midlevel to the use of violence and intimidation by the police and armed forces to repress groups and communities who seek to organize politically and express their grievances (Nef, 1995, pp. 100-101); and at the macro- or global level to the coercive influence and intimidation which international organizations such as the International Monetary Fund (IMF), the transnational corporations and the United States government exercise over the Latin American governments to secure favorable policies and gain concessions that promote their interests at the expense of the majority of the population governed by these governments (Henwood, 1995).

The Integration of Latin America into the Global Capitalist System

Any serious attempt to explain the extreme inequalities and ubiquitous forms of injustice that characterize the Latin America societies inevitably leads to a critical examination of the exploitative relations of capitalist production and distribution that predominate throughout the region. As Cardoso and Faletto noted in their classic study, "the system of production and institutions of appropriation" in Latin America are closely linked with "the strong inequalities" and "processes of domination" in the region (Cardoso and Falleto, 1979, p. x). Therefore, these interdependent linkages can best be analyzed if the concepts of capital, inequality and injustice are applied in an integrative manner to the analysis of contemporary Latin America.

It is difficult to avoid the conclusion that the primary cause of the extreme social and economic inequalities in Latin America and elsewhere in the world is the result of the worldwide expansion of capitalism (Amin, 1992). The classical Marxist perspective on this question is convincing. The motive forces associated with the accumulation of wealth that underlie the capitalist system drive individual capitalists and capitalist ("private") enterprises to expand their accumulative activities and overcome all geographic, cultural and political barriers that obstruct their path to accumulating wealth (Magdoff, 1992). These same forces also motivate individual capitalists and capitalist enterprises to concentrate and centralize their control over the various means whereby wealth is accumulated. As a result, individual capitalists and capitalist enterprises have extended their efforts to accumulate wealth to every corner of the planet and they have increasingly integrated the world's economies into a single global economic system as a result of their continuing attempts to concentrate and centralize their control over the accumulation process.

The nature of the Latin American region's integration into the global capitalist economy has reinforced the extreme forms of inequality and widespread injustice that prevail in this part of the world. A critical analysis of the effects of capitalism reveals that it has created extreme inequalities in the region as well as in the entire world. In fact, the globalization process stimulated by the worldwide expansion and development of capitalism has consistently favored only a limited proportion of the Latin American population while the vast majority have had to suffer the adverse effects of this process.

In the last two decades, nearly every major aspect of contemporary economic, political and social life in Latin America has been affected by the region's accelerated integration into the global capitalist system. The contemporary Latin American economies have become integral components of a global economic system that is dominated not by nation-states, but by the large transnational corporations that constitute the main global actors in this system. Since the 1960s, the global expansion of these transnational corporations has greatly undermined the former national organization of economic relations and contributed to the global concentration and centralization of the capital accumulation process. The Latin American economies are being integrated into the global capitalist economy as "captive markets" and the source of cheap human and natural resources for the North American-based transnationals, which find themselves increasingly challenged at the global level by the major European- and Asian-based transnational corporations (Henwood, 1993, pp. 23-28). Efforts to develop national capitalism (capital accumulation within the territorial confines of a single nation-state) and/or improve "national" competitiveness are still possible. However, such efforts face increasing difficulties since they run counter to the increasingly global nature of the world economy and the global interests and actions of the transnational corporations (Radice, 1989, p. 68).

The contemporary capitalist class in Latin America are what can be called a "weak bourgeoisie" (Fiori, 1995, p. 98). The close ties of these local entrepreneurial elites to the global capitalists who control the transnationals operating in their countries make it extremely unlikely these local business elites will undertake any kind of national capitalist project. Moreover, the only "competitive advantages" the Latin American capitalists have at their disposal to compete in the world economy are cheap labor (maintained by keeping wages low through high levels of unemployment and political repression) and certain valuable natural resources. They lack the technology, skilled labor, large domestic consumer markets, and financial capital possessed by capitalists in the major capitalist countries of the world. Since they lack the means to compete on equal terms with the transnational capitalists, they have had little choice but to join with them as their local junior partners. Thus, the Latin American business elites have thrown open the doors of their economies to the transnational corporations who are interested in the cheap labor, natural resources, finance capital and consumer markets in the Latin American countries (Petras and Morley, 1992, pp. 16-29).

Together the local elites and the transnational capitalists have promoted major structural changes in the Latin American economies in order to facilitate the increased integration of the region into the global capitalist economy. These structural changes and the mutual interests of this alliance are cloaked in "neoliberal" ideology, which has its ideological roots in the eighteenth and nineteenth century thought of liberal thinkers such as Adam Smith and John Locke. However, the promotion of this ideology is in fact primarily a product of the contemporary global strategy of the transnationals as well as the policies of the Reagan, Bush, and Clinton administrations in the United States, and the Thatcher and Major governments in the United Kingdom (NACLA, 1993, p. 16). This ideology has been used to justify the strategy of economic "restructuring" and the "adjustment" policies followed by most of the Latin American states since the 1980s.

As a result of the debt crisis experienced by countries such as Mexico, Bolivia, and Argentina during the 1980s, the IMF, the World Bank, and other international lending agencies such as the Inter-American Development Bank (IDB)—imposed "free market" structural adjustment policies on the Latin American governments to make sure that they dedicated sufficient funds to the payment of their international debts (Weeks, 1995). These neoliberal adjustment policies have involved completely opening up the domestic markets of the Latin American states to transnational capital, the promotion of so-called nontraditional exports to earn as much foreign exchange as possible to pay off the debts, and the deregulation of local capital and commercial markets. They have also involved unpopular fiscal "austerity measures" aimed at reducing public services and privatizing many public utilities and enterprises so that public funds can be diverted to debt payments.

These policies have in general slowed the rate of economic growth and brought about a drastic reduction of government services as well as public employment. They have resulted in the wholesale denationalization of these countries' major utilities and public enterprises, and abolished the protective tariffs and other forms of support previously enjoyed by local industries. National currencies have also been devalued and pegged to the U.S. dollar, and the growth of exports (particularly the so-called nontraditional exports such as fruit, vegetables, flowers, and some manufactured goods) have been promoted at the expense of the production of food crops for domestic consumption. As a result, even though the upper classes and their government agents incurred the huge debt burden amassed in the 1970s and early 1980s, the lower classes have been saddled with paying for these debts in the 1990s (Weeks, 1995, p. 125).

Harsh austerity measures have been adopted by most of the governments in the region in order to reduce their expenditures on education, health and other social services so that they can service the combined private and public sector debts of their countries. These measures have adversely affected the income and living standards of not only the lower classes but also important sectors of the middle class. The consequences of these policies, in tandem with the effects of the global economic recession of the 1980s and early 1990s, have been graphically described by Juan de Dias Parra, head of the Latin American Association for Human Rights:

> In Latin America today there are 70 million more hungry, 30 million more illiterate, 10 million more families without homes and 40 million more unemployed persons than there were 20 years ago ... There are 240 million human beings who lack the necessities of life and this when the region is richer and more stable than even, according to the way the world sees it. (Halebsky and Harris, 1995, p. 4.)

In addition to the human suffering caused by the neoliberal economic policies, these measures have also jeopardized the limited process of political democratization that has been taking place in the Latin American societies since the end of the 1980s. These unpopular, "neoliberal" policies were initially introduced in most cases by the repressive military regimes that held sway throughout Latin America in the 1970s and 1980s. However, the elected civilian governments that succeeded these regimes in the late 1980s and early 1990s have continued these unpopular measures. Their continuance of these measures, along with other factors, has prevented these regimes from implementing policies to combat the more obvious inequalities and injustices suffered by the impoverished majority of the population in these countries (Nef, 1995, pp. 101-104).

Even a cursory examination of countries such as Chile, Costa Rica, and Mexico, which have faithfully followed the IMF's and IDB's policy guidelines, reveals that their publicized achievements in macroeconomic growth have been accomplished at the cost of holding down the real wages of their salaried work forces, the downsizing of their public services, the reduction of social benefits, as well as the rapid growth of the "informal" sector in their economies composed of self-employed street vendors, hired hands, workers in small workshops, day laborers, repairmen, prostitutes, domestic servants, and the like (NACLA, 1993, p. 17).

Export-oriented modern capitalist farms and agro-industrial complexes, many of which are tied to transnational corporations, have replaced most of the former large estates and plantations that dominated the Latin American countryside for centuries (Kay, 1995, pp. 22-25). In addition, the traditional peasant sector is declining as a result of the peasantry's increasing reliance on wage-earning sources of income and their migration to the cities. The increasing integration of Latin American agriculture into the global capitalist economic system has benefited only a privileged minority of the rural population, while the peasantry have been largely excluded from the benefits (Vilas, 1995, pp. 140-141). Thus, the exclusionary nature of the capitalist transformation of Latin American agriculture has increased the impoverishment of the rural population and accelerated the migration of the rural poor to the cities in search of employment.

The presence of the large informal sector helps to keep wages low and the costs of reproducing the urban labor force to a minimum for both the local businesses and the transnational corporations. Thus, the capitalists are able to maximize their profits by paying low wages to their workers and few if any benefits (Vilas, 1995, pp. 140-141). In this regard, the so-called informal sector of the economy represents a type of subsidy for the capitalist enterprises in the formal sector.

The global process of capitalist restructuring and integration and the neoliberal reforms undertaken by the Latin American governments have reconfigured the labor market, increased the transfer of income from the lower classes to the upper classes, and greatly weakened the position of the working class in Latin America (Vilas, 1995, pp. 146-150). In general, the working class and other lower class elements (i.e., the peasantry, lower middle class strata, the impoverished participants in the informal sector, etc.) have been forced to bear the costs of the economic crisis of the 1980s and the global process of capitalist restructuring that has been taking place since the 1970s.

An analysis of the ecological effects of capitalism in Latin America makes it clear that the global capitalist system has not only placed large numbers of Latin American workers, peasants and informal sector income earners in a precarious situation it has also placed the natural environment of the region in danger (Dore, 1995). In order to repay their international debts and comply with the neoliberal dictates of the international lending agencies, the Latin American countries have followed economic development strategies which have been antithetical to the preservation of their natural environment. In fact, the so-called free market strategies advocated by the World Bank and other international development agencies, despite the lip service they give to environmental protection, have accentuated the degradation of the natural environment in Latin America.

The contemporary emphasis on exports in order to service the international debt of the Latin American countries, the neoliberal efforts to deregulate the economy in these countries and the reduction of government expenditures on programs such as reforestation have contributed to the already well-established pattern of environmental despoilation characteristic of capitalist agriculture, mining, and manufacturing in Latin America. Under the present conditions of deregulation and so-called free market economics, the transnational corporations are attracted to Latin America because they can pollute, dispose of wastes, and extract natural resources with little fear of state interference (Kelly, 1995). Thus, the degradation of the ecology of the Amazon Basin as well as many other important environmental crises in Latin America are the direct result of the expansion and intensification of global capitalism in the region.

Inequality in Contemporary Latin America

One of the most disturbing realities of contemporary Latin America is the extreme degree of economic, political, and social inequality that characterizes the societies of this region. The previous discussion has attributed this inequality for the most part to the nature of capitalist development. The extent of this inequality in contemporary Latin America is perhaps best revealed by the distribution of income between the upper and lower income-earners in the Latin American societies.

The highest 20 percent of income earners account for between 40 and 70 percent of the total annual income earned in the Latin American countries, while the lowest 40 percent of income earners account for between 5 and 20 percent of the total income earned in these countries (Vilas, 1995, pp. 154-155). Moreover, the polarization of the population between the "haves" and the "have-nots" is increasing in most parts of Latin America. A concomitant of such income disparity is the fact that 40 percent of all Latin American households live below the poverty line—defined in terms of the income required to satisfy basic needs for food, housing and clothing (Cardoso and Helwege, 1992). In fact, half of this group does not have an income sufficient to satisfy even their basic food needs.

Between 1980 and 1990, the number of poor people in Latin America increased from 120 to 200 million, and in Central America 80 percent of the population live below the poverty line (Nef, 1995, p. 96). And between 1990 and 1993, the poverty rate in Honduras increased from 68 to 78 percent, while in postrevolutionary Nicaragua over 70 percent of the work force are unemployed. This change can be attributed to the restructuring of the Latin American economies and while the rural and urban poor have suffered the most from these structural adjustments, the middle class is disintegrating as the gap between the superrich and the superpoor grows.

The growing spatial and social polarization that exists in the urban areas of Latin America stems from the increasing concentration of wealth in the hands of the privileged elites who typically reside in the cities and from the continuing migration to these urban areas of impoverished members of the rural population. Sixty percent of the rural population in Latin America are poor, and over a third of the urban population live in poverty (Halebsky, 1995, p. 54). The extent of poverty has increased in the largest cities as a result of recent wage declines, downsizing in the private sector, the reduction of the public sector work force, and the decline of public services and subsides.

Moreover, rates of illiteracy and infant mortality, although they have improved somewhat over the last several decades, are still unacceptably high—particularly in the rural areas. Generally speaking, the rural population exhibits rates of illiteracy that are 50 to 75 percent greater than the population in the urban areas (Wilkie and Contreras, 1992, Table 900). And somewhat more than one out of every 20 children who are born in Latin America die within a year of their birth, a rate six times as great as that in the advanced industrial nations (United Nations, 1992, Table 15). For most of the population, access to doctors, medicine, and hospitals are severely limited. Disparities are especially striking between the rural and urban areas. Basic services such as running water, sewage, and electricity are unavailable for much of the rural population (Grindle, 1986, Tables 6.5 and 6.6).

Another striking condition of inequality in Latin America is the sharp disparity in land holdings. These are deeply rooted in historical inequities and exploitative institutions, and they have been aggravated by the expansion of capitalist market relations, the widespread commercialization of agriculture, the development of agro-industries, and the concomitant displacement of large numbers of small farmers and poor peasants from the land. The general picture is one of a very small number of landholders who possess a very large proportion of the land. For example, in seven Latin American countries, less than one percent of the landowners (all with land-holdings of 1,000 hectares or more) own 42 percent of the land, whereas 62 percent of the landowners (with landholdings of ten hectares or less) own only four percent of the land (Cardoso and Helwege, 1992, Appendix D).

As previously indicated, probably no other sector of the Latin American population has suffered more inequality and injustice than the indigenous peoples of the region (Kearney and Varese, 1995). For the last five centuries, the indigenous peoples of Latin America have suffered almost every indignity and abuse imaginable. Since the European conquest of the region, Latin American societies have been based on the maximization of labor exploitation along ethnic lines, and the differential treatment of ethnic groups by both capital and the state has created a complex "ethno-class" structure. The indigenous peoples have generally occupied the lowest rung of this structure of extreme economic and social inequality, and until very recently they have been excluded or marginalized form the political process.

In sum, economic and social inequality is extreme throughout Latin America, and recent transformations in the global capitalist system and the economies of the Latin American states have for the most part contributed to the already polarized structure of class, gender and racial/ethnic differentiation in these societies. However, in spite of unfavorable economic conditions, there is opposition and resistance to the maintenance of the existing ethno-class structure from an increasing number of social groups and organizations—including the new social movements organized by women, indigenous peoples, the residents of the urban shanty towns, gays and lesbians, workers opposed to the traditional clientelistic trade unions, and middle-class environmentalists.

Social Injustice in Contemporary Latin America

The use of force is the main form in which domination and subordination have been exercised in Latin America (Nef, 1995, pp. 82-92). The historical origins of the contemporary Latin American societies lie in military conquest, the forced subjugation of the indigenous peoples of the region under European colonial rule, and the subsequent authoritarian domination of the population by dictatorial regimes. Thus, the contemporary politics and social life of the region are to a large extent the legacy of European colonial domination, the ideological domination of the Catholic church, a tradition of militarism and armed conflict as well as the institutionalization of numerous class, gender and racial/ethnic inequities.

Contemporary Latin Americans have inherited state structures based on political authoritarianism and the exclusion of large sectors of the population from the governmental process, as well as chronic forms of political violence, frequent military coups and dictatorships that both provoke popular insurrections as well as brutally suppress them (Boron, 1995, pp. 13-24). In other words, the political and social hierarchies in Latin America are inherently unjust, and these hierarchies are preserved by structures and practices that are unjust in terms of both universal and local standards of fairness and justice (which are frequently espoused but not practiced).

The ruling elites in Latin America have generally served as intermediaries between the dominant external power and the local population (Nef, 1995, pp. 83-89). Paternalistic, authoritarian, and clientelistic relations of subordination between the local elites and the masses at the national and subnational levels have gone hand in hand with the subordination of the Latin American societies to external colonial or neo-colonial elites interested in the exploitation of the natural resources, labor and capital of these societies. Moreover, military dictatorships, military repression of popular protests and insurrections, foreign military invasions, and the frequent intervention of the military in the governmental process have been a continuing and prominent feature of the political scene. In fact, the importance of the military and the use of military force have been the natural outgrowth of a system of social relations based largely on the subordination and exploitation of the majority of the population.

The apparent demilitarization and democratization of the Latin American states in recent years have been viewed by many observes as a welcome sign that the region is overcoming its past and undergoing a democratic political transformation. However, the civilian regimes that have replaced the former military dictatorships "have been neither truly democratic nor sovereign" (Nef, 1995, pp. 91-104). Although they possess the formal trappings of democracy and sovereignty, the current civilian regimes in Latin America for the most part exclude the popular classes from effective participation in the political process. Their decisions are also subject to the de facto veto of the military as well as the external dictates of the IMF, the World Bank, the U.S. government and the transnational corporations (Petras and Morley, 1992, pp. 179-198).

The Prospects for Social Justice in Latin America

The role of the state in regulating the economy has significantly declined as a result of the privatization of state assets, the deregulation of many economic activities, and the drastic reduction of government expenditures and public employment. Nevertheless, a considerable degree of centralized state power and an authoritarian governmental bureaucracy still remain in all the Latin American countries. Moreover, the neoliberals' rhetoric about limiting the role of the state in the economy in fact redirects the state's role in the economy away from serving the needs of the popular classes toward the special interests of the upper classes. As one astute observer has put it:

> We are witnessing efforts to alter the direction of state activity, and not in fact a movement to liquidate the centrality of its "economic function" [and] ... this shift in direction may well be paralleled with more openly activist roles for the state in the process of economic concentration and the further hierarchicalization of economic and social relations. Already measures have been taken to reduce the role of the state in providing welfare, basic needs, unemployment relief, and so on. This legitimizes the social and economic inequality of capitalism under the guise of disinvolvement. (Thomas, 1989, p. 344.)

Despite the neoliberal rhetoric in contemporary governmental and business circles in Latin America, there is "a necessary interdependence and complementarity between state and market" in these countries as in all capitalist societies (Thomas, 1989, p. 344).

The elected civilian governments that have replaced the military dictatorships have restored the formal aspects of political democracy and freed civil society from the more repressive and brutal forms of political injustice that existed during the military regimes of the 1970s and 1980s. There has also been a notable decline in the level and extent of political violence. Governmental stability has apparently begun to take hold, although deviations from this pattern occur with disturbing frequency.

One of the most disturbing features of the contemporary political scene is the lack of governmental responsiveness to the needs of the majority of the population even though the formal mechanisms of democratic politics have been established throughout most of the region. As one astute Latin American intellectual has observed:

> policies aimed at deregulating markets, at privatization and liberalization, have had as one of their consequences the extraordinary reinforcement of the bargaining power of a handful of privileged collective actors, whose demands gain direct access to the upper echelons of the government and the central bureaucracy. Therefore, the quality of democratic governance is not only impaired by the deterioration of the material foundations of citizenship: these fragile democratic experiments are also endangered by the fact that, deaf to the reasonable and legitimate expectations of the

underlying population, they tend to magnify the strength of the dominant classes and, as a result, to further reinforce the role of naked, noninstitutionalized power relations. (Boron, 1995, p. 211.)

In most countries, the urban working class, the peasantry, rural workers, the lower sectors of the salaried middle class, the members of the large informal sector, and the indigenous communities have been largely excluded or marginalized from the political arena. Taken together, these various classes and sectors represent anywhere from two-thirds to three-quarters of the population, depending upon the demographic profile of each country.

Past efforts to organize and unite these classes and sectors for the purposes of representing their interests in the centers of state power have proved politically difficult and quite dangerous. In addition to the violent reaction of the military and right-wing paramilitary groups, the political mobilization of these sectors of the population has been obstructed by traditional forms of political co-optation—such as clientelism, patronage and corporatism—which the political elites have used quite effectively in most cases to subordinate and divide the members of these classes and sectors of the population.

Many of the former progressive members of the intelligentsia in Latin America have in recent years assumed a relatively moderate political position. As a result, they have distanced themselves from the popular classes and sectors mentioned above, and they have often accommodated their views to the prevailing neoliberal orthodoxy (Petras and Morley, 1992, pp. 145-175). Many of the former leftist political parties and organizations (such as the unions) have assumed a low profile on the political scene (although there are notable exceptions such as the Workers Party in Brazil). Other leftist organizations and movements have fallen into considerable organizational and ideological disarray.

Revolutionary movements and insurgent groups such as those which existed in Nicaragua and El Salvador during the 1970s and 1980s have been forced to give up their anti-imperialist and revolutionary struggles for national liberation, popular democracy and social justice. The revolutionary regime in Cuba has endured the collapse of the Soviet Block and the continued economic and political embargo of the United States, but it has been forced by the end of the Cold War and the "triumph" of global capitalism to seek increasing accommodation with the main actors in the global capitalist system (Blanco, 1995). In fact, were it not for the uncompromising hostility of the U.S. government, the Cuban regime would probably have already succeeded in accommodating itself to the global capitalist economy.

The direction that Latin America will take in the coming decades of the twenty-first century is not clear. The region could continue to follow the current course of increasing integration into the global capitalist economy under the continuing influence of neoliberal ideology and moderate-conservative civilian regimes. On the other hand, there are also indications of growing discontent with these regimes, both among the popular classes who have received few if any benefits from them as well as among the right-wing critics of these regimes, and their allies in the armed forces, who fear that even the limited democratization that has taken place in Latin America has gone too far.

The Left and other progressive forces in Latin America have been weakened and disoriented by major developments at the global level, such as the demise of the revolutionary movements in Central America and other parts of Latin America, as well as their own failure to develop an effective strategy for mobilizing the population against the neoliberal project of the right-of-center civilian regimes throughout the region. The unsuccessful outcome of the Nicaraguan revolution and the revolutionary movements in Central America during the 1980s appears to have foreclosed, at least for the time being, a strategy based upon a popular revolutionary insurrection. However, the progressive political forces in the region could change Latin America's current course of development in the direction of greater political democracy, rising standards of living and social justice, if they could devise an effective strategy that would allow them to successfully mobilize the majority of the population in this direction (Harris, 1995, pp. 293-296).

Most of the progressive parties and movements in Latin America recognize that they are seriously handicapped by their failure to offer an effective alternative to the reigning neoliberal project. As a result, they have established an ongoing cross-national dialogue aimed at developing a new identity and strategy for the contemporary era. The main impetus for this dialogue was the São Paulo Forum which was formed in July 1990 by representatives from over 40 leftist political parties and organizations (Robinson, 1992).

The globalization process has provoked the active resistance of many previously passive communities and groups who now see their survival increasingly threatened by the economic and cultural effects associated with the accelerated integration of their societies into the global capitalist economy. The global media have contributed to this phenomenon through the international diffusion of information about the political mobilization of traditional communities and ethnic groups in different parts of the world, e.g., the former Soviet Union, Yugoslavia, and others (Robertson, 1992, pp. 130-131, 166-172). This global diffusion process has created a demonstration effect in the sense that the activation of an increasing number of groups has been inspired by what they learn from the global media about other groups like themselves. Thus, globalization has stimulated the political mobilization of oppressed groups and communities that have been previously subordinated, suppressed, and/or marginalized.

Throughout Latin America one can find grass-roots movements that have arisen among formerly quiescent ethnic groups, indigenous communities and the most exploited sectors of the population. Some specific examples are the increasing ethnic awareness and mobilization of Afro-Brazilians, the political mobilization and rebellion of the indigenous population in the Mexican state of Chiapas, and the organization and resistance of the rubber tappers led by Chico Mendes in the Amazonia region of Brazil.

Like the more conventional political parties, trade unions and peasant organizations, the new social movements in Latin America have established themselves as a force with which to be reckoned on the local and national levels (Hellman, 1995). However, many of these movements tend to be based upon clientelistic and hierarchical relations that are a reflection of the larger political environment based upon patronage and bossism. Thus, in most cases they have not succeeded in transforming the day-to-day nature of power relations or contributed as much as might be hoped to the construction of a more just and democratic social order.

On the other hand, many of the new movements have departed from the older movements and parties by using new tactics and by seeking the support of international public opinion. Thus, Judith Hellman notes that: "human rights as a transnational concern in which domestic and foreign activists work together to influence international public opinion is not only new in its conception, but like the feminist, gay and green movements, relies to a large extent on a network of international communications that has only become feasible in the computer age" (Hellman, 1995, p. 174). Some of these new social movements not only maintain international linkages with movements like themselves in other countries, they also maintain linkages with progressive political parties, international nongovernmental agencies and international religious organizations who are willing to form alliances with them in order to promote their specific issues as well as the more general goals of social justice, economic redistribution and political democratization. These alternative structures and relations of power have emerged in opposition to the existing structures, processes and relations of global capitalism, inequality, and injustice in Latin America.

Conclusion

In the previous pages, I have attempted to provide a global perspective on the major structures, process and relations that have shaped and are shaping the course of political, economic, and sociocultural development in contemporary Latin America. Using an integrative conceptual framework centered on the "metaconcepts" of capital, inequality, and injustice, I have identified and critically examined the interrelationships between certain basic structures and processes of "uneven modernity" in Latin America, the influence of past occurrences on contemporary circumstances, as well as the effects of global conditions and local forces on the direction of current developments in the region.

The conceptual perspective provided by the combined use of these three key concepts reveals the exploitative relationships, social inequalities, and unjust relations of dominance and subordination that predominate in contemporary Latin America. This perspective also has identified potential forces of progressive change that could transform the existing structures and relations of capital, inequality, and injustice in Latin America, and replace them with a new social order based on equitable and sustainable development as well as genuine popular democracy and social justice.

NOTES

1 This article is a revised and updated version of the author's contribution to a volume of original essays he recently coedited with Sandor Halebsky (Harris, 1995).
2 Cardoso, who is now the President of Brazil, has distanced himself from this perspective. See Fiori (1995, pp. 98-99).
3 For a discussion of the diversity of postmodernist viewpoints in Latin America, see the essays in Beverley, Oveido, and Aronna (1995).

REFERENCES

AMIN, S.
  1992 *Empire of Chaos.* New York: Monthly Review Press.
BAMBIRRA, V.
  1976 *El Capitalismo Dependiente Latinoamericano.* Mexico City: Siglo Veintiuno.
BEVERLEY, J., J. OVEIDO, and M. ARONNA, eds
  1995 *The Postmodernism Debate in Latin America.* Durham, N.C.: Duke University Press.
BLANCO, J.
  1995 "Cuba: Crisis, Ethics and Viability." Pp. 185-201 in: *Latin America Faces the Twenty-first Century: Reconstructing a Social Justice Agenda*, edited by S. Jonas and E. McCaughan. Boulder, Colo.: Westview.
BORON, A.
  1995 *State, Capitalism and Democracy in Latin America.* Boulder, Colo.: Lynne Riener.
CARDOSO, F. and E. FALETTO
  1979 *Dependency and Development in Latin America*, Berkeley and Los Angeles: University of California Press.
CARDOSO, F. and A. HELWEGE
  1992 *Latin America's Economy: Diversity, Trends, and Conflicts.* Cambridge: MIT Press.
CHILCOTE, R. and J. EDELSTEIN
  1986 *Latin America: Capitalist and Socialist Perspectives of Development and Underdevelopment.* Boulder, Colo.: Westview Press.
DORE, E.
  1995 "Latin America and the Social Ecology of Capitalism." Pp. 253-278 in: *Capital, Power and Inequality in Latin America*, edited by S. Halebsky and R. Harris. Boulder, Colo.: Westview.

FIORI, J.
1995 "Brazil: Cardoso Among the Technopols." Pp. 95-104 in: *Free Trade and Economic Re-structuring in Latin America*, edited by F. Rosen and D. McFadyen. New York: Monthly Review Press.

GRINDLE, M.
1986 *State and Countryside*. Baltimore: Johns Hopkins University Press.

HALEBSKY, S.
1995 "Urban Transformation and Survival Strategies." Pp. 53-80 in: *Capital, Power and Inequality in Latin America*, edited by S. Halebsky and R. Harris. Boulder, Colo.: Westview.

HALEBSKY, S. and R. HARRIS, eds
1995 *Capital, Power and Inequality in Latin America*. Boulder, Colo.: Westview.

HARRIS, R.
1995 "The Global Context of Contemporary Latin America Affairs." Pp. 279-304 in: *Capital, Power and Inequality in Latin America*, edited by S. Halebsky and R. Harris. Boulder, Colo.: Westview.

HELLMAN, J.
1995 "The Riddle of New Social Movements: Who They Are and What They Do." Pp. 165-184 in: *Capital, Power and Inequality in Latin America*, edited by S. Halebsky and R. Harris. Boulder, Colo.: Westview.

HENWOOD, D.
1993 "Impeccable Logic: Trade, Development and Free Markets in the Clinton Era." *NACLA Report on the Americas* 26 (May): 23-28.
1995 "Clinton's Trade Policy." Pp. 32-37 in: *Free Trade and Economic Restructuring in Latin America*, edited by F. Rosen and D. McFadyen. New York: Monthly Review Press.

KAY, C.
1995 "Rural Latin America: Exclusionary and Uneven Agricultural Development." Pp. 21-52 in: *Capital, Power and Inequality in Latin America*, edited by S. Halebsky and R. Harris. Boulder, Colo.: Westview.

KEARNAY, K. and S. VARESE
1995 "Latin America's Indigenous Peoples: Changing Identities and Forms of Resistance." Pp. 207-232 in: *Capital, Power and Inequality in Latin America*, edited by S. Halebsky and R. Harris. Boulder, Colo.: Westview.

KELLY, M.
1995 "The Politics of Toxic Waste." Pp. 263-271 in: *Free Trade and Economic Restructuring in Latin America*, edited by F. Rosen and D. McFadyen. New York: Monthly Review Press.

LARGUIA, I.
1995 "Why Political Feminism?" Pp. 89-93 in: *Latin America Faces the Twenty-first Century: Reconstructing a Social Justice Agenda*, edited by S. Jonas and E. McCaughan. Boulder, Colo.: Westview.

LAUDERDALE, P. and A. OLIVERIO
1995 "Justice, Ethics and Liberation." *International Journal of Comparative Sociology* 26: 131-148.

MACKINNON, C.
1989 *Toward a Feminist Theory of the State*, Cambridge: Harvard University Press.

MAGDOFF, H.
1992 *Globalization to What End?* New York: Monthly Review Press.

MARINI, M.
1974 *Dialectica de la Dependencia*. Mexico City: Ediciones Era.

NACLA (North American Congress on Latin America)
1993 "A Market Solution for the Americas." *NACLA Report on the Americas* 26 (February): 16-17.

NEF, J.
1995 "Demilitarization and Democratic Transition in Latin America." Pp. 81-108 in: *Capital, Power and Inequality in Latin America*, edited by S. Halebsky and R. Harris. Boulder, Colo.: Westview.

PETRAS, J. and M. MORLEY
1992 *Latin America in the Time of Cholera: Electoral Policies, Market Economics and Permanent Crisis*. New York: Routledge.

RADICE, H.
1989 "British Capitalism in a Changing Global Economy." Pp. 67-81 in: *Instability and Change in the World Economy*, edited by A. MacEwan and W. Tabb. New York: Monthly Review Press.

ROBERTSON, R.
1992 *Globalization: Social Theory and Global Culture*. Newbury Park, Calif.: Sage Publications.

ROBINSON, W.
1992 "The São Paulo Forum: Is There a New Latin American Left?" *Monthly Review* 44 (December): 1-12.

SCHUURMAN, F.
1992 "Introduction." Pp. 23-29 in: *Beyond the Impasse: New Directions in Development Theory*, edited by F. Schuurman. London: Zed Press.

THOMAS, C.
1989 "Restructuring the World Economy and Its Political Implications for the Third World." Pp. 340-356 in: *Instability and Change in the World Economy*, edited by A. MacEwan and W. Tabb. New York: Monthly Review Press.

UNITED NATIONS
1992 *United Nations Demographic Handbook*. New York: United Nations.

VASCONI, T.
1978 *Gran Capital y Militarización en America Latina*. Mexico City: Ediciones Era.

VILAS, C.
1995 "Economic Restructing, Neoliberal Reforms, and the Working Class in Latin America." Pp. 137-164 in: *Capital, Power and Inequality in Latin America*, edited by S. Halebsky and R. Harris. Boulder, Colo.: Westview.

WEEKS, J.
1995 "The Contemporary Latin American Economies: Neoliberal Reconstruction." Pp. 109-136 in: *Capital, Power and Inequality in Latin America*, edited by S. Halebsky and R. Harris. Boulder, Colo.: Westview.

WILKIE, J. and C. CONTRERAS
1992 *Statistical Abstract of Latin America*, 29. Los Angeles: UCLA Latin American Center.

Upheaval from the Depth

The "Zapatistas," the Indigenous Civilization, the Question of Matriarchy, and the West[1]

CLAUDIA VON WERLHOF*

ABSTRACT

In this article the central concepts of the new Zapatista movement in Mexico are analyzed: dignity, politics, the government, democracy, power, autonomy, law and rights, justice, freedom, the land, community, the "dead" (history), the prophecies of the upheaval, and the "army." This is done from the point of view of a feminist theory of society that is based on the analysis of the "housewifeization" of labor, the "colonization" of life and nature, the "continuing" process of "primitive accumulation," and "patriarchy" in the capitalist world system. In this analysis, formulated as "questions to Ramona," the Zapatistan leader, I ask about a possible "subsistence perspective" of the movement and an attitude of "dissidence" of the people that would correspond to the "deep Mexico," newly emerging as a possibly "matriarchal" civilization.

WITH THIS ARTICLE I neither want to participate in a specifically "Mexican" debate of social scientists, nor in the discussion of "Subcommandante Marcos's" personality. My "questions to Ramona," the Zapatistan leader, stem instead from my experiences during 30 years of research and theoretical efforts on the so-called "Third World," especially Latin America, on capitalism as a "one-world" system, on peasants' and women's issues; they stem from the search for a society and culture that would no longer exploit and destroy people and nature (Wallerstein, Evers, and Smith, 1984; Werlhof, 1983, 1984).

The respective findings that Maria Mies, Veronika Bennholdt-Thomsen, and I have been publishing for many years and in different countries, including Mexico and the United States (see Mies, Bennholdt-Thomsen, and Werlhof, 1983, 1988, 1995; compare also Werlhof and Neuhoff, 1982; Werlhof, 1985a, 1985b, 1985c, 1985d, 1986a), center mostly around:

* Institute of Political Science, Department of Social and Economical Sciences, University of Innsbruck, Austria.

- the *"housewifeization"* of labor as the real "model" of capitalistic exploitation in contrast to "normal" ("proletarian") wage labor,

- the *"colonization"* of all spheres of life and nature, which takes place as a politics of "divide and rule," externally as well as internally,

- the *"continuing" process of "primitive accumulation"* that shows the real face of capitalism as a "necessarily" violent economic and political process that is rooted in the inclusion of all forms of commodity production (including the ones that are not organized in the form of wage labor), and of "subsistence production" (being unpaid) so that part-time wage laborers, peasants, the "marginalized mass," and the housewives as "producers" of labor power can be seen as integrated into the process of capital accumulation,

- the *"subsistence perspective"* as the only possible way out of the dilemma of exploitation and destruction—as it is expressed in the activities and debates of a growing number of social movements around the world, getting organized at the "periphery of the periphery" (see Bennholdt-Thomsen, 1977, 1980a, 1980b, 1981, 1982, 1984, 1988, forthcoming; Mies,1991; Mies and Shiva, 1993; Werlhof, 1985e, 1991, 1996).

The processes of "globalization" and the application of neoliberal politics in all parts of the world are producing results that must be interpreted as the "best proof" of our findings. It is *not* housewives and peasants who are 'disappearing" from the Capitalist World System (Werlhof, 1986c), but "proletarian" wage labor as the socially declared "model of reproduction" and supposed fundament of accumulation and exploitation.

Seen from this reality it is no longer surprising that the most radical struggles against capitalism and for a new society are coming from "below" the wage labor's sphere, and are those struggles that the left could never accept as "class struggles." And, indeed, in these struggles people do not want to seize power over capital and/or the state anymore, but develop a perspective that is totally "dissident" with the economic and political system as a whole. Therefore, the *"dissidence"* of the people, be it with "development," be it with commodity production, be it with all forms of coercion, violence, social hierarchies, and forms of domination in general, has become another major theme in my work (Werlhof, 1996; Werlhof, Schweighofer, and Ernst, 1996; Werlhof, ed., 1996). Moreover, I wondered whether the Zapatistas—as vanguards of a worldwide dialogue on "dissidence" in modern society—had also considered the question of "patriarchy" in their struggle against domination.

The Power of the State and the Power of the People as Their "Dignity"

When in January 1994 I heard for the first time about the rebellion of a so-called "Zapatista-movement" in the Mexican State of Chiapas, and when I saw the pictures of armed men with masks, I thought: "No, please not again!" After having experienced the politics of armed men in the sixties and seventies in Latin America, especially in El Salvador, I belong to those who react allergically to all forms of violence (see Werlhof, 1975; Topitas, 1994). Didn't the guerilla, the "armed struggle," and generally the intent to overcome the system by using its own means, fail everywhere, and didn't it only double the existing violence (see Debray, 1975)? Veronika Bennholdt-Thomsen, who had done research on Chiapas for years, told me that the case was different this time, the rebellion being an indigenous upheaval "from below," and not politics "from above," like the guerilla activities initiated by urban intellectuals. In addition, I noted that the rebels included many women, about 30% (see Gorman, 1995).

Is the Zapatista-rebellion, which already has been described as the "first insurrection of the 21st century" (see Topitas, 1994, p. 14), the "social quake" after the earthquake of Mexico City in 1985 (see Werlhof, 1986b)? And why did it start in the countryside, where already the first insurrection of the 20th century, the Mexican Revolution, had started too? And what does it mean that both upheavals are connected with Emiliano Zapata, the leader of the Mexican Revolution, who still seems to be alive in the minds of the people, at least in the South East of Mexico today? (Zapata, the "campesino," wanted Mexico to be a free country of free peasants without private property and without a central state power.) And wasn't the Ejido-system a success of the Mexican Revolution, being at least a guarantee for the peasants' access to the land in many parts of Mexico since that time? In Chiapas this reform has not yet occurred; indeed, here one would still need a Zapata. The actual reform of Article 27 of the Mexican Constitution has cancelled the old agrarian reform resulting from the revolution. "By law we are not supposed to have access to the land anymore," the peasants say (see González Esponda and Polito Barrios, 1994, p. 240). This is due to the fact that the Mexican land is left to the new "partners" of the North: it is Mexico's present to the United States and Canada, who are now accepting Mexico as a member of the "First World," inserting it into the North American Free Trade Agreement (NAFTA). Thus, the insurrection of the Zapatistas started on the same day that the Mexican government capitulated to the North. On the first of January 1994, the day that was heralded to the Mexican people as the day of their biggest triumph, was the moment that the rebels cried out "Now it's enough!" ("Ya basta!"). It is, indeed, the first rebellion against "neoliberal" politics and its globalization, a politics that is doing away with the last remains of the sovereignty of the single nation-states (see Bennholdt-Thomsen, 1994, p. 260).

Upon reading the speeches of "Subcommandante Marcos," I noted that he had changed sides: he not only knows what he is criticizing, but also where he wants to go, and from this place he already is looking "back." Instead of striving towards "height," he is rooting in "depth." (Guillermo Bonfil Batalla's "Deep Mexico: A Denied Civilization" [1989] seems to have played a certain role in the Zapatista movement.) Marcos not only expresses what he himself is thinking, but also what the indigenous peasants and women are thinking, to whom he is lending his voice—he, who in reality would belong more to the whites, the urban people and the intellectuals. Marcos, the "indianized" mestizo, is speaking in all languages, the white one, the indigenous one, and his own. But he is always telling the same story, so that it can be heard and understood in all parts of Mexico and in the whole world: "The prophecy of the South-East is valid for the whole country" (see Secret Revolutionary Indigenous Committee, 1994, p. 121).[2] As an intellectual Marcos is reaching the minds, and as a poet he is reaching the souls of the people. The internal sovereignty he is expressing indicates that the government may still seem to be leading the situation militarily, but no longer spiritually. The rebels are much superior in the latter, and the state's power appears unworthy of belief, if not ridiculous (see Esteva, 1995).

Without any wrong compromise, Marcos is showing what could be thought around the world, and full of compassion and love he is showing, too, what could be felt and done around the world. The rulers do not know this sort of veracity—the humor, the self-irony and the readiness even to die for a life in "dignity"—and all this combined with the renunciation of taking over state power, political power—the power that comes from outside, from above, from the "height," from the armed one, from the "foreign" power (foreign to the people), even from the power that one's self could possibly exercise. "Does (political) power not attract you?" a journalist asks Marcos. His answer: "It is frightening me" (see Marcos, 1995). But the people of the movement would not renounce their own power, the power of the living, their acting and thinking full of "dignity," as they say. Dignity stems from the connection with the depth, the roots. "We do not want charity, nor presents, but the right to live with the dignity of human beings, with the wisdom and justice of our old people and our ancestors" (see Dietrich, 1994, p. 130). And so, we in the West "staring at the 'unworthy poverty' of others ... did not pose the question of our own dignity anymore for a long time... This way we are thrown back to our own reality by them ... in order to find the place of our own dignity again" (Dietrich, 1994, p. 142). "Dignity" is the central concept of the Zapatista movement. With their call for dignity they have obtained a spiritual victory that is recognized everywhere in Mexico and elsewhere.

In Mexico, the political power is not only put into question through neoliberalism, but also through another power, the one of the "words" (Esteva, 1995). At least, the few guns of the Zapatista "army" could not have split the "Party of the Institutionalized Revolution" (PRI) that has been ruling monolithically since the Mexican revolution. And there is also no other explanation for the fact that millions of Mexicans are actively sympathizing with the rebels, though they neither want to be a political party, nor to attain power. Marcos said: "We don't strive for duties, nor glory, nor honour. We only want to be the frontage to a new world; a new world and a new form, to make politics, a new form of politics in which the people are the government, a politics of men and women who obey to the orders of the people" (see Esteva, 1995, p. 206). Did the people want their politics to consist of laying their destiny in the hands of international financial capital and the drug mafia? From the pint of view of the Zapatistas this is exactly what is happening by uniting Mexico with the "first world." Didn't the Mexican state in this way freely or consciously give up its political power? Consequently a new power is emerging, the proper power of the people themselves. Those who still think that social movements have only "demands" cannot imagine what all this means. For most people it is still unthinkable that striving for money, political power, rights, or general participation in progress and development does not contribute to solve the real problems. Rather the contrary is true, and therefore these are not demands of the Zapatistas.

Marcos said: "Call upon all people to resist, so that nobody will taken from those who give by ordering. Write on your banners that you are not selling yourself. . . . That all the alms coming from the ruling are sent back. . . . Don't give up! These were the words coming out of the hearts of our deads, since always. We saw that truth and dignity were in their words. . . . We are not going to accept anything. . . . Even when we see that others sell themselves to the fist who is oppressing them. . . . Democracy! Freedom! Justice!" (see Secret Revolutionary Indigenous Committee, 1994, pp. 123-124). The Mexican government tried to prove to the international public that the conflict would be solved by using money and/or violence (see González Esponda and Polito Barrios, 1994, p. 244). In the meantime it is obvious that none of it works. "If the dignity of the Mexicans has no price, then what about the power of the ruling?" (See "Secret Revolutionary Indigenous Committee," 1994, p. 124.)

Why, then, "democracy, freedom and justice," knowing how used up, neglected and mendacious they have become (not only) in Mexico? "Are the Zapatistas naive?," many observers were asking. And in this way they were confessing that they knew that the Western system in the form of the "modern" Mexico as the "fictitious" one (see Bonfil Batalla, 1989) has finally reached the end of its possibilities . What is it then that the Zapatistas want?

Questions to Ramona

In 1995 I went to Mexico and Chiapas to better understand the Zapatista movement. I visited many people, men and women, from and around the movement, and discussed with them the questions treated in this article. I am formulating them as "questions to Ramona." Ramona is one of the leading heads of the Zapatista movement and is representing the "Women's Committee" of the indigenous communities. My questions to Ramona are rhetorical questions about the "word," the language used by the Zapatistas, their concepts and pictures. I want to know how she is understanding the situation and what it means for the women, for the indigenous communities of today, for the indigenous patriarchy and possibly also matriarchy (the "deep" Mexico) and, last not least, for our situation in the West.

Politics

Ramona, what do you understand by politics? You are saying that the politician should be a "servant" of the community. He should not govern by ordering, but by obeying (see Esteva, 1995, p. 106; Topitas, 1994, p. 14). For you "political participation," therefore, is more than just electing politicians who are then "free" to practice politics as "a confrontation between the political organizations," without taking into consideration the political "proposals" from the people themselves (see "Secret Revolutionary Indigenous Committee," 1994, p. 120). Does being elected then mean that you neither want to elect a dominating group, nor desire that the people themselves be dominating ("democracy")? Isn't it more likely that you want "politicians" who are "only" exercising what the people really want and who there-fore precisely have *no* political "power"? If the politician is "not good," he has to be "dismissable" (see Marcos, 1994, p. 38). Do you mean by this the old concept of politics—that cannot be expressed by the Greek concept of "polis" anymore—that normally is attributed to presumably "primitive" premodern and even pre-patriarchal societies (see Canetti, 1986; Clastres, 1976)? In these cases politics and communi-ties had not yet been divided, the public sphere had not yet been dissolved from the private one, no social classes did exist, over which one would have to have domi-nated, and which consequently could not have been allowed to determine common politics.

Do you think that your so-called "authority," the elected politician of the com-munity, can be compared to the "hero" ("heros") of the matriarchal community, its "king" or mediator to the "rest of the world" (see Göttner-Abendroth, 1980)? Do you think that the political proposals of the people should also stem from the community of women and children, whose acceptance would also be needed to make politics "possible"? Would it, from your point of view, be up to the women to define the contents of politics, whereas its practical exercise, especially the mediation between internal and external groups, would generally be the task of the men (Illich, 1982, 1983)? And how could you—how could we—reach this goal, knowing that reality, in your communities, too, is partly or totally different from what you yourself are proposing?

The Government

You say that the government that is elected should be like "the shadow of a tree" (see Esteva, 1994a, p. 77). For me this is a wonderful picture. If you want, you move to the protecting shadow of a tree. Isn't it a motherly picture? The tree is spreading its coat around all those who are sitting under its boughs and at its feet. The tree is more giving than taking. She reminds us of the tree of life, the tree of love and recognition, the family tree, the common ancestress. It is true, one is sitting at its feet, and it is elevated above us, but nevertheless there is no hierarchy in the sense of domination, control, the right to use violence. Here, nothing is going to be manipulated, but everything welcomes "conviviality" (see Illich, 1978), and not mutual rivalry and competition. Those gathering under the tree are like "relatives" to each other. Therefore they would neither plunder the tree nor cut themselves off from the tree. The tree is central for the community, it can be found in its middle, it is the place where everybody like to be, where there is home and safety. Is the tree like the pasture-ground of the animals, a word that was basic to our concept of ethics, customs, and morals?[3] This would be, not doubt, the "good" in contrast to the "bad" government, as you say. It is the government of the mother "over" her children, the people, but in a completely nonpatriarchal, nondominating sense (see Vegetti-Finzi, 1992). Do you agree with me?

Democracy

"Politics" and the "government" express what you understand by "democracy." As you are always stressing, you really want a democracy, though the word "kratos," domination, is included in it. Do you want the domination, too? I cannot imagine so, because you seem to think of a direct democracy from below that is also staying below and does not get separated from the base in order to be independent from it within a special sphere, the so-called public sphere. Political power and domination as a result of the "abstraction" of power from the single individuals and their own power as such, as we experience it in modern democracy (Werlhof, 1996, pp. 12-26), is not what you mean. Isn't it that you say that the "democracy, of which the president of Mexico is speaking, is a disdain in our eyes" (see "Political Direction," 1994, p. 156)? You are criticizing how power and money are concentrated, and debts and poverty distributed, in the ruling democracies of today. You are saying that this would be a dictatorship of power and money, as is typical for "party democracy", and in this way the promises of democracy could never be fulfilled. And it would be impossible, too, to transform the representative democracy (again) into a direct one, the way you understand it. A communal conviviality would, in any case, be impossible with the actual democracy—that, paradoxically, always appears as a condition for the former. You are saying that there is a growing tendency for the transformation of democracy into dictatorship, instead of dictatorships being just the opposite of democracy, as we all are normally told. And therefore you are saying that the people finally should decide for democracy, but the one, of course, that cannot lead into dictatorship. Which are the "democratic" experiences in history or from today that you have in mind?

Power

"Power" in your language is "a flower which is walking in the hands of the people" (see Esteva, 1995). This picture, again, is rather female, similar to that of the tree, taken from life in and with nature. Power as a flower is again not frightening. On the contrary, this power is decorating the people, it belongs to them, it brings them together and it unites them with the world. Your picture is expressing what I call the proper power of the living beings themselves. It is exactly the power that modern politics is extracting (abstracting) from the people to get them under control, directing their proper power, transformed into "political power," that is turned against them afterwards (see Werlhof, 1996, p. 126-144). "Power," then, is not a living power anymore, but a dead one, a killing one. So you too are refusing such an abstract, political "power," as one that is detrimental to conviviality, and that is separating the people and staying external to them. Don't you think, too, that such a power does not help solving the problems, because no real help or salvation can ever come from outside, but only from inside and from below, from the locality? There is no need of a central power—this is what you, like Zapata and Pancho Villa, have in mind. It seems to me that you are trying to avoid the repetition of experiences that you have had, when external and foreign interests have been carried through within the communities. Therefore you are now proposing a change in the election law, so that the propositions of the communities have to be recognized, even if they have not gone through the "political power," namely elections and political parties. How are you going to take care that the power remains a flower in the hands of the people, especially the women, given the realities of politics?

Autonomy

"Autonomy" is one of the words you like most (see "Peasant Communities," 1994, p. 245). But in your language autonomy means something totally different than in our language. In our language autonomy means independence from others as an individual who strives for living without any bonds with other individuals or groups. Such an "egologics" presumably is completely alien to you (see Keller, 1986; Ernst, 1996). It is an autonomy that stems from the machine-model of a society, in which the individual is just an interchangeable spare part (see Bammé *et al.*, 1983). Whereas we understand by autonomy individual independence from nature and society, you mean by autonomy the economic independence of communities from the central state, as self-suppliers, and political self-determination (see Bennholdt-Thomsen, 1994, pp. 264-265). This means that you are organizing your economy in the way of a subsistence agriculture, or you would need the latter as a basis at least. But you do not speak about that. And the question for me is, *who* would provide the economic basis for an autonomy in your sense? Would this be done by all the members of the community together, or would it rest upon the women again and as always, without even being recognized (Bennholdt-Thomsen, 1994, pp. 267-268)? If you are denying the meaningfulness and "fertility" of women's work, taking it automatically for granted, your "autonomy" then would be built again on the patriarchal sexual division of labor of the "white man." Thus, where you are trying to get rid of all forms of colonialism, you would, paradoxically, keep its "internal basis." If the women remain "the last colony" (see Mies, Bennholdt-Thomsen, and Werlhof, 1988), you would retain a sort of "Trojan-horse," being a permanent threat to your autonomy and the rest of your further achievements.

Do you agree with me? I know that the discussion about the autonomy of the indigenous communities in the meanwhile has been extended to all parts of Mexico (see Esteva, 1994a). This shows how far the decay of the Mexican political system and its institutions has already gone. But nowhere have I read of a discussion about the basis of your "autonomy."

Law and Rights

In the negotiations with the government you are concentrating on carrying through your own legal system. You think of a local legal system, which does not necessarily have much to do with the universal, abstract law system of the West. In contrast to this you want to reintroduce and exercise your own local indigenous rights. Indeed, rights are not just an invention of the West or modern times. Indigenous ideas about rights that presuppose neither abstract legal norms, nor the formal "posing" of positive rights (see Ernst, 1993; Göttner-Abendroth, 1988), are also discussed in the West (see Lauderdale, 1993, 1996). Like the concept of a matriarchal society your legal system does not know imprisonment and it needs no legal apparatus and especially no police or military force. Gustavo Esteva told me that a man who would kill another man would in your community not be put in jail, but would have to take care of the family of the killed person for the rest of his life—the idea being that the perpetrator would be made responsible for the consequences of his act, and thus one would no longer need a criminal law.

But there are many people who feel that the concrete legal practice within the communities could eventually lead to hurt the so-called "human rights" (see Esteva, 1995). And indeed, in many indigenous communities patriarchal social relations under certain conditions allow the men, for example, to rape women of the community, to marry them against their will, to keep them in economic dependence, and to exploit them as a labor force. Therefore you have formulated the "revolutionary women's rights" from 1993 that have been called the "first upheaval" before the "general upheaval" (see Topitas, 1994, pp. 82, 93, 103). Now, the question is, does this proposal contradict the men's concept of law and rights?

On the other hand, it has to be asked whether something like equality, emancipation and "human rights for women" are enough, or can help at all. We women from the West can tell you that this needs to be doubted. Violence against women occurs despite the formal acceptance of so-called human rights that expressly include women. Never have the law or rights protected women effectively against violence. This is because the so-called human or "natural" rights are fundamentally perceived as men's rights over women and nature (see Bloch, 1991; Gerhard *et al.*, 1990). So the claim for the Western human rights will be a disappointing experience for women, if not a boomerang. Therefore, I think the solution of the problem has to be found within the communities themselves. Violence against women can never be legitimate, if you think about democracy, power, and politics, the way you do. From your point of view there can be no justification of the violence against women, be it in indigenous law or be it in Western law.

Law and rights have had too much to do with patriarchy since its inception (see Werlhof, 1996, pp. 27-60). Therefore one has to dig deeper into the question. One would have to recognize women's rights and especially mother-rights the way they are in societies without patriarchal social relations of domination (see Werlhof, Schweighofer, and Ernst, 1996). So, especially with respect to the question of law and rights, you would have to profoundly criticize your own indigenous understanding of them. If not, it is likely that you would simply reintroduce a new structure of domination in the communities, or to confirm the old one. In any case, the right of women to have access to the land (see Topitas, 1994, p. 95) is an appropriate and very important one to start with, because in patriarchy it has typically been denied to them (see Mies, Bennholdt-Thomsen, and Werlhof, 1988).

Justice

"Democracy! Freedom! Justice!" These are your central and often-repeated political concepts. Justice has, of course, much to do with law and rights. By justice you understand veracity, credibility and honesty. Bishop Samuel Ruiz, who loves you so much, expressed it in the following way: "There is no justice between poverty and wealth. . . . There is a world of domination and of subjection, and . . . the one doesn't exist without the other. . . . As long as we thought that we would have to treat equal spheres, we thought that we had to help on one side. . . . But, since we found out, that it is a question of justice, we have to take a decision. One cannot be with the people who are below, without telling the dominant people very clearly, that they have to come down. . . . The mighty have to get down from their throne, and the powerless have to raise themselves" (see Ruiz, 1994, p. 192). This shows that "your" Bishop does not think about justice anymore the way the West is doing it. Since Roman law, the West defines justice as "suum cuique," which essentially means to give the rich what belongs to them, and the poor what belongs to them (namely nothing). In this concept of justice the equality or comparability of social relations is presupposed, as if they were independent from one another. Justice under these conditions starts from a status quo of relations of domination, and confirms what from your point of view is injustice. If I understand you well, you finally want to stop the *injustice of equality* between the dominating and the dominated by revealing the fact of domination itself as untruthful, unworthy of belief, and dishonest, so that it will have to disappear before something like a real justice could come into being.

I like this very much, but I think the same has to be applied to the relationship of dominance of men over women. Justice as equality of men and women does not help as long as women are the dominated. If there is to be justice for women, then men have to step down from their throne of power over women, and the women have to rise up—not on the throne, but simply to (be) themselves.

Freedom

Your idea of freedom means "to be free like the wind" (see Esteva, 1994b, p. 76). Freedom cannot be limited by fences and orders. It is the freedom to move, the inner freedom, the freedom of the spirit (wind, air, bird). What a difference to our Western definition of freedom! Our freedom is the freedom of private property: with private property we can do what we want. This freedom is unlimited, too, but its foundation and consequences are different. They consist in their own opposite: the unfreedom of the owned and the impossibility to stop the liberty of destruction. You can see this most clearly with respect to the question of ecology. When land is private property, it can also be destroyed, and often enough it is not possible to limit this destruction by law. The same is valid for the question of private property of living people. In our case they are not called slaves anymore, but wives (see Reddock, 1995). Though the wife formally has a right to her physical integrity, this right is simply not observed in most cases (see Werlhof, 1996, pp. 27-60). The unfreedom of the one is seen as the basis for the "freedom" of the other one. The person who is "posed" or set unfree, cannot successfully claim the same freedom for him- or herself. This would be illogical. The only possibility to become free would consist in building his/her freedom on the basis of the unfreedom of others again. Therefore, Western freedom cannot be something good for women (nor men, nor nature), and I ask myself why men are still so proud of this freedom, be it in the West, be it in Mexico. Your freedom, the one of the wind, is not conceivable in the West. The beautiful thing about it is that the freedom of the wind can never become unfreedom for others, because it is a spiritual form of freedom that exists by nature and cannot really harm anybody—even if it is a little bit stormy. This freedom can be taken by everybody without any permission, it is always there. There is—on the other hand—also no coercion to be free, and no one has to be liberated from unfreedom.

To find your freedom, we in the West would first have to get rid of our freedom of private property. Only then the respect for the freedom of others and the world would have a chance to come into being without having to be produced or to be fought for. This freedom could exist without having to put rules on anybody, and without having to be regulated by anybody. What about the state of freedom in your communities today?

The Land

"Land and freedom!" This is what you wanted all the time, since colonialism (see Bennholdt-Thomsen, 1994, p. 264). Indigenous people belong to the land, and the land belongs to them. It is their basis. You will get what you need for your "autonomy" by producing yourself what you need. Some feminist colleagues and I call this subsistence production (see Mies, 1991; Werlhof, 1985e). Therefore, the land is nothing external to you, but it is the place that you are rooted, the depth from which you have emerged. You call the land "your mother." It is the mother of all human beings, animals and plants. She has birthed them. She is nursing them; she is body, spirit and soul in one. From this point of view the privatization of land, especially now in the neoliberal economical system (see Topitas, 1994, p. 241), can never be accepted by you. How can your mother be divided, sold, and transformed into private property of people who are not even there (see Deloria, 1973)? Therefore you are proposing that land is not a commodity, but it is a "communality," communally owned by all the indigenous peoples and peasants in general.

"Land or death!" This is again the question for you, in contrast to us in the West, who believe that this question will never be important for us again. How silly we are! We too knew the communal land, the "Allmende" as we called it— or the "commons" (see Illich, 1982; Boehme, 1988). To remember this tradition may be seen as the only possibility, to return to a situation where the land is not destroyed anymore. Only when you depend on the land on which you live would you bother about its well-being and an "ecological" way of life, in which a subsistence production and a politics of "regionalization" as an alternative to the capitalistic economy are viable (see Bennholdt-Thomsen, 1994). How could "autonomous" self-supplied communities remain subjugated in the long run? Freedom *through* the land is an inexpressible taboo for those interested in domination. Land doesn't need domination; to the contrary, it dissolves it. But we in the West think that there is no life in freedom without dominating the land (including the peasants, the women, and the colonies worldwide). What a long way *we* in the West still have to go to get to our roots.

Community

You say that where there is community, there is the "good life." No good life without community. Community means living together, respecting one another, sharing things, not having to be sad because of loneliness and living without real troubles, because there is always someone who would help in case of necessity, "Community" is one of the heart and the soul. It is even a "cosmic" community where the relationship with nature is reappearing as human culture (see Klingler-Clavigo, 1995). This is a community of the "deep" Mexico, as Guillermo Bonfil Batalla is describing it.

Of course, we know that the indigenous communities of today have been re-organized by the catholic church in colonial times and after, and that they, even on the basis of the ejido, do not represent this lovely picture anymore. The subjection of women especially has been responsible for this decay of the community. But you still know, at least, what you mean by community. In the West this is not the case anymore. In the meantime, we have destroyed practically all forms of community, and in the end we are dissolving the nuclear family, too. Whereas we have been forced to live as individuals and "egos," you have maintained a concept of "the indigenous" as "communal man" (and woman?), who lives in a community and not in a general competition of each against each (see Illich, 1982). In comparison with you, we have lost our roots and our community and do no longer know what a life of dignity and truth would feel like. And many people don't even want to know this anymore. But soon we will again need the community more than any other thing in the world. And this is when our individualistic model of life will have come to an end. It is already becoming too expensive.

Your concept of community is, again, very female. Wouldn't it have to be central to every community to care about the next generation—and this means to look from the perspective of the women and children in the community, and not from the perspective of a male public sphere that is defined independently from the "private" one? So the question remains how to build a community that would not be based on the subjugation of women and children, but would, in contrast, be centered (positively) around them.

The Dead

If "culture is the way how humans are human" (Ruiz, 1994, p. 190), then culture is also the way how the dead are dead. In your case the dead belong to the living. You say: "We are the dead of all the times" (see Dietrich, 1994, p. 134). You feel connected with the people beyond their time on earth. You remember what they lived for. And you even take this as a legacy for your actual life. If the people have to make a decision, Marcos says, "they turn to the mountains and to the places where the dead are living. And they ask their dead, if they would have died for the construction of a hospital, for a road or for credits with which their votes are bought, or if they would have raised themselves for freedom, democracy and justice, the 1st of January" (Dietrich, 1994, p. 135). So, you are asking your dead, whether the living should fight for the goals for which they, the dead, have died: from hunger, killed by the landowners, tortured by the military, wasted away by pain and misery. And the dead have told the living that they should lead a life of dignity, because otherwise their death would have been in vain. The dead said that the living should not simply die, but fight for their lives, and this would be their responsibility to those who had already died (Marcos, 1994). And now, as the government is going to practically uproot you by taking your land away (because in the new liberal economic order it seems to be cheaper that you die than continue to live), there is your responsibility with the dead. You, finally, have to start to fight.

When the dead are speaking to the living as if they were still alive—like for example Zapata himself, who is not dead for you—it is also possible to say, vice versa, that you the living call yourselves "the already dead." For there is a continual relationship between the living and the dead, between life and death. So if you are the dead who have returned from memory, then there is nothing that still can be given to you, nobody can buy you, nothing is important for you—besides the subsequent reestablishment of your (that is, the dead's) dignity. Therefore you are strong enough to resist wrong promises and offers, and you have a measure for the veracity of your acting. The dead belong to your roots and to your dignity, which nobody can take away from you. And, as you have died already, you are invulnerable and have left behind all fear, greediness, and selfishness. "All for all, nothing for ourselves."

It is this culture of not allowing one to be divided from one's own experiences— your historical consciousness (see Topitas, 1994, p. 184), the culture of the memory passing over times and distances (see Assmann, 1992), this not being cut off of past or of future generations, a sort of magical consciousness of the connectedness of all life and of life and death—that gives you such a spiritual superiority over Western thinking. If culture is the maintenance of this connectedness, instead of using the principle of "divide and rule," like in the West, then it is we in the West who, with our resulting fear of death and life equally, have no culture anymore. Western progress on the one road of evolution has lost its culture. And if you don't think only of your dead, but also act in coincidence with your thinking—because the word has to become acting, as your concept of "k'op" says (García de León, 1994, p. 148)—then the connectedness is maintained in this way as well. The proper power of the living, the dignity of each and the capacity to cooperate with others, to build community, thus comes full circle. If you, in contrast to us, favor the connectedness of thinking, acting, and feeling, and if you do not experience them as contradicting each other, but as one proper and common power that has different sides, then it is exactly this connectedness that people feel when your people are speaking. Because then you are already proving by your words that the belief in an external political power (which is directed against the people) is silly, and that it is not even necessary to offer a sort of "counter-power." It now becomes clear why you, like Zapata and Pancho Villa, really do not want to seize power: You have maintained your culture, you don't need it—contrary to left movements and the guerillas.

And again, this rather immediate relationship with death and the dead appears to be very female, because in a cyclical movement one is returning to those from whom one has emerged, or they return to us. It is this cyclical, textile-like metaphorical understanding of the world that is so typical for non-Western or premodern societies (Meier-Seethaler, 1993).

The Prophecy of the Upheaval

In this sense your insurrection has its own logic and is a real upheaval from "the depth" of your culture. You are doing what the dead were saying. But at which point does cultural resistance transform into rebellion and even an upheaval? Finally, the prehistory of your rebellion embraces not only the last ten years of this century, but 500 years of colonization. "Maintaining the memory of the precolonial epoch as a part of one's own history which is reaching up to the present, colonization is becoming relative. It is perceived as a moment within this history which has a beginning and will have an end. This way, colonialization is obtaining a transitory historical dimension; it ceases to be an unrevertable and eternal natural destiny. It is becoming just a further chapter which only has to be finished in order to be able to turn a new page" (see Bonfil Batalla, 1994, pp. 173-174). "All the colonialized people are conscious that the true history has been proscribed by the colonialist. . . . But in spite of all this, they know that their history exists and their presence as a people is the obvious proof for it. One's own history is not only necessary to explain the presence, but also to lay the ground for the future. Future in these cases means, first of all, liberation, regaining the right of self-determination" (p. 172).

This explains why the Mexican revolution did not mean the end of colonization for you. An new insurrection was unavoidable. In 1982, when the volcano Chichonal in Chiapas erupted, your historian Antonio García de León was already prophesying the rebellion: "The eruption occurred in order to range as a further announcement within the parts of this immense puzzle in the landscape of this slow battle of movements, of this apparently immovable chronology which can only be measured by centuries. Its tremendous shake. . . did only announce the impatience of the original and subterranean forces which where pushing to get again to the surface" (see García de León, 1994, p. 128). The oldest prophecies of your upheaval are said to go back to the Mayan calendar. Only we in the West who understand history as nothing else than a past that will never come back and a future that is simply an extension of today, only we "evolutionists" could be surprised. I wonder which is, finally, the heritage we in the West would have to remember (see Ganser, 1996).

The "Army"

For Marcos the Zapatista Liberation Army is "the heart of the movement" (see Esteva, 1995, p. 208). I don't know any other army that would call itself a "heart." "To follow one's heart" means, as you say, to find one's own dignity. So is your army the first in the world that wants to lead the people to their dignity? Or are you an army at all? "We are the product of 500 years of struggle.... We are the heirs of the real founders of our nation, we, the ones without possessions... invite all of you to join this call as the only way not to starve in the face of the insatiable thirst for power of a dictatorship which lasts more than 70 years, ... of sellers of the fatherland ... who are taking away from us everything, absolutely everything..." (see General Command of the Zapatista Liberation Army 1994, p. 20). And again Marcos, who has set up this army with years of work: "The question is, that they want to kill us.... On the 1st of January we did not march out for a war to kill or to be killed. We left, instead, to be heard.... It was neither suicide nor adventure" (Marcos, 1994, p. 27). And: "We believe that our war can serve those ... who suffer like we..." (Topitas, 1994, p. 156). The army as guardian and servant: It wants to serve like "politics"?

The paradox of this "army" can only be understood if one knows from where it stems, and the circumstances under which it came into being. "It was the people themselves who said: Let's start now! We don't want to wait any longer, because we are all starving.... So the struggle started" (Topitas, 1994, p. 159). The whole people had been asked before and the communities themselves proposed the insurrection. The army is well accepted in the civil population. They know that the rulers fear the union between the armed and the civil population. The armed people say: "We are peaceful people. We have a lot of patience. If not, we would have started with our rebellion a long time ago" (see Topitas, 1994, p. 156). Behind this you find the concept of "k'op" again. You cannot decide to start an insurrection and not realize it afterwards. This would be "illogical" (p. 183). And you saw "that it is bad to die without having fought" (p. 36). It was the last alternative; everything else had already been tried.

Is there anything like a "symbolic" army, an army that is expressing the wish and the will for resistance, but that is not "really" an army in the sense of the military concept? If you equate "army" and "war" with struggle, only then are you able to explain the paradox of "an armed liberation army which has invented a resistance which is strictly free from violence and has eliminated the traditional guerilla with its violent concept of power from the project" (see Dietrich, 1994, p. 137). Today our problem is that—after such a long militaristic history full of wars—we think that struggle is always the same as war, violence, and militarism.We don't know a struggle anymore that would not contain militaristic forms of conflict. And this means that we have left to the state and to the military the responsibility to deal with conflicts, and we behave as if in this way we will have been liberated from conflicts altogether. We behave as if the (so-called "legal") violence that the state/military uses would be justified and "necessary" on the one hand, and as if we, on the other hand, would have nothing to do with it. This way we fancy to be peaceful, because we have left violence to others.

Maybe it makes sense to characterize your army this way. It wants to bother about something that can neither be delegated nor displaced. We could distinguish between the institutionalized army of the state (which can also be directed against the proper people—that is to say an abstract apparatus that does not stem from below but from above) on one hand, and the "guerilla" that wants to seize power, on the other hand, and finally the so-called "popular resistance" as a third possibility (see Virilio and Lothringer, 1984, pp. 110-111). Distinguishing between the regular army and the guerilla, including terrorist groups, on one side and popular resistance on the other side, the Liberation Army would undoubtedly belong to the tradition of popular resistance (compare Virilio and Lothringer, 1984). It doesn't omit the question of death, it stems from its own milieu, and it is using no special means besides several guns, which is not very special if one thinks about the norms of modern military equipment. Furthermore it has to do more with civil disobedience and peaceful resistance than with a so-called "armed struggle" (see Ebert, 1983). Its members are not socially atomized and "deterritorialized" urban individuals, but "are able to do something" independent from "technocratic situations" where only terror is possible. You do not use terrorist strategies. You try to avoid situations of violence, but you have arms in order to show that you are going to defend yourself. Marcos is repeating again and again, that it is his aim to make the army superfluous and to abolish it when the threat has ceased to exist. This struggle would never be won through gunshots. Nevertheless, an ambivalence remains. It is so difficult to avoid a further "patriarchalization," especially in the case of crisis, and every fighting party is in a crisis. Where there are arms "male bonding" is to be expected, which has the tendency to become independent and to produce the legitimation for its continuation (see Völger and Welck, 1990). This has been the case in indigenous movements, too (see Münzel, 1978).

The participation of women in armed conflicts is a special problem. Indeed, it belongs to the oldest traditions of humankind, that women are actively defending their communities, especially the life of their children, without hesitating. They have even been feared because of this attitude (see Eisler, 1987; Aliti, 1993; Loraux, 1992). But under the conditions of today one has always to take into account that the "equality" of women in the army, from which Marcos is speaking, could in the end also be a step in the opposite direction. Does the struggle-experience of the women contribute to a new, modernized form of patriarchalization? Or does it improve the conditions for the re-invention of even matriarchal relationships in the community—as would be more likely in the case of a people's resistance? Isn't it that nearly all popular upheavals in history, including the ones that lead to the big revolutions, have been started and in their beginning even guided by women (see Mies and Reddock, 1978)? Will the experience of women in the Zapatista Liberation Army result in greater awareness, so that women could begin to bother about the huge problems in the community more actively and without any fear of conflicts? Or will they only have learned in a new way to subject themselves and to obey—even if they may have commanded in the army, too? Could the popular resistance in the end be transformed into a new model of domination, and will it then only have contributed to its training (see Topitas, 1994, pp. 47, 163)? On the other hand, what was the alternative?

The Question of Matriarchy and the West: What Is a "Civilization"?

My last two major questions have, to my knowledge, not been discussed much in Mexico yet. One question refers to a so-called "matriarchy" in Mexico, and the other to the issue of "Western civilization." The question of matriarchy is the question of the character of the Central American "civilization," which in the form of the "deep Mexico" seems to have become a social vision again. Has this civilization or culture been an essentially "female" or nonpatriarchal one? Guillermo Bonfil did not pose this question, he didn't even realize it. So should the "beautiful indigenous cause" only end up in a local "post"-capitalistic neopatriarchy? Does one want to miss the chance to overcome relationships of dominance and violence at the "lowest" level, too? To avoid this, these relationships have to be discussed (see Bennholdt-Thomsen, 1994). Or has even the "deep" Mexico been organized in a patriarchal way, and were even the Mayas at the time, when the West knew their societies were no longer matriarchal (compare Popol Vuh, 1993)? Would a "matriarchal" society in Central America still have to be "discovered"?

In your language, Ramona, your thinking and acting, I could not find a patriarchal tradition. Your pictures and concepts seem to me much more "matriachal": they do not claim domination of any kind. Your language remains bound to concrete experience and thus is not abstract. It speaks of "general" problems and conflicts in life, but it is never "universalistic." It is a language that could be valid for the world in its totality, without being "totalitarian" at all. It remains rooted in the "depth" and from there it directs itself against the ruling and the mighty, without wanting to replace them, and it points in the direction of a (worldwide possible) culture, free from domination. Your language is friendly, positively related to life and nature, it is erotic and tender, motherly and very near to the earth, full of love and soul, and last not least, supported by a tremendous spiritual freedom. This language does not stem from the darkness of historical patriarchies, including the modern capitalistic ones. But patriarchy—besides capitalism—is the reality today, in your indigenous communities as well (see Bennholdt-Thomsen, 1988; Gunn Allen, 1986). And might not a new "deep" but patriarchal Mexico finally attract everything you have wanted to do away with since colonial times?

Guillermo Bonfil spoke of the existence of *two* different civilizations, the Western and the Central American, as if they could be analyzed independently from one another. He said that the latter had been subjugated by the former. But what if the subjugated (part of a) civilization is really going to liberate itself from the subjugating one? What kind of civilization will be the result? And what will then happen to the subjugating civilization? If (part of a) civilization is able to exist independently from the other one, then the question arises, whether the subjugating (part of the) civilization would be capable of independence from the subjugated one or not. Why did it subjugate another civilization? If it did it because it could not develop on its own, it is not deserving the name "civilization" as such. How can something that is not (or does not want to be) self-sufficient—the subjugating civilization—carry the same name as something that has been self-sufficient—the subjugated civilization?

In case your indigenous civilization should again emerge as an independent one in Mexico, the actual situation would suddenly be completely per- (or better) reverted: The indigenous civilization would be recognizable as the independent, the Western as the dependent one. It was the West that needed colonialism—cheap raw materials, labor power and international markets—to become a "Western civilization" (see Mies, Bennholdt-Thomsen and Werlhof, 1988). What will happen to "Western civilization" if the colonial situation that it is based upon broke down not only in Mexico but elsewhere too? Does Western civilization break down when there are no colonies anymore? Does "Western civilization" mean to have colonies? Is "Western civilization" defined by the fact that it has subjugated other civilizations and is nourishing itself from them? Or would the West become a real civilization only if there are no colonies anymore? And would this civilization then be still a "Western" one? What we define as "Western civilization" is a product of modern times and colonialism. By "Western civilization" we do *not* refer to the Middle Ages or an old, European-type civilization that no longer exists (see Gimbutas, 1982). Whereas you will be able to relate to your own traditions, we in the West are standing empty-handed. We invented so many heights, but have lost our "depth." Where are our own roots and forces, the heritage of our culture and former civilizations that might not have been parasitic and maybe not patriarchal (nor capitalistic, of course) either?

The decay of Western power in Mexico (the end of the "fictitious" Mexico, as G. Bonfil says) also means the decay of power and civilization in the West. Therefore, we in the West have to ask the same questions as you. The difference is that we do not know how to do this without subjugating others. But whereas we are not even really asking these questions, you are already preoccupied with the answers. With your upheaval—which is not only an insurrection—and with the perspectives it has in relation to the global economic crisis and neoliberalism as a form to globalize this crisis, the relations suddenly appear to be turned upside down. Now it is the West that is weak. Does it destroy non-Western or your civilization completely, is it going to decay because it is losing its basis? Does it let the non-Western civilization be independent, to also decay? There is only one solution: The reconstruction of a non-Western civilization in the West and all over the planet. And this cannot mean replacing the external colony by an "internal" one (or maintaining it). When women remain to be treated as "the last colony," it would only repeat internally what had just perished externally.

NOTES

1 This is a revision and translation of "Fragen an Ramona: Die Zapatisten, die Indianische Zivilisation, die Matriarchatsfrage und der Western," in Werlhof (1996), pp. 189-224.
2 All quotations are translations by the author.
3 The words *ethos*, *nomos*, and *mos* originally meant the same: the pasture ground (see Illich *et al.*, 1993).

REFERENCES

ALITI, Angelika
    1993 *Die wilde Frau. Rückkehr zu den Quellen weiblicher Macht und Energie*. Hamburg: Hoffmann & Campe.
ASSMANN, Jan
    1992 *Das kulturelle Gedächtnis*. München: C.H. Beck.
BAMMÉ, Arno, Renate GENTH, Guenther KEMPIN, and Guenter FEUERSTEIN
    1983 *Maschinen-Menschen, Mensch-Maschinen*. Reinbek: Rowohlt.
BENNHOLDT-THOMSEN, Veronika
    1977 "La Conciencia Campesina Derivada del Desarrollo Capitalista en México." *Revista del México Agrario* 10 (3): 11-26.
BENNHOLDT-THOMSEN, Veronika
    1980a "Investment in the Poor: Analysis of World Bank Policy" Parts 1 and 2. *Social Scientist* 8 (7): 1227-1243; 8 (8): 2012-2027.
BENNHOLDT-THOMSEN, Veronika
    1980b "Towards a Class Analysis of Agrarian Sectors: Mexico." *Latin American Perspectives* 7 (4): 100-114.
BENNHOLDT-THOMSEN, Veronika
    1981 "Marginalidad en América Latina. Una Crítica de la Teoría." *Revista Mexicana de Sociología* 43 (4): 1505-1546.
BENNHOLDT-THOMSEN, Veronika
    1982 "Subsistence Production and Extended Reproduction: A Contribution to the Discussion about Modes of Production." In: *Journal of Peasant Studies* 9 (4): 241-254.

BENNHOLDT-THOMSEN, Veronika
1984 "The Sexual Division of Labour in Capitalism." Pp. 252-271 in: *Households and the World Economy*, edited by Immanuel Wallerstein, Hans-Dieter Evers, and Joan Smith. New York: Sage.

BENNHOLDT-THOMSEN, Veronika
1988 *Campesinos: Entre Producción de Subsistencia y de Mercado*. México: UNAM/CRIM.

BENNHOLDT-THOMSEN, Veronika
1994 "Die Zapatistas und Wir." Pp. 257-268 in: *Ya Basta! Der Aufstand der Zapatistas*, edited by Topitas. Hamburg: Verlag Libertäre Assoziation.

BENNHOLDT-THOMSEN, Veronika, ed.
Forthcoming *Juchitán, la Ciudad de las Mujeres*. Oaxaca (México): Instituto Oaxaqueno de las Culturas.

BOEHME, Hartmut
1988 *Natur und Subjekt*. Frankfurt: Suhrkamp.

BLOCH, Ernst
1991 *Naturrecht und menschliche Würde*. Frankfurt: Suhrkamp.

BONFIL BATALLA, Guillermo
1989 *México Profundo: Una Civilización Negada*. México: Grijalbo.

BONFIL BATALLA, Guillermo
1994 "Geschichten, die noch nicht Geschichte sind." Pp. 169-174 in: *Ya Basta! Der Aufstand der Zapatistas*, edited by Topitas. Hamburg: Verlag Libertäre Assoziation.

CANETTI, Elias
1986 *Masse und Macht*. Frankfurt: Fischer.

CLASTRES, Pierre
1976 *Staatsfeinde: Studien zur Politischen Anthropologie*. Frankfurt: Suhrkamp.

DEBRAY, Regis
1975 *Kritik der Waffen. Wohin geht die Revolution in Lateinamerika?* Reinbek: Rowohlt.

DELORIA, Vine, Jr.
1973 *God Is Red*. New York: Gosset and Dunlop.

DIETRICH, Wolfgang
1994 "Die wütende Erde Mexikos." Pp. 125-143 in: *Ya Basta! Der Aufstand der Zapatistas*, edited by Topitas. Hamburg: Verlag Libertäre Assoziation.

EBERT, Theodor
1983 *Gewaltfreier Aufstand*. Frankfurt: Waldkircher Verlagsgesellschaft.

EISLER, Riane
1987 *The Chalice and the Blade*. San Francisco: Harper and Row.

ERNST, Werner
1993 "Formale Form als Rechtsgewalt." in: *Ethica: Wissenschaft und Verantwortung* 1 (2): 163-184.

ERNST, Werner
1996 "Metapsychologie und egologisches Subjekt." Pp. 80-110 in: *Herren-los: Herrschaft-Erkenntis-Lebensform*, edited by Claudia von Werlhof, Annemarie Schweighofer, and Werner Ernst. Frankfurt, Paris, New York: Peter Lang.

ESTEVA, Gustavo
1994a "Basta!" Pp. 65-78 in: *Ya Basta! Der Aufstand der Zapatistas*, edited by Topitas. Hamburg: Verlag Libertäre Assoziation.

ESTEVA, Gustavo
1994b *Crónica del Fin de Una Era*. México: Editorial Posada.

ESTEVA, Gustavo
  1995 *Fiesta: Jenseits von Entwicklung, Hilfe und Politik.* 2d ed. Frankfurt/Wien: Südwind.
GANSER, Renate
  1996 "Der Springende Punkt: Vom natürlichen zum künstlichen Gedächtnis; Erinnerung zwischen Herschaft und Widerstand." Pp. 111-132 in: *Herren-los: Herrschaft-Erkenntis-Lebensform,* edited by Caudia von Werlhof, Annemarie Schweighofer, and Werner Ernst. Frankfurt, Paris, New York: Peter Lang.
GARCÍA DE LEÓN, Antonio
  1994 "Aspekte der Vorgeschichte der Zapatista-Bewegung." Pp. 148-150 in: *Ya Basta! Der Aufstand der Zapatistas,* edited by Topitas. Hamburg: Verlag Libertäre Assoziation.
GENERAL COMMAND OF THE ZAPATISTA LIBERATION ARMY
  1994 "Erklärung aus der 'Selva Lacandona.'" Pp. 20-22 in: *Ya Basta! Der Aufstand der Zapatistas,* edited by Topitas. Hamburg: Verlag Libertäre Assoziation.
GERHARD, Ute, Mechtild JANSEN, Andrea MAIHOFER, Pia SCHMID, and Irmgard SCHULTZ, eds.
  1990 *Differenz und Gleichheit: Menschenrechte haben (k)ein Geschlecht.* Frankfurt: Ulrike Helmer Verlag.
GIMBUTAS, Marija
  1982 *The Goddesses and Gods of Old Europe.* Berkeley: University of California Press.
GONZÁLES ESPONDA, Juan, and Elizabeth POLITO BARRIOS
  1994 "Bauernbewegungen in Chiapas." Pp. 230-244 in: *Ya Basta! Der Aufstand der Zapatistas,* edited by Topitas. Hamburg: Verlag Libertäre Assoziation.
GORMAN, John
  1995 "Understanding the Uprising: Two on Chiapas." *Native Americas* (fall): 62-63.
GÖTTNER-ABENDROTH, Heide
  1980 *Die Göttin und ihr Heros.* München: Frauenoffensive.
GÖTTNER-ABENDROTH, Heide
  1988 *Das Matriarchat I: Geschichte seiner Erforschung.* Stuttgart, Berlin, Köln: Kohlhammer.
GUNN ALLEN, Paula
  1986 *The Sacred Hoop. Recovering the Feminine in American Indian Tradition.* Boston: Beacon Press.
ILLICH, Ivan
  1978 *Fortschrittsmythen.* Reinbek: Rowohlt.
ILLICH, Ivan
  1982 *Vom Recht auf Gemeinheit.* Reinbek: Rowohlt.
ILLICH, Ivan
  1983 *Gender.* New York: Pantheon Books.
ILLICH, Ivan, Sigmar GROENVELD, Lee HOINACKI, and Bernhard HEINDL
  1993 *The Hebenshausen Declaration on Soil.* Man.: Hebenshausen.
KELLER, Catherine
  1986 *From a Broken Web: Separation, Sexism, and Self.* Boston: Beacon Press.
KLINGLER-CLAVIGO, Margit
  1995 Kosmovision in Konflikt. Interview, 22 November. Frankfurt: Hessischer Rundfunk.
LAUDERDALE, Pat
  1993 "Alternativas al Castigo: Una Percepción Indígena del Derecho." *Opciones* 20: 9-17.
LAUDERDALE, Pat
  1996 "Indigene Nordamerikanische Alternative zur Vorstellung von Recht und Strafe in der Moderene: Was die Natur uns lehrt." Pp. 133-156 in: *Herren-los: Herrschaft-Erkenntnis-Lebensform,* edited by Claudia von Werlhof, Annemarie Schweighofer, and Werner Ernst. Frankfurt, Paris, New York: Peter Lang.

LORAUX, Nicole
   1992 *Die Trauer der Mütter: Weibliche Leidenschaft und die Gesetze der Politik.* Frankfurt: Campus.
MARCOS, Subcommandante
   1994 "Marcos zur 'Moderne.'" Pp. 27-38 in: *Ya Basta! Der Aufstand der Zapatistas,* edited by Topitas. Hamburg: Verlag Libertäre Assoziation.
MARCOS, Subcommandante
   1995 "Interview" (of Subcommandante Marcos). *Focus* 41: 351.
MEIER-SEETHALER, Carola
   1993 *Von der göttlichen Löwin zum Wahrzeichen männlicher Macht: Ursprung und Wandel großer Symbole.* Zürich: Kreuz.
MIES, Maria
   1991 *Patriarchy and Accumulation on a World Scale: Women in the International Division of Labor.* 4th ed. London: Zed Books.
MIES, Maria, and Vanda SHIVA
   1993 *Ecofeminism.* London: Zed Books.
MIES, Maria, Veronika BENNHOLDT-THOMSEN, and Claudia von WERLHOF
   1983 *Frauen, die Letzte Kolonie.* Reinbek: Rowohlt.
MIES, Maria, Veronika BENNHOLDT-THOMSEN, and Claudia von WERLHOF
   1988 *Women, the Last Colony.* London, New Delhi: Zed Books.
MIES, Maria, Veronika BENNHOLDT-THOMSEN, and Claudia von WERLHOF
   1995 *Women and the World System* (in Japanese). Tokyo: Fujiwara.
MIES, Maria, and Rhoda REDDOCK, eds
   1978 *National Liberation and Women's Liberation.* The Hague: Institute of Social Studies.
MÜNZEL, Mark
   1978 *Die Indianische Verweigerung. Lateinamerikas Ureinwohner zwischen Ausrottung und Selbstbestimmung.* Reinbek: Rowohlt.
"PEASANT COMMUNITIES OF THE 'SELVA LACANDONA'"
   1994 Pp. 245-250 in: *Ya Basta! Der Aufstand der Zapatistas,* edited by Topitas. Hamburg: Verlag Libertäre Assoziation.
"POLITICAL DIRECTION OF THE ZAPATISTA LIBERATION ARMY"
   1994 Pp. 156-162 in: *Ya Basta! Der Aufstand der Zapatistas,* edited by Topitas. Hamburg: Verlag Libertäre Assoziation.
POPOL VUH
   1993 *Das Buch des Rates.* München: Eugen Diederichs.
REDDOCK, Rhoda
   1995 *Women, Labour, and Politics in Trinidad and Tobago: A History.* London: Zed Books.
RUIZ, Samuel
   1994 "Interview mit Bischof Samuel Ruiz." Pp. 187-192 in: *Ya Basta! Der Aufstand der Zapatistas,* edited by Topitas. Hamburg: Verlag Libertäre Assoziation.
"SECRET REVOLUTIONARY INDIGENOUS COMMITTEE"
   1994 Pp. 119-124 in: *Ya Basta! Der Aufstand der Zapatistas,* edited by Topitas. Hamburg: Libertäre Assoziation.
TOPITAS (Angela HABERSETZER, Annette MASSMAN, Beate ZIMMERMANN, Danuta SACHER, Gaby SCHULTEN, Herby SACHS, Theo BRUNS, and Ulrich MERCKER, eds)
   1994 *Ya Basta! Der Aufstand der Zapatistas.* Hamburg: Verlag Libertäre Assoziation.
VEGETTI-FINZI, Silvia
   1992 *Mondkind: Psychologie von Frauenphantasien und Mutterträumen.* Reinbek: Rowohlt.

VIRILIO, Paul, and Sylvère LOTHRINGER
   1984 *Der reine krieg*. Berlin: Merve.
VÖLGER, Gisela, and Karin von WELCK, eds
   1990 *Männerbande, Männerbünde. Zur Rolle des Mannes im Kulturvergleich*, 2 vols. Köln: Rautenstrauch-Joest-Museum.
WALLERSTEIN, Immanuel, Hans-Dieter EVERS, and Joan SMITH, eds
   1984 *Households and the World Economy*. New York: Sage.
WERLHOF, Claudia von
   1975 *Prozesse der Unterentwicklung in El Salvador und Costa Rica* (Processes of underdevelopment in El Salvador and Costa Rica). Saarbrücken: Breitenbach.
WERLHOF, Claudia von
   1983 "Production Relations without Wage Labor and Labor Division by Sex: Collective Cooperatives in New Irrigated Farming Systems in Venezuela." in: *Review* (The Household and the Large Agricultural Unit, New York: State University, Fernand Braudel Center) 7 (2): 315-359.
WERLHOF, Claudia von
   1984 "The Proletarian Is Dead. Long Live the Housewife? The Economic Crisis and War Danger as Problems of a Restructing of the International and Sexual Division of Labor." Pp. 131-147 in: *Households and the World Economy*, edited by Immanuel Wallerstein, Hans-Dieter Evers, and Joan Smith. New York: Sage.
WERLHOF, Claudia von
   1985a"El Desarollo Agroindustrial y el Nuevo Movimiento Campesino en Venezuela." *Boletín de Estudios Latinoamericanos y del Caribe* 39 (Amsterdam): 3-43.
WERLHOF, Claudia von
   1985b"El Proletario Ha Muerto. Viva el Ama de Casa?" *El Gallo Ilustrado* (weekly supplement of "El Día", Mexico D.F.) (18 August): 12-17.
WERLHOF, Claudia von
   1985c"La Mujer y la Economía Política." *El Gallo Ilustrado* (1 December): 16-20.
WERLHOF, Claudia von
   1985d"Vía Campesina en Venezuela: La Teoría y la Práctica de un Nuevo Movimiento Social en las Zonas Rurales de un País Petrolero." *El Gallo Ilustrado* (10 November): 7-10.
WERLHOF, Claudia von
   1985e*Wenn die Bauern wieder kommen: Frauen, Arbeit und Agrobusiness in Venezuela*. Bremen: Peripheria-Verlag/Edition CON. (Forthcoming in Spanish, Cuando los campesinos vuelven: La cuestión agraria y femenina vistas desde Venezuela.)
WERLHOF, Claudia von
   1986a"El Proletario Ha Muerto. Viva el Ama de Casa?" *Homines, Revista de Ciencias Sociales* 10 (1) (Universidad Interamericana de Puerto Rico, San Juan): 2245-2258.
WERLHOF, Claudia von
   1986b"La Burla del Progreso." *El Gallo Ilustrado* (22 June): 3-4.
WERLHOF, Claudia von
   1986c"Porqué los Campesinos y las Amas de Casa no Desaparecen en el Sistema Capitalista Mundial" (Why peasants and housewives do not disappear in the capitalist world system, Washington: meeting of the *American Sociological Association*). *El Gallo Ilustrado* (9 February): 2-10.
WERLHOF, Claudia von
   1991 *Was haben die Hühner mit dem Dollar zu tun? Frauen und Ökonomie* (What does the chicken have to do with the dollar? Women and economy). München: Frauenoffensive.

WERLHOF, Claudia von
   1996 *Mutter-Los: Frauen im Patriarchat zwischen Angleichung und Dissidenz* (Mutter-Los: Women in patriarchy between alignment and dissidence). München: Frauenoffensive.
WERLHOF, Claudia von, and Hans-Peter NEUHOFF
   1982 "The Combination of Different Production Relations on the Basis of Non-Proletarianization: Agrarian Production in Yaracuy, Venezuela." *Latin American Perspectives* 34: 79-103.
WERLHOF, Claudia von, ed.
   1996 *Beiträge zur Dissidenz* (Contributions to dissidence). Frankfurt, Paris, New York: Peter Lang.
WERLHOF, Claudia von, Annemarie SCHWEIGHOFER, and Werner ERNST, eds
   1996 *Herren-los: Herrschaft-Erkenntnis-Lebensform.* Frankfurt, Paris, New York: Peter Lang.

Indigenous North American Jurisprudence[1]

PAT LAUDERDALE*

ABSTRACT

This article explores differences between indigenous North American and contemporary Western perspectives on jurisprudence. It examines the impact of state law arising from a paradigm of control and standardization of behavior and contrasts it with indigenous "law" which reflected an emphasis on nature, diversity, and freedom. The research here suggests that political organization is a central variable affecting particular types of punishment and forms of law. The study raises central issues regarding the roles of criminal and civil law as well as different forms of sanctioning. The article proposes an agenda for future research explicating indigenous civil law which can be examined in a variety of specific social contexts varying in scale, complexity, degree of formalization, and historical and comparative setting.

SOCIOLOGISTS USUALLY study law by examining its relationship to basic sociological variables such as class, gender, age, and race, or to social institutions such as the economy, family, education, religion, and polity. A focus upon an indigenous perspective is noteworthy primarily because of its absence, especially in regard to research on jurisprudence (Oliverio and Lauderdale, 1990). Modern jurisprudence in the United States focuses upon nonindigenous perspectives on law, nature, and punishment with a preponderance of criminal sanctions.

This paper proposes an alternative research agenda based on indigenous North American jurisprudence with its emphasis on civil sanctions and the diffusion rather than the consolidation of political power. First, the current law and order paradigm emerging from the separation of people and nature continues to focus upon repressive punishment in a manner that exacerbates inequality and injustice. Second, the rediscovery of civil sanctions and civil law with their emphasis on restitution as a means for addressing some of the underlying sources of inequality and injustice is examined. Third, it is suggested that civil law, if it is based on indigenous jurisprudence with its respect for diversity, will be useful in understanding the changing roles of kinship, individual responsibility, group rights, time, and nature. Civil refers to processes that attempt to restore relationships rather than permanently separate or

* School of Justice Studies, Arizona State University, Tempe, AZ 85287-0403, U.S.A.

stigmatize.[2] The sociological approach employed here examines law, nature, and punishment from different levels of analysis and degrees of abstraction.[3]

Law and Order versus Law-ways

Despite the cultural diversity among North American Indian Nations, there was a commonality in the use of civil rather than criminal sanctions. The common ground of indigenous jurisprudence stems from the respect for all life forms rather than the modern separation of humans from nature.

From a sociological perspective, modern jurisprudence, the study of law and legal philosophy and the use of its ideas in law to regulate conduct, differs significantly from law-ways, the "law" of indigenous North Americans (compare Whitt, 1995; Medicine, 1993; Black, 1976, 1993; Deloria, 1992; Garland, 1990; Friedman, 1985; Luhmann, 1985; Inverarity, Lauderdale, and Feld, 1983; Unger, 1976).[4] Even recent laws that intend to protect the environment are usually shortsighted and fragmented.[5] One of the reasons that law in modern societies is fundamentally different than the law of many North American indigenous people is because the jurisprudence created by the modern nation-state assumes that law and nature should be separated. A common feature of diverse indigenous cultures, however, was that law and nature were bound together; indigenous nations were comprised of peoples who shared a common culture, heritage, language, geography, political system, desire for common interaction, and indigenous jurisprudence. Law was not considered to be contained within the realm of nation-state structures, autonomous from other social institutions, interpreted only by legal specialists.

For most North American Indians law was accessible to everyone since the oral tradition allowed it to be carried around as part of them rather than confined to legal institutions and inaccessible experts who largely control the language as well as the cost of using the law (Deloria and Lytle, 1983; Monture-Okanee, 1993; see also Reid, 1970, p. 70).[6] North American Indian law-ways based on oral traditions have continued to preserve much of the diversity embedded in the cultures of many North American Indians (Deloria, 1973; Monture-Okanee, 1993).

The recent call for cultural diversity being implemented in part through recent laws is a conundrum (Goldberg, 1993, p. 220). Corporate culture of the modern state, for example, now acts as if it has discovered diversity, yet it is only a rediscovery and is typically practiced in a bureaucratic manner, rather than in indigenous forms where diversity, especially respect for the diversity of nature, was inherent (Fitzpatrick, 1992; also for a broader comparative analysis of diversity, see Lauderdale and Cruit, 1993). The modern state attempts to control and dominate nature and then defines this process as progress. Rather than learning the diverse lessons of nature, the modern linear, univariate plan is one of controlling and dominating nature—whether it be rain forests, animals/humans or natural technologies (compare Deloria, 1992, especially pp. 2-3, 93-95 on nature;[7] Hosmer, 1991).

The European tradition, especially the philosophical justifications of Hobbes, emphasized "the state of nature" from which humans separated themselves from nature in order to dominate it (compare Werlhof, 1991). Although the liberal philosophical tradition following Kant and Locke was more concerned with the relationship between, for example, freedom and nature, much of their concern revolved around human nature and led to questions about race or utopian naturalism (Goldberg, 1993, pp. 17-32). And, the melting pot ideology of the later Euroamericans instructed U.S. citizens to ignore diversity or to homogenize it whenever possible. In contrast, from an indigenous perspective, Deloria notes that "if all things are related the unity of creation demands that each life form contribute its intended contribution. Any violation of another entity's right to existence in and of itself is a violation of the nature of creation and a degradation of religious reality itself" (Deloria, 1973, p. 299). The care for and examination of nature provided the lessons which demonstrated the relevance and importance of diversity.

Indigenous law-ways embodied ideas and methods of practicing social diversity and responsibility. Social responsibility, rather than the modern imposed notion of individual rights by the state, served as the cornerstone of law (compare Thomas and Lauderdale, 1987; Monture-Okanee, 1993). Law that emerged from this jurisprudence contrasts with contemporary North American law which focuses on achieving order through hierarchical structures, privilege and conformity. In modernity, social and political stability is viewed as a result of law and order.

Eurocentric Justice: The State and Punishment

The expansion of criminal law and punitive sanctions for the past 900 years occurred primarily as a consequence of the growth of centralized state control (Schaefer, 1968; Samaha, 1987; Inverarity, Lauderdale, and Feld, 1998). The state in the United States legitimated its control and expanded its jurisdiction by deconstructing indigenous solidarity, experiential education and family and community welfare, as it constructed national citizenship, formal education, and limited forms of government welfare for individuals. The concepts of nation-state and citizen were presented as major sources of solidarity and identity, emphasizing an abstract concept of nationalism. Formal education, especially higher education, with rigid hierarchical organization, unbridled competition, and dichotomous conceptions of students such as bad versus good, was touted typically as superior to experiential learning. The state centralized welfare amidst claims of its progressive care, yet modern forms of state welfare often have created varying levels of stigma for recipients and the state has created new and disproportionate forms of repressive punishment.

Victim compensation programs also have been transformed into rituals of retribution under the banner of restitution. The meaning of restitution has changed
into stigmatization as offenders often are treated as demonic with only commodity
value and victims become less concerned about *restoring* relationships or community (compare Ross, 1993; Moore and Mills, 1990). In the modern penal system,
the state has become the principal claimant regarding criminal action. Redress-
ing major social problems through the legal system often reinforces the dominant
assumptions on which it is based (Youngbear-Tibbets, 1991; Lawson and Morris,
1991; Lauderdale, McLaughlin, and Oliverio, 1990; Scales, 1986). The expansion
of the process of rationalization in production—couched in formal, predictable pro-
cedures and rules—for example, has spread beyond the workplace and influenced
the direction of legal change.

A common argument articulated in defense of the modern system of punishment
is to deter future similar wrongdoing and to educate the community. The criminal
act, therefore, becomes the occasion for but not necessarily the reason for ceremo-
nial punitive measures. Whether the modern system's emphasis is on physically
punishing, morally rehabilitating or imprisoning the offender, the actual levying of
punishment is primarily for political purposes (Foucault, 1979, especially p. 49).
This political emphasis, still relevant to modern sanctioning, stands in stark contrast
to models of conduct based on nature. Imprisonment in its modern form, for example, is a human creation. Similarly, pseudospeciation, a human invention that leads
people to define their own species as another in order to extinguish life for narrow
political purposes, is not a lesson taken from nature (Erikson, 1984).

The modern punitive system is also anomalous in other terms. In the United
States, for example, the expansion of criminal law and punitive sanctions led to
an approximate 50 percent increase in the population of jails from 1985 to 1990.
State and federal prison populations increased at an average annual growth rate of
approximately 13 percent, totaling over one million in 1996, approximately three
times the population of U.S. prisons in 1982. Thirty-eight states are now under federal district court orders for prison conditions and overcrowding. State expenditures
for corrections will probably become the largest of any item on state budgets. The
states will need at least $45-50 billion more to construct and operate the additional
prison space over the next five years. The U.S. Federal Bureau of Statistics reported
in 1996 that of the more than one million Americans in jail or prison, the most
conservative cost of simply housing them for one year is $16 billion. It typically
costs between $55,000 and $100,000 to build one new prison bed; plus $20,000
to $35,000 per year to feed and house an inmate.[8] Tuition at the most prestigious
colleges in North America are just a fraction of those costs. And, the incarceration
rate in the U.S. is 455 per 100,000 while the closest incarceration rate of comparable countries is South Africa with 311. Hungary is third with 117 per 100,000.
And, there is a disproportionate number of minorities in U.S. prisons, e.g., in 1990

approximately 50 percent of the state and federal prisoners were reported as "black" people (Inverarity, Lauderdale, and Feld, 1998).[9]

Repressive punishment offers no incentive for the victim to become involved in the justice process other than to satisfy feelings of revenge which in the end are considered insignificant in the face of further legitimizing the status quo. Moreover, efforts to bring about equality and social justice directed to underlying transformations in society and the world system typically are ignored or viewed as unrealistic and policymakers return to their focus upon legal regulation.

One of the most popularized reactions to this issue has been to claim that the relatively recent increase in litigation in the United States is an indicator of more justice, or in the words of Friedman (1985), "total justice." The claim rests on data which reveal the significant increase in regulation and an incorrect interpretation suggesting that this increase was a function of individual citizens pushing for the regulations and/or the expansion of victims' rights. While this claim was popular in the 1980s, systematic research suggests, however, that such significant increases came primarily from large corporations who were bringing legal charges against small corporations and individual citizens, and state managers who were attempting to use new regulations to control major crises.

Stookey (1990) examines the issue from both consensus and conflict perspectives on litigation. He notes that one approach emphasizes the role of litigation in gaining consensus. The other focuses upon litigation's role in economic and political competition and domination. He proceeds to test the perspectives using a data base of 28,000 trials, and while he does not ignore the role of the consensus, the data and conclusions largely reflect the competition and domination aspects of new regulation. The pervasive issue of disproportionate access to law also is a central issue, as repeat users of the law such as large multinational corporations are dominant at most levels of litigation (Stookey, 1990; Nader, 1980; Lauderdale and Cruit, 1993; Inverarity, Lauderdale, and Feld, 1998).

Hunt (1993) suggests a central difference between regulation and law, where law is concerned with equity and social justice. He notes that there is ample evidence of the expansion of regulation, but the expansion of regulation may be at the expense of restorative law.

A jurisprudential shift from criminal to civil law entails a change in the substantive uses of law as well as our view of the role of law, not simply an alteration in the form or amount of law. Also, much of the tort law in the U.S. legal system and its peculiar forms of compensation are far removed from the original intent of most civil law and often appear in substance as retribution.[10]

Civil Law and Indigenous Jurisprudence

The closest approximation to the law-ways or common law of most indigenous North Americans is civil law. Civil law is more amenable to incorporating essential principles of unity and collectivity. It has the potential to provide a more equitable, less oppressive arena in which to negotiate and regulate major social problems, including those of a violent nature. The civil process has the potential to consider the positions and perceptions of the victim and the offender. This process focuses upon the paying of damages and the receipt of compensation reflecting both the problematic behavior of the offender and the suffering endured by the victim. Civil proceedings can carry far less degradation to the parties involved and de-emphasize the moral condemnation or stigma of criminal sanctions. This civil approach is especially relevant to victims of domestic violence, for example, who often become stigmatized because of their relationship with the offender. Civil sanctions are alternatives to repressive punishments both for the specific parties involved and also the broader system of law and justice. The civil emphasis on restoring relationships, especially at the community level, is critical. However, these civil alternatives are often suffocated before they reach any public policy agenda.[11]

Despite ethocentric reports which portray premodern or indigenous law as "primitive," there is systematic documentation that in the infancy of modern jurisprudence people depended upon the Law of Tort for protection against violence or fraud (Milsom, 1969, pp. 353-356; Garland, 1990; Maine, 1961).[12] And these analyses are similar to Durkheim's position on this matter when he noted that consolidation of power by the government leads to more repressive rather than restitutive sanctions (Durkheim, 1899). More recently, Garland (1990) examines evidence leading to the conclusion that cultures with nonabsolutist political organization tend to have a preponderance of lenient punishments while absolutist cultures have a preponderance of severe punishments.[13] This research is crucial because it explicates why we should reject dichotomous approaches that claim that all indigenous law was restitutive or repressive (see Inverarity, Lauderdale, and Feld, 1983, especially page 157 on Spitzer, 1975). In essence, political organization is central to our understanding of when particular types of punishments and what forms of law are more likely to be imposed.

External forces (such as the U.S. military or degree of colonization) changed indigenous negative sanctioning significantly in form, duration, and intensity; nonetheless, North American indigenous justice reflects civil rather than a criminal application of law (Harring, 1994). Phillip Deere's (1978) statement is accurate today:

> All over our Country, historians, anthropology people, dug up the earth to find the history of the Western hemisphere. But they have not found any jail house. They have not found any prisons. . . . How did different Nations of people speaking so many different languages live without these institutions? (p. 10)

Such discoveries on the absence of prisons have led to numerous accounts of the cause of what is now considered a modern anomaly. Smith and Roberts (1954) in their study of the Zuni, for example, noted that imprisonment seemed only to appear around 1900 as mandated by orders of the U.S. military. Even by this time period Smith and Roberts note that "Imprisonment is not a usual form of legal sanction at Zuni, and it is imposed only for the purpose of holding an offender temporarily pending trial or for the purpose of compelling him to perform labor in situations in which he is unable to pay a fine or damages."[14] Prisons in the United States emerging from a centralized authority are modern inventions.

The written history of the North American Indian cultures continues to be embroiled in great controversy, in part because it is continually rewritten by individuals and institutions with quite varying agendas and perspectives. Writers such as James A. Clifton argue that the North American Indian has been invented for political convenience, in particular to use ideals of the noble and wise native to criticize modernity (compare Clifton, 1990). The larger controversy includes claims that (1) recent attempts to find the essence among the Indian Nations has led to romanticizing these premodern cultures;[15] (2) the record of the Aztecs and Mayans, often viewed (from modernity) as the "Greeks and Romans of the New World," indicate that these cultures had strikingly similar versions of modern law and methods of punishment and that they can be seen as representative of indigenous culture;[16] (3) Indian "tribes," prior to colonization, were as different as modern groups—some inflicted severe punishments while others viewed such punishments as unthinkable; or (4) the written history of Indians from the 18th, 19th, and part of the 20th centuries is a close approximation to earlier indigenous life, and that historical account reveals the most accurate depiction of the cultures. Relying exclusively on anthropological studies of North American Indians, however, when analyses often are based on reservation life which approximated concentration camps, is problematic.

Obviously, colonization has had dramatic effects on indigenous cultures (compare Wright, 1951; Thornton, 1990; Jaimes, 1992).[17] Yet, Harring (1994) presents a systematic study that explicates how Indian peoples "retain whole systems of legal understanding that are significantly evolved from their traditional ways, reflecting a century of innovation and social change, but that are nevertheless distinct" (p. 292).

Useful findings and controversy continue, primarily because of issues of generalization and/or heuristic method. The Hurons, for example, have been described consistently as a culture which did not have social classes, a government independent from their kinship system, or private property. The Zunis were noted for their political structure based on "a council of the oldest men" (papas) rather than a chief who decided on issues of victim compensation but not on retribution. As Smith and Roberts (1954) state from their translation of a Zuni report:

The old law was that whoever killed another should not be punished because that was the prerogative of the gods, and if he were punished by the people, the gods would not punish him further (p. 50).[18]

The Comanches, at present, disagree over the historical interpretation of "chief" with some arguing that the concept was adopted or affixed only in the past two hundred years. It is premature to draw definite lines of convergence or divergence based on such evidence and variations from other Indian nations, however, these alternatives to most modern political organization and their origins are important (compare Champagne, 1992; Warrior, 1995). Specifically, for example, the issue of generalization may depend, in important areas, on a comparative analysis of words which are Indian-derived such as caucus or powwow and the relevance of onomatopoeic research.[19] Nonetheless, one distinct characteristic of most indigenous cultures especially prior to colonization, was the lack of repressive punishment as the mode of control or domination (Allen, 1986; Weatherford, 1990; compare Grinde and Johansen, 1991).

An examination of many indigenous societies also suggests that struggles to achieve equality before efficiency are neither unique, nor are egalitarian policy solutions a modern invention. Many indigenous confederations and nations in North America such as the Iroquois, Cheyenne, and Laguna had flexible leaders who possessed policy-making power that led to a greater implementation of what modern states claim to be social justice (Allen, 1986). There is increasing evidence that the Iroquois confederation, which included the Mohawk, Onondaga, Seneca, Oneida, Cayuga, and later the Tuscarora nations, was the primary model for civility in modern political forums such as the United Nations (Grinde and Johansen, 1991; Weatherford, 1990). The Haudenosaunee (Iroquois) confederation also is noted for a major characteristic, the absence of punitiveness and the presence of discipline as the mode of social control.

Spirituality and ritual were central to North America Indian cultures, and not separate from practical everyday life (Allen, 1986; Thornton, 1987; Weatherford, 1990; Mander, 1992; Fixico, 1993). The concept of a sacred society persists; it is not unique either in comparison to other sacred societies of the past (Celtic society) or the present (Tibetan society). These forms of spirituality and ritual seem to provide a different sense of identity than that of *modern individual* imposed by the state as well as a different sense of subsistence and security. What system of knowledge helps us understand the reemergence of the American Indian Movement, the protests of the Amazonian Indians or the Basques in Spain, and conflicts in general—Shiite and Sunni Muslims, Protestant and Catholic Irish, Sikhs and the Indian state, Xhosas and Zulus in South Africa, Southern and Northern Italians, French and English-speaking Canadians, China and Tibet, Turks and Greeks in Cyprus, and Palestinians and Israelis? Some of the North American Indian experiences may prove most instructive.

Despite numerous attempts of holocaust proportion to destroy indigenous people, some of them and important parts of their traditional law have persisted (Thornton, 1990; Snipp, 1989; Fixico, 1993; Nagel and Snipp, 1993). Social organization and cultural values based on learning the lessons of nature are central to this persistence.[20] Clearly, future work needs to continue explicating specific indigenous cultures prior to colonization (compare Wilmer, 1993).[21] Moreover, issues concerning the relatively small size of the Native North American Nations and their homogeneity are important considerations. Despite comparable size and homogeneity of numerous modern subcultures or similar groups, they typically do not possess the social organization or cultural values of the indigenous North Americans who lived symbiotically with nature (Wilmer, 1993; Deloria, 1973, p. 295). A central part of the indigenous organization and values examined here is the diffusion of political power.

Suggestions for Future Research

The sociological perspective employed in our analysis of indigenous jurisprudence here focuses upon the encompassing commonalties or differences among indigenous North Americans, suggesting an agenda for future research on broader issues of indigenous life (Deloria and Lytle, 1983, p. 150; Weatherford, 1990, pp. 140-149). This research can explicate the origins and reasons for important practices such as (1) "counting coup," in which warriors touched the enemy or took weapons of the enemy rather than life; (2) eschewing punishment since it might lead to destructive intolerance or a climate of violence; (3) promoting diversity, diffusion of power, and social responsibility; and (4) developing forums for collective and civil approaches to conflict.[22] These practices are related when we examine them within the context of nature (Allen, 1986; Weatherford, 1990; Werlhof, 1991). Moreover, Harring stresses that North American Indian legal history is a part of the legal culture in the United States in its own terms, as tribal law, a jurisprudence independent of U.S. law (Harring, 1994). This jurisprudence guards against the domination of nature.

We can situate current findings on indigenous jurisprudence within larger debates on the role of research in examining the limits of state control, the environmental crises, the meaning of justice and modernity, and approaches to and indicators of knowledge. And, in general, this research strategy should help explicate social processes such as norm formation, power realignment, economic consolidation, solidarity enhancement, and deviance creation, in terms of other abstract features, which are then examined in a variety of specific social contexts varying in scale, complexity, degree of formalization, and historical and comparative setting. In this light, the research may prove useful in explicating concepts such as justice which are rife with cultural relativism at the world system level. Current theorists, for example, often consider most oral history to be imprecise, archaic, and/or romantic; yet, the passing of some indigenous knowledge via the oral tradition included precise knowledge concerning childbirth, natural medicines, living in concert with nature, and the continuation of a high quality of life (in comparison with current Eurocentric standards).[23]

We may also need to reconsider other fundamental relationships. As is evident from Thornton's *American Indian Holocaust and Survival*, the date of nadir for the North American buffalo, from some 60 million to less than 1,000, and the nadir for the North American Indian, from at least 7 million to less than 400,000, were both circa 1895. Yet, most of the dominant scholarly explanations for their simultaneous demise are, at best, spurious and, at worst, grossly linear (Thornton, 1990). In contrast, indigenous jurisprudence does not ignore symbiotic relationships regardless of their historical context.

Current research on premodern Celtic culture and earlier work on Latin America has produced some interesting similarities with work on indigenous North American culture (compare Campbell, 1981; Warrior, 1995; Weatherford, 1990; Werlhof, 1991; Wilmer, 1993). One important similarity concerns the kinship structure of many indigenous cultures. Law emerging from this structure was not used as a social technique or as a simple moral standard for society (Werlhof, 1991). Critically important aspects of indigenous law are surviving (Grinde and Johansen, 1991; Harring, 1994; Mander, 1992; Wilmer, 1993).[24] The foundations for these laws include analyses of respect for diversity rather than simply tolerance, and a critical examination of fundamental concepts such as kinship, individual responsibility, group rights, time, and nature.

There are at least 3,000 indigenous nations living within the less than 200 nation-states in the modern world. Systematic analyses of their diverse jurisprudence can contribute significantly to current understanding of law and justice. Indigenous people are beset with problems that developers take for granted, including free expression of language and religion, the right to live within self-determined cultures and traditions, and basic sustenance such as clean water, air, and land (Lam, 1996). Many of the indigenous nations are approached by developers who want to ostensibly modernize them by establishing economic incentives via waste disposal companies, mining corporations, energy producers and other development schemes that have proven in the past to be polluting. The so-called homogenous development proposals seem unable to respond to indigenous people throughout the world who are still experiencing the full presence of injustice in the form of poverty, landlessness, dispossession, political and religious oppression, and genocide.[25]

In an astute analysis of the transformation of law during his explication of *Crow Dog's Case*, Harring states that "the criminalization of American Indians and other native peoples has largely been ignored by scholars" (Harring, 1994, p. 24).[26] Harring presents the strikingly disproportionate arrest and jailing of these indigenous peoples in light of the impact of colonization and U.S. law when indigenous law-ways regarding, for example, landholding were characterized as "communistic." While colonization and the U.S. legal system gradually transformed many indigenous civil approaches into criminal law and punishment, Harring (1994) reminds us that:

> The Indian tribes had their own laws, evolved through generations of living together, to solve the ordinary problems of social conflict. This legal tradition is very rich, reflecting the great diversity of Indian people in North America (p. 10).[27]

Contemporary research presents different reports of this survival. Ross (1994), for example, suggests that an indigenous justice-as-healing approach seems to be gaining on the case-processing, primarily reactive Western justice paradigm; however, Miller (1995) is less convinced of this movement. Research such as Miller's suggests that peace-making and tribal courts often are transformed ("developed") gradually into bureaucratic reactive models unless care is paid to traditional codes. An important part of these codes is their grounding in tradition, including the diffusion rather than the concentration of political power, and the connection with nature.

One of the most interesting features of indigenous jurisprudence is its substantive reliance on the interrelatedness of nature. As a point of departure it inspires creativity, including those instances when it requires respect for principles of diversity, compared to the constraining foundation of most modern jurisprudence in which law's primary function is to limit, constrain, and punish.[28] Today's call for diversity and acceptance of diversity is indeed limited when it is built within the constraints of modern jurisprudence which often views diversity as deviance if it does not conform to societal norms and definitions. The imprisonment and repressive punishment of people and the contemporary justifications for such action are not lessons taken from nature. Future research on indigenous jurisprudence has the potential to provide us with more civil lessons.

NOTES

1 I would like to thank Randall Amster, Joane Nagel, Annamarie Oliverio, Manuel Pino, James Riding In, and Morris Zelditch Jr. for their thoughtful comments. This work was supported in part by a Fulbright Research and Teaching grant. I also thank Janet Soper and Chrys Gakopoulos from the College of Public Programs at Arizona State University and Cecilia Ridgeway from the Department of Sociology at Stanford University for providing technical support for this work. Conversations with Karol Maloy, Arnold Red Elk, and William Quetone were the initial reason for pursuing the ideas. I also appreciate the encouragement of Vine Deloria Jr. I am responsible for any misinterpretations in the analysis. This paper is a translation and revision of my 1995 article, "Recht und Natur." *Kontroversen* 8: 37-55.

2 In this sense, equity law is more similar to civil than criminal law. Prior research suggests that European uses of civil law, e.g., Roman Civil Law, have other meanings and focus upon other processes. Furthermore, "civilized" forms of punishment have various meanings, and the term civilized is exceedingly polemical (compare Garland, 1990).

3   The approach here also has been called critical social theory. However, that label has become ambiguous. Our focus on degrees of abstraction for example originates with Mills's approach to sociological investigations (1959, pp. 34-73). Mills noted that "Much that has passed for 'science' is now felt to be dubious philosophy" (p. 16), and we examine the study of law in contemporary research with that statement as a warning (see also Deloria, 1995); one that emerged from examining evidence from different degrees of abstraction and levels of analysis. This sociological approach continues to be developed in the social sciences in work such as Inverarity, Lauderdale, and Feld (1983); Garland (1990); and to some extent Hunt (1993).

4   Indigenous law in this paper refers to traditional law, i.e., the analysis attempts to explicate traditional law prior to the impact of various forms of Eurocentric influence, and traditional law that has withstood the attacks of colonization in its varied forms and compare it to the mode of contemporary law. Contemporary law is often called modern law usually to claim its superiority over traditional law. The claim is under review, especially since many characterizations of traditional law are contaminated by different episodes of colonization.

5   The laws assume that the environment is external to, outside of, people and that people have the right to control the environment solely for their ends. The anthropocentric perspective attempts to control and dominate nature, i.e., people and all forms of environment (Fitzpatrick, 1992, especially p. 30; Merchant, 1989). The claim of progress and civilization as part of culture is conjecture, as is the imposition of backward and primitive to nature. In this context, the term primitive is a result of ethnocentrism and the term nature is confusing. Nature has never been backward.

6   Reid, building on Robert Lowie's research, notes that unwritten laws of customary use are followed far more willingly than written codes.

7   This edition of *God Is Red* contains a few of these important changes to the original, i.e., 1973, edition. (There also is another more recent printing by Fulcrum Publishing.)

8   These figures are even more striking in light of the per capita income in various parts of Indian country. The *County and City Data Book* (U.S. Department of Commerce, 1994) reports the per capita income in the **lowest county in the United States** at $5,559, and the per capita income for Pine Ridge, South Dakota at $3,585.

9   The word "Black" is used in the "Prisoners Under State and Federal Correctional Authority" section of the *Statistical Record of Native North Americans* (Reddy, 1993). Using pigmentation as an ostensible measurement is another reflection of the significant problems in studying the issue of punishment (also, see Dixon, 1966, for a recent analysis of organizational issues in one specific area, i.e., sentencing). In contrast to the bureaucratic practices above, see Green (1993) for the disproportionate number of American Indian arrests and a thoughtful analysis of this aspect of social control.

10 On early forms of civil law, see Maine (1961) and Garland (1990). Early forms of correctional measures also have been transformed dramatically. The era of the birth of Anglo-American prisons initially focused upon how to **correct** inmates through solitary reflection, religious instruction, and productive labor (Fisher, 1995).

11 The dramatic increase in victims' rights legislation and victim assistance programs in the 1980s appeared at first to recapture civil sanctioning, however, the programs ignored major groups of victims such as those of white-collar crime (Moore and Mills, 1990), and the *rituals* played out in many of the programs were more similar to the repressive punishment described by Durkheim over one hundred years ago (Inverarity, Lauderdale, and Feld, 1983). The political structure of the state and state managers during that time period, i.e., the 1980s, might explain part of this transformation of restitutive processes into repressive rituals.

12 Milsom notes in a discussion of the origins of modern criminal law that the "starting point is the law of tort." He states that "criminal law grew from the methods evolved by the crown for prosecuting

pleas of the crown at its own suit." These pleas of the crown "were originally matters in which the crown had an interest ... and they included 'civil' claims involving royal rights." It should be noted that Cocks (1988, p. 198) suggests that Maine analyzed the law not in purely conceptual terms but "by reference to social and historical facts." For an explication of how this specific point impacts on the preponderance of civil law, compare Cocks with Milsom and Garland. For a comparison with case law, see Llewellyn and Hoebel (1941, pp. 47-50). Llewellyn and Hoebel distinguish between what they define as primitive law "tort" and the modern notion of "crime," which in their view only involves "the range and clarity of available administrative machinery."

13 Garland (1990) also suggests the importance of understanding the complex variables that lead to historical periods of severe punishment, e.g., the sixteenth and seventeenth centuries in England and the United States where servants, apprentices, children and wives were treated with a "casual cruelty" and the penal systems were cruel and brutal both in terms of severity and duration of punishments (pp. 230-231). Most systematic research indicates that there is no simple linear or evolutionary civilization of punishment in modern societies.

14 Smith and Roberts (1954) also mention that except for witchcraft, the premeditated killing of another human "seems originally to have been, in our terms, 'civil' rather than 'criminal'. The perpetrator was to be held liable for damages to the family of the victim but not for any kind of retribution at the hands of the body politic" (p. 50). For an analysis of the dialectical issues in maintaining restitutive sanctions, see Hagan, 1966, pp. 104-105 (Courts of Indian Offenses not authorized by the Secretary of the Interior until 1883). On witchcraft and its varying appearance and punishment during times of social crises, see Ben-Yehuda (1985) and Smith and Roberts (1954, pp. 46-48).

15 The other side of the gross romantic dichotomy suggests the United States is evolving into the restitutive punishments of organic society. Durkheim originally suggested the idea of organic society and the preponderance of restitutive sanctions in his early work then rejected it in his later revisions because his analysis of new data noted the crucial variable of level of centralization of power.

16 These cultures, however, "developed" concentration of power and repressive punishments (also see Rugeley 1996 on Mayan caste war and Bauer 1992 on the Inca state).

17 Colonization and attempts to "develop" North American Indians into the Euroamerican model of modernization have had disastrous impacts (Thornton, 1987; Deloria, 1992).

18 Smith and Roberts refer to the gods as the "body politic" and the source as their "informant." Compare Weatherford (1990).

19 Onomatopoeic research in this context also may provide insights into learning specific lessons from nature. Some of the classical experimental and control group logic of today's science can be traced to such lessons. However, this topic is beyond the scope of the present paper. Charney's (1993) work reveals once again how ostensibly simple indigenous language may in fact communicate complex relationships and understanding.

20 Compare the Native American Rights Fund legal advocacy regarding repatriation, especially the issue of returning human remains from museums; and Riding In (1992).

21 Also, see Deloria's (1973, p. 295) suggestion regarding Druidism and land.

22 The various indigenous meanings of warrior, for example, will require an examination of concrete actions of diversity, an examination that includes more than tolerance for diversity. The actions of Leonard Peltier during and after his trial, for example, are a conundrum from most Eurocentric perspectives.

23 Also, Deloria's (1995) use of oral traditions presents another important critique of migration studies on the Bering Strait.

24 Taken together, this current research on indigenous people throughout the world broadens our understanding of Deloria's (1973) presentation in *God Is Red* of the role of healing ceremonies via religion. The more recent research provides insights into the relationship among healing ceremonies, religion, and indigenous law.

25 While indigenous peoples often resist state-centered development because it destroys their culture and nature, these varying deviant labels are imposed by the larger states (Lam, 1996). Economically developed nation-states understand the commonality of their interests because if they change the labels of indigenous people from deviants to diverse people, confirm rights of sovereignty, and grant independence to the native nations they might subvert worldwide development plans that are linear and homogenous. Also, see Whitt (1995, especially pp. 20-22).

26 Harring notes that American Indians are arrested at a rate that "approaches 40 per 100 of population per year, compared to about 5 per 100 for black Americans and just over 1 per 100 for white Americans." Also, see Green (1993) for an analysis of American Indians; and LaFree and Drass (1996) on the issue of the impact of income inequality on arrest rates for African Americans and whites.

27 Harring (1994) also mentions important monographs and dissertations on American Indian law during various historical periods that rarely are integrated into contemporary legal scholarship. The works examine some of the legal decisions emerging from a civil, i.e., restoration, approach based upon the collective social experiences of a particular indigenous culture. Also, see his discussion of civil approaches (especially pp. 104-106). Compare with Goldberg-Ambrose (1994).

28 Furthermore, on modern jurisprudence, Garland (1990) notes that punishment sanctioned by law is "inescapably marked by moral contradiction and unwanted irony—as when it seeks to uphold freedom by means of deprivation, or condemns private violence using a violence which is publicly authorized" (p. 292).

REFERENCES

ALLEN, Paula Gunn
    1986 *The Sacred Hoop: Recovering the Feminine in American Indian Traditions*. Boston: Beacon Press.
BAUER, Brian
    1992 *The Development of the Inca State*. Austin: The University of Texas Press.
BEN-YEHUDA, Nachman
    1985 *Deviance and Moral Boundaries*. Chicago: The University of Chicago Press.
BLACK, Donald
    1976 *The Behavior of Law*. New York: Academic Press.
BLACK, Donald
    1993 *The Social Structure of Right and Wrong*. New York: Academic Press.
CAMPBELL, Joseph
    1981 "Indian Reflections in the Castle of the Grail." Pp. 3-30 in: *The Celtic Consciousness*, edited by R. O'Driscoll. New York: George Braziller.
CHAMPAGNE, Duane
    1992 *Social Order and Political Change: Constitutional Governments Among the Cherokee, the Choctaw, the Chickasaw, and the Creek*. Stanford, Calif.: Stanford University Press.
CHARNEY, Jean Ormsbee
    1993 *A Grammar of Comanche*. Bloomington, Ind.: University of Nebraska Press.

CLIFTON, James A., ed.
  1990 *The Invented Indian*. New Brunswick, N.J.: Transaction Books.
COCKS, R.C.J.
  1988 *Sir Henry Maine*. New York: Cambridge University Press.
DEERE, Phillip
  1978 "Operations Guide (Cheyenne River Swift Bird Project)." *LEAA, U.S. Department of Justice* (1978): 10.
DELORIA, Vine, Jr.
  1973 *God Is Red*. New York: Grosset and Dunlap.
DELORIA, Vine, Jr.
  1992 *God Is Red*. 2d ed. Golden, Colo.: North American Press.
DELORIA, Vine, Jr.
  1995 "The Bering Strait and Narrow." *Winds of Change* (winter): 56-59.
DELORIA, Vine, Jr., and C.M. LYTLE
  1983 *American Indians, American Justice*. Austin: University of Texas Press.
DIXON, Jo
  1996 "The Organizational Context of Criminal Sentencing." *American Journal of Sociology* 100 (5): 1157-1198.
DURKHEIM, Emile
  1899 "Two Laws of Penal Evolution." *Economy and Society* 2: 285-313.
ERIKSON, E.H.
  1984 "Reflections on Ethos and War." *The Yale Review* 73: 481-486.
FISHER, George
  1995 "The Birth of the Prison Retold." *Yale Law Review* 104 (6): 1235-1324.
FITZPATRICK, Peter
  1992 *The Mythology of Modern Law*. London: Routledge.
FIXICO, Donald L.
  1993 "Encounter of Two Different Worlds: The Columbus-Indian Legacy of History." *American Indian Culture and Research Journal* 17: 17-31.
FOUCAULT, Michel
  1979 *Discipline and Punish*. New York: Vintage Books.
FRIEDMAN, Lawrence
  1985 *Total Justice*. New York: Russell Sage Foundation.
GARLAND, David
  1990 *Punishment and Modern Society*. Chicago: University of Chicago Press.
GOLDBERG, David
  1993 *Racist Culture*. Cambridge, Mass.: Blackwell.
GOLDBERG-AMBROSE, Carole
  1994 "Of Native Americans and Tribal Members: The Impact of Law on Indian Group Life." *Law & Society Review* 28 (5): 1123-1143.
GREEN, Donald E.
  1993 " The Contextual Nature of American Indian Criminality." *American Indian Culture and Research Journal* 17: 99-119.
GRINDE, Donald A., Jr., and Bruce E. JOHANSEN
  1991 *Exemplar of Liberty*. Los Angeles: American Indian Studies Center.
HAGAN, William T.
  1966 *Indian Police and Judges*. New Haven, Conn: Yale University Press.

HARRING, Sidney L.
  1994 *Crow Dog's Case*. New York: Cambridge University Press.
HOSMER, Brian
  1991 "Creating Indian Entrepreneurs." *American Indian Culture and Research Journal* 15: 1-28.
HUNT, Alan
  1993 *Explorations in Law and Society*. New York: Routledge.
INVERARITY, James, Pat LAUDERDALE, and Barry C. FELD
  1983 *Law and Society*. Boston: Little, Brown.
INVERARITY, James and Pat LAUDERDALE
  1998 *Law, Justice and Society*. New York: General Press.
JAIMES, M. Annette, ed.
  1992 *The State of Native America: Genocide, Colonization, and Resistance*. Boston: South End
       Press.
LAFREE, Gary and Kriss A. DRASS
  1996 "The Effect of Changes in Intraracial Income Inequality and Education Attainment on
       Changes in Arrest Rates for African Americans and Whites, 1957 to 1990." *American
       Sociological Review* 61: 614-634.
LAM, Maivan C.
  1996 "The Legal Value of Self-Determination: Vision or Inconvenience?" Pp. 79-142 in: *People
       or Peoples; Equality, Autonomy, and Self-Determination: The Issues at Stake of the Interna-
       tional Decade of the World's Indigenous People*, edited by American Indian Research Society
       of Quebec. Montreal: International Center for Human Rights and Democratic Development.
LAUDERDALE, Pat and Michael CRUIT
  1993 *The Struggle for Control*. New York: SUNY Press.
LAUDERDALE, Pat, S. MCLAUGHLIN, and A. OLIVERIO
  1990 "Levels of Analysis, Theoretical Orientations, and Degrees of Abstraction." *American Soci-
       ologist* 21: 29-40.
LAWSON, Paul E. and C. Patrick MORRIS
  1991 "The Native American Church and the New Court: The *Smith* Case and Indian Religious
       Freedoms." *American Indian Culture and Research Journal* 15 (1): 79-91.
LLEWELLYN, K.N. and E. Adamson HOEBEL
  1941 *The Cheyenne Way: Conflict and Case Law in Primitive Jurisprudence*. Norman: University
       of Oklahoma Press.
LUHMANN, Niklas
  1985 *A Sociological Theory of Law*. London: Routledge & Kegan Paul.
MAINE, Henry
  1961 *Ancient Law*. London: J.M. Dent and Sons Ltd.
MANDER, Jerry
  1992 *In the Absence of the Sacred*. San Francisco: Sierra Club Books.
MEDICINE, Beatrice
  1993 "North American Indigenous Women and Cultural Domination." *American Indian Research
       and Culture Journal* 17: 121-130.
MERCHANT, Carolyn
  1989 *Ecological Revolutions*. Chapel Hill: University of North Carolina Press.
MILLER, Bruce G.
  1995 "Folk Law and Contemporary Coast Salish Tribal Code." *American Indian Culture and
       Research Journal* 19 (3): 141-164.

MILLS, C. Wright
    1959 *The Sociological Imagination*. New York: Oxford University Presss.
MILSOM, S.F.C.
    1969 *Historical Foundations of the Common Law*. London: Butterworths.
MONTURE-OKANEE, Patricia A.
    1993 "Ka-Nin-Geh-Heh-Gah-E-Sa-Nonh-Yah-Gah." *Canadian Journal of Women and the Law*
        6 (1): 119-131.
MOORE, Elizabeth and Michael MILLS
    1990 "The Neglected Victims and Unexamined Cost of White-Collar Crime." *Crime and Delin-
        quency* 36: 408-418.
NADER, Laura, ed.
    1980 *No Access to Law*. New York: Academic Press.
NAGEL, Joane and C. Matthew SNIPP
    1993 "Ethnic Reorganization: American Indian Social, Economic, Political, and Cultural Strategies
        for Survival." *Ethnic and Racial Studies* 16: 203-235.
OLIVERIO, Annamarie and Pat LAUDERDALE
    1990 "Indigenous Jurisprudence." Pp. 59-78 in: *The Implementation of Equal Rights for Men and
        Women*, edited by Fanny Tabak. Onati: Onati International Institute for the Sociology of
        Law.
REDDY, Marlita A., ed.
    1993 *Statistical Record of Native North Americans*. Detroit, Mich.: Gale Research.
REID, John Phillip
    1970 *A Law of Blood: The Primitive Law of the Cherokee Nation*. New York: New York University
        Press.
RIDING IN, James
    1992 "Without Ethics and Morality: A Historical Overview of Imperial Archaeology and American
        Indians." *Arizona State Law Journal* 24 (1): 11-34.
ROSS, Marc H.
    1993 *The Culture of Conflict: Interpretations and Interests in Comparative Perspective*. New
        Haven, Conn.: Yale University Press.
ROSS, Rupert
    1994 "Duelling Paradigms? Western Criminal Justice versus Aboriginal Community Healing."
        Pp. 250-265 in: *Continuing Poundmaker & Riel's Quest*, compiled by Richard Gosse, James
        Youngblood Henderson, and Roger Carter. Saskatchewan, Canada: Purich Publishing.
RUGELEY, Terry
    1996 *Yucatan's Maya Peasantry and the Origins of the Caste War*. Austin: The University of
        Texas Press.
SAMAHA, J.
    1987 *Criminal Law*. 2d ed. St. Paul: West Publishing.
SCALES, A.
    1986 "The Emergence of Feminist Jurisprudence: An Essay." *Yale Law Journal* 95 (7): 1373-
        1403.
SCHAEFER, S.
    1968 *The Victim and His Criminal*. New York: Random House.
SMITH, Watson and John M. ROBERTS
    1954 "Zuni Law: A Field of Values." *Peabody Museum of American Archeology and Ethnology*
        43: 46-121.

SNIPP, C. Matthew
   1989 *American Indians: The First of This Land.* New York: Russell Sage Foundation.
SPITZER, Stephen
   1975 "Punishment and Social Organization: A Study of Durkheim's Theory of Penal Evolution."
      Law and Society Review 9: 613-635.
STOOKEY, John A.
   1990 "Trials and Tribulations: Crises, Litigation and Legal Change." *Law & Society Review* 24:
      497-519.
THOMAS, George and Pat LAUDERDALE
   1987 " World Polity Sources of National Welfare and Land Reform." Pp. 198-214 in: *Institutional
      Structure*, edited by G. Thomas, J.W. Meyer, F.O. Ramirez, and J. Boli. Newbury Park, Calif.:
      Sage.
THORNTON, R.
   1987 *American Indian Holocaust and Survival.* Norman: University of Oklahoma Press.
THORNTON, R.
   1990 *The Cherokees.* Lincoln: University of Nebraska Press.
UNGER, Roberto M.
   1976 *Law in Modern Society.* New York: Free Press.
U.S. DEPARTMENT OF COMMERCE
   1994 *The Country and City Data Book.* Washington D.C.: Bureau of the Census.
WARRIOR, Robert
   1995 *Tribal Secrets.* Minneapolis: University of Minnesota Press.
WEATHERFORD, J.
   1990 *Indian Givers.* New York: Ballantine Books.
WERLHOF, Claudia von
   1991 *Male Nature and Artificial Sex.* Wien: Wiener Frauenverlag.
WHITT, Laurie Anne
   1995 "Cultural Imperialism and the Marketing of Native America." *American Indian Culture and
      Research Journal* 19 (3): 1-31.
WILMER, Franke
   1993 *The Indigenous Voice in World Politics.* Newbury Park, Calif.: Sage.
WRIGHT, Muriel H.
   1951 *A Guide to the Indian Tribes of Oklahoma.* Norman: University of Oklahoma Press.
YOUNGBEAR-TIBBETS, Holly
   1991 "Without Due Process." *American Indian Culture and Research Journal* 15 (2): 93-138.

Conclusion
Balancing the Scales of Justice

RANDALL AMSTER and PAT LAUDERDALE

In THIS BOOK we have tried to shed light on global issues of injustice and inequality that often are visible only in the shadows, focusing in particular on the experiences of historically marginalized peoples and their struggles for justice, equity, and freedom. We have stressed a grounded analysis for a number of reasons. At the outset, this volume ought to be read as a critique of the modern rationalist paradigm and its abstract, universalistic conception of justice as a transcendent ideal, and to that end the chapters address issues of injustice with a concreteness often lacking in much of the philosophical and legal scholarship surrounding the study of justice. In addition, we resist the monolithic notions of "indigenous peoples" or "marginalized peoples" that sometimes pervade the field, maintaining instead that each locus of inquiry raises unique problems and even within a particular setting or specific group there are often disparate issues.

Thus we return to the difficulty posed by the McWorld versus Jihad dichotomy that we noted in the opening paragraph of the introduction to this volume. Such vulgarizations imply a choice of strategies limited to assimilation or secession, and fail to acknowledge the more complex dialectical relationship between the universal and the particular, corporate monoculture and bioregional diversity, or abstract rights versus concrete and individual identities. By way of illustration, in the last century Burke was closely associated with nationalism and particularism, while Marx was critical of such political agendas and called for one type of universalism. A close reading of Marx, Weber, and Durkheim, however, suggests their distaste for the (current) vulgar dichotomy of particularism versus universalism, which is reminiscent of the false dichotomy of functional versus conflict theories in sociology in North America in the 1960s. Although we recognize deeply the global reach of technology, cultural capital, and the world market, it may be the case that in the coming millennium the world will witness the integration of wisdom and knowledge, with the periphery teaching the center how to live in reciprocal balance with the natural environment and create sustainable communities in the spirit of justice and equality.

Despite the benefits of the critical, grounded approach to justice studies suggested here, we would be remiss if we fail to acknowledge the concomitant difficulties with such an approach and the questions that remain unaddressed by the chapters in this volume. In a sense, the potential for wider resistance movements to the burgeoning global monoculture premised on corporate capital and rational statist bureaucratization is perhaps hampered by the failure to account for the similarities among claimants and their claims, and although we stop short of offering any grand, unified pronouncements of marginalized peoples and their struggles for justice, we leave it to the reader perhaps to discern such potential connections and commonalities. To that end, further work in this area would benefit from an even deeper grounding, indicated by the inclusion of more research that could give voice to various peoples and their plights, and perhaps further delineate the existence of common threads and themes. In essence, we are offering a methodological critique that we hope will resonate for those "in the field" doing critical, comparative work on justice issues in the world system.

The chapters collected in this book, while in combination yielding a potent and provocative analysis of the persistence of injustice in the world system, should each be read in light of their own analytical and methodological scope. In their chapter on women's suffrage and reproductive rights, Francisco Ramirez and Elizabeth McEneaney undertake an event history analysis to illuminate women's struggles for justice and equitable treatment. Such an approach can be strengthened by the inclusion of narratives and stories by women and men from some of the nations studied, emphasizing the unique aspects of the struggle for equality in particular geographic settings. In his piece on political assassinations in the Middle East, Nachman Ben-Yehuda offers a similar analysis that can be extended fruitfully by more ethnographic work which will uncover motivations and perceptions of justice and social control. Similarly, in their chapter on state disintegration and human rights in Africa, Julia Maxted and Abebe Zegeye take a macroscopic (statist) perspective on justice issues that could be enlarged by focusing on the same issues from the perspective of the affected individuals themselves. A consideration of similar issues in other regions of the world might also be heuristic. An interesting expansion of Richard Harris's neo-Marxian analysis of capitalism in Latin America could explain fully the problems with postmodernism in making the case for the continuing vitality of the meta-narrative analytical tool loosely denoted as "political economy." Annamarie Oliverio's comparative analysis of terrorism in the United States and Italy manifests a provocative research approach that can be expanded by alternative methods of analysis. And Claudia von Werlhof's analysis of the Zapatista rebellion in southern Mexico can be strengthened by explicating why matriarchy is still a form of domination/hierarchy, and perhaps by ascribing to the Zapatistas a different metaphorical point of origin than "the Depths"—beneath Ramona's mask and the masks of other indigenous peoples who struggle for justice, equity, and autonomy, are common people who have faced destruction and death for centuries. Finally, a useful extension of Pat Lauderdale's consideration of indigenous North American jurisprudence could include comparisons with other indigenous cultures throughout the world, as well as a more rigorous grounding in the methods and practices of such peoples and not only the theoretical tensions between the western and indigenous jurisprudential paradigms.

There is also the tendency (in sociology in general, and in this volume in particular excepting perhaps von Werlhof's discussion of the Zapatista land rebellion and Lauderdale's analysis of indigenous world-views) to offer an anthropocentric analysis of the social, political, and economic realms, as if ecological and environmental issues are irrelevant or unimportant to such matters and are better left to other disciplines. We think it is problematic to bifurcate nature and society, particularly where such a separation connotes the domination by humans of the environment, as in the discourse of late capitalism and its central emphases on overproduction and overconsumption. Ecological concerns are germane to any analysis of human conduct and interaction, precisely because we are still part of nature, having never in fact left the womb of the garden despite the revisionist assumptions proffered in Leviathan and its progeny and manifested today in a pervasive consciousness of human superiority and unlimited entitlement to the fruits of nature. To fail to address or account for our separation from the natural environment is to court the prospect of repeating the mistakes of the past even while ostensibly aiming to serve scientific, progressive, or liberatory aims. Again, we offer such ideas and comments as signposts for careful readers and future researchers.

We also note the proclivity in much social theorizing (e.g., systems analysis in particular) to elevate the state as the primary unit of analysis, to the exclusion of other forms of governance and sites of social arrangement. The state is but one such level from which to view social problems, and while it presents an interesting case in many respects, we should take care not to limit ourselves to its artificial boundaries. In some instances it might make sense to focus on smaller units such as local communities, or larger units such as multinational corporations or global regions, or in some cases on amorphous or geographically ambiguous units as might be the case with studying people whose history is the product of dislocation and diaspora. The point worth noting is that the state, and governments in general, offer but one view of governance and sometimes operate to preclude meaningful analyses of other conceptions of organization and political control. In some of the prophesies of indigenous peoples, for instance, there is a prediction that native people of North and South America will unite in the near future, with matrons re-emerging along with the centralization of power—that is, not by the consolidation of power at the acme of hierarchies or the current misnomer of centralization, but with political decisions made directly in the center.

Finally, a brief word about hegemony, ideology, universalism, and "totalizing discourses." There is a tendency to overuse or misuse such concepts in discussing and critiquing capital, the state, and modernity. (As an aside, we also wonder whether concepts such as radical democracy and multiculturalism are different hegemonic terms for a new universalism.) But this linguistic shortcoming should not obscure the important lessons of a comparative, global study of justice nor the reasons for emphasizing such "buzzwords" in the first place. Whatever criticism is brought to bear on our terminological conundrum, it must be recalled why we were compelled to compile (and you, the reader, perhaps to consume) this work in the first instance: The continuing alteration of the global landscape by the forces of late capital and high technology have profound consequences for the lives of real people, their traditional customs and ways, and a certain ecological wisdom that is in peril of being trampled if not altogether lost. We hope at this juncture to offer a critique of corporate rationality, nation-statism, and forms of domination in the world system from the perspective of those who have been and still are marginalized and threatened by these pervasive processes, and let that critique speak for itself. People around the globe whose lives hang in the balance—and not rarefied wordplay—are central to the comparative sociologist's domain, a fact that is sometimes obscured by the necessities of academic life and the paper treadmill on which we all too often get stuck. If nothing else, perhaps this book will (ever so slightly) nudge the scales of justice to weigh more carefully those very lives in the balance.

CONTRIBUTORS

Randall Amster J.D. (1991), Brooklyn Law School, is a doctoral student in the School of Justice Studies, Law and the Social Sciences, at Arizona State University. He was formerly the Associate Managing Editor of the *Brooklyn Law Review*, in which he published an article analyzing the culpability standard in federal civil rights legislation. His present research interests focus on anarchism, ecology, and resistance.

Nachman Ben-Yehuda received his Ph.D. from the University of Chicago. His studies have focused on the sociology of deviance vis-à-vis politics, morality, and ideology. His most recent book (University of Wisconsin Press: 1995) is entitled *The Masada Myth*, in which a political myth is analyzed in the context of deviance.

Richard L. Harris is Associate Professor of Global Studies at the Center for Collaborative Education and Professional Studies, California State University at Monterey Bay. He is one of the coordinating editors of the quarterly academic journal *Latin American Perspectives*, and he has published numerous books and articles on African politics, Latin American political and economic development, Marxism, socialism, democracy, revolution, and comparative public administration. His most recent publications are *Capital, Power and Inequality in Latin America* (Westview: 1995), and *Marxism, Socialism and Democracy in Latin America* (Westview: 1992).

Pat Lauderdale is a professor in the School of Justice Studies and is director of the Justice Studies, Law and Social Sciences Ph.D./J.D. Program at Arizona State University. His recent work includes *The Struggle for Control: A Study of Law, Disputes and Deviance*, with Michael Cruit; comparative articles on indigenous jurisprudence; and a forthcoming revision of *Law and Society* with James Inverarity.

Julia Maxted studied Geography at St. Catherine's and Nuffield Colleges, Oxford. A former Research Fellow at the Centre for Research in Ethnic Relations, University of Warwick, she is currently teaching in the Black Studies and Sociology Departments at the University of California, Santa Barbara. Her research interests focus on processes of social and spatial exclusion.

Elizabeth H. McEneaney is a doctoral candidate in the Department of Sociology at Stanford University. Her dissertation is a comparative-historical analysis of changes in curricular content in science and mathematics. She is also working with David Frank on an analysis of worldwide trends in legislation pertaining to homosexual relationships. She is co-author, with Susan Olzak and Suzanne Shanahan, of *Poverty, Segregation, and Race Riots, 1960-1993*, forthcoming in the *American Sociological Review.*

Annamarie Oliverio's research agenda is in the area of law and social sciences, including the state and the production of hegemony and terrorism, the therapeutic state, and women and politics. This article was completed in 1996 while she was a visiting scholar in the Department of Sociology at Stanford University. She is co-author of a forthcoming article on therapeutic states in the *International Journal of Politics, Culture, and Society*, and is author of the forthcoming book *The State of Terror* (SUNY Press: 1997).

Francisco O. Ramirez is Professor of Education and (by courtesy) Sociology at Stanford University. He is the author of numerous articles on the political incorporation of women and on the institutionalization of mass schooling. He is the co-author of *Institutional Structure: Constituting State, Society, and the Individual* (Sage: 1987). He is also studying the discursive and organizational links between science and development.

Claudia von Werlhof is Professor of Political Science and Women's Studies at the Institute for Political Sciences at the University of Innsbruck in Austria. She is a founder of International Women's Studies and Women's Research, has also done field research in Latin America for many years and has, together with M. Mies and V. Bennholdt-Thomsen, developed a general feminist critique of developmentalism and capitalist patriarchy. She is author and co-author of numerous books that have been published in German, English, Spanish, and Japanese, including *Women: The Last Colony.*

Abebe Zegeye has written extensively on society and the environment in Africa and is currently a Visiting Professor at the University of California, Santa Barbara. His latest publication is *Ethiopia in Change* (British Academic Press). He is co-editor of *Social Identities: Journal for the Study of Race, Nation and Culture.*

INDEX